The Gender Gap

The Gender Gap

A Congregational Guide for Beginning the Conversation about Men's Involvement in Synagogue Life

Edited by Hara Person
with Carolyn Bricklin, Owen Gottlieb, and Melissa Zalkin Stollman

Doug Barden, Consulting Editor

A Joint Project of the Men of Reform Judaism and URJ Press

URJ Press
New York, New York

All rights reserved. No part of this book may be reproduced, stored in a
retrieval system, or transmitted without express written permission from URJ Press.
This excludes brief quotations used only for the purpose of review.

For permission to reprint, please contact URJ Press at:

URJ Press
633 Third Avenue
New York, NY 10017-6778

(212) 650-4124
press@urj.org

Library of Congress Cataloging-in-Publication Data

The gender gap : a congregational guide for beginning the conversation about men's involvement in synagogue life / edited by Hara Person, with Carolyn Bricklin, Owen Gottlieb, and Melissa Zalkin Stollman ; consulting editor, Doug Barden.
   p. cm.
 Includes bibliographical references.
 ISBN-13: 978-0-8074-1058-5 (pbk. : alk. paper)
 ISBN-10: 0-8074-1058-6 (pbk. : alk. paper)
  1. Jewish men--Religious life--United States. 2. Masculinity--Religious aspects--Judaism. 3. Masculinity--United States. 4. Sex role--Religious aspects--Judaism. 5. Reform Judaism--United States. I. Person, Hara. II. Bricklin, Carolyn. III. Gottlieb, Owen. IV. Stollman, Melissa Zalkin. V. Barden, Doug.
 BM725.G47 2007
 296.7081--dc22
                              2007041705

© 2008 by URJ Press

This book is printed on acid-free paper.
Manufactured in the United States of America

10 9 8 7 6 5 4 3 2 1

Contents

Permissions	ix
Foreword *by Doug Barden*	xi
Introduction to *The Gender Gap by Carolyn Bricklin and Owen Gottlieb*	xv

Section I: Notes from the Field

Introduction	3
Questions for Discussion	4
Jewish Men on My Mind	5
by Mindy Portnoy	
Man Enough	11
by Stephen S. Pearce	
Connecting Men to Judaism: The Need for a Comprehensive Cultural Shift	15
by Michael Holzman	
Where Do We Go from Here? One Woman's Perspective . . .	19
by Elyse Goldstein	
Reform Jews Examining Ways to Retain Their Young Men	23
by Debra Nussbam-Cohen	

Section II: Young Men and Their Needs

Introduction	29
Questions for Discussion	30
Jewish Learning and Multiple Intelligences	31
by Evie Rotstein	
A Letter to My Sons	35
by Dana Jennings	
Bar Mitzvah with a Side Order of Testosterone	37
by Jeffrey K. Salkin	
Teenage Boys and Girls: A Jewish World Apart	39
by Leonard Saxe and Shaul Kelner	
Change It Up!—Creating an Appealing Youth Program for Your Male Teens	41
by Melissa Zalkin Stollman	
Teen Brotherhood	47
by Jason Freedman and Bobby Harris	
A Look at Jewish Camping	49
by Daniel G. Zemel	
Ten Suggestions for Reaching Young Men	51
by Michael Holzman	

Section III: *L'Dor vaDor*: From Generation to Generation

Introduction	55
Questions for Discussion	56
Remedy for an "Absent" Father	57
by Jerry Kaye	
Torah for a Jewish Father	61
by Michael Holzman	
The Gift of Fierce Father Love	65
by Allan C. Tuffs	
The Real Man	69
by Joel Soffin	
Journeying Together: Obligations of the Jewish Father	73
by Michael Geller	

Section IV: Involving Men

Introduction	79
Questions for Discussion	80
To Restore the Brother of Brotherhood	81
by Sheldon Zimmerman	
Men's Stories: The Longing for Holiness	87
by Art Grand	
Getting in Touch with My Masculine Side	91
by Kenneth Milhander	
Lech Lecha: New Pathways for Jewish Men	95
by Shawn Israel Zevit	
Men and Leadership in Reform Congregations: More Questions Than Answers	101
by Dale Glasser	
The Role of Men in the Social Action Arena	107
by Marla J. Feldman	

Section V: Gender-Sensitive Worship

Introduction	113
Questions for Discussion	114
Praying in the Velvet Sea	115
by Kevin Kleinman	
A Different Worship Experience: Experimenting with Same-Sex Services at Eisner Camp	119
by Lisa Lieberman Barzilai and Greg Weitzman	
Not for Men Only: A Model for Worship with Men in Mind	123
by Victor S. Appell and Jonathan Comisar	
The Reluctant Man: A Conversation with Susan Weidman Schneider	127

Section VI: Adult Education: Men Welcome

Introduction	133
Questions for Discussion	133
Jewish Men and Adult Jewish Learning	135
by Lisa D. Grant	
For What Do Men's Souls Hunger?	141
by Howard Jaffe	

Our Roles as Fathers	144
The God of My Father	148
A True Homecoming	151
by Jerry David	
Yes, We Are Our Brother's Keeper, and He Is Ours!	155
by Dan Moskovitz	

Section VII: Gender Boundaries Blur: Alternative Masculinities

Introduction	163
Questions for Discussion	163
Gender, Stereotypes, and Sexuality	165
by Craig Rosen	
Girls and Boys: What About Everyone Else? Supporting Our Trans Community	169
by Rachel Van Thyn	
Conclusion—Beginning the Discussion: A Guide for Congregational Conversations	173
by Doug Barden	
Endnotes	181
Bibliography	185
Biographies of Contributors	191

Permissions

Every attempt has been made to obtain permission to reprint previously published material. The authors gratefully acknowledge the following for permission to reprint previously published material:

ACHIM MAGAZINE: "Journeying Together: Reflections on the obligations of the Jewish Father" by Michael Geller (Fall 2002), "Where do we go from here? One Woman's Perspective" by Rabbi Elyse Goldstein (Fall 2004), "Ten Suggestions for Reaching Young Men" by Rabbi Michael Holzman, "Torah for a Jewish Father" by Rabbi Michael Holzman (Fall 2002), "Getting in Touch with my Masculine Side" by Rabbi Kenneth Milhander, "Man Enough" by Rabbi Stephen S. Pearce, Ph.D. (Spring 2007), "Bar Mitzvah with a Side Order of Testosterone" by Rabbi Jeffrey K. Salkin, "The Gift of Fierce Love" by Rabbi Allan C. Tuffs (Fall 2002), "Lech Lecha: New Pathways for Jewish Men" by Rabbi Shawn Zevit Israel (Fall 1999), and "To Restore the Brother of Brotherhood" by Rabbi Sheldon Zimmerman (1994). Used by permission of the authors and Men for Reform Judaism.

HOWARD JAFFE: "Our Roles as Fathers—Programming" and "The God of My Father" by Rabbi Howard Jaffe previously published in *The Outreach and Membership Idea Book* (URJ Press, 2005). Used by permission of Rabbi Howard Jaffe.

THE NEW YORK TIMES: From The New York Times, February 4, 2006 © 2006 The New York Times, Inc. All rights reserved. Used by permission and protected by the Copyright Laws of the United States. The printing, copying, redistribution, or retransmission of the Material without express written permission is prohibited.

REFORM JUDAISM MAGAZINE: "Teen Brotherhood" by Jason Freedman and Bobby Harris, "A Letter To My Sons" by Dana Jennings, "Remedy for an 'Absent' Father" by Jerry Kaye, "The Reluctant Man: A Conversation with Susan Weidman Schneider" by Susan Weidman Schneider, and "The Real Man" by Rabbi Joel Soffin from Fall 2006. Used by permission of the authors and Reform Judaism Magazine.

SH'MA: "Living Words" by Rabbi Mindy Portnoy reprinted with permission from the author and *Living Words III: Best High Holiday Sermons of 5761*. The volume is published by *Sh'ma: A Journal of Jewish Responsibility* (www.shma.com). "Teenage Boys and Girls: A Jewish World Apart" by Shaul Kelner and Leonard Saxe, *Sh'ma: A Journal of Jewish Responsibility*, May 2001. Used by permission of the authors and *Sh'ma: A Journal of Jewish Responsibility*.

Foreword

The Men of Reform Judaism (MRJ, formerly the North American Federation of Temple Brotherhoods [NFTB]) and its parent body, the Union for Reform Judaism (URJ), is pleased to share with you *The Gender Gap: A Congregational Guide for Beginning the Conversation about Men's Involvement in Synagogue Life*. We hope that congregations will find this book a helpful addition to the recent series of books that have focused on the issue of increasing the participation of men of all ages in our congregations.

In January 2006, I published a monograph entitled *Wrestling with Jacob and Esau: Fighting the Flight of Men; A Modern Day Crisis for the Reform Movement* that dealt with a very widespread phenomenon: the disengagement of men from Jewish life. The monograph argued that this phenomenon affects our professionals (e.g., rabbis, cantors, and educators), our young teenage males, and the adult men of our community. My goal in writing the piece was to place the issue of the disengagement of men on the front burner of the cultural gatekeepers of our Movement—namely, the rabbinic and lay congregational leaders; the Movement's youth group leaders; the camp directors; the regional and national staff of URJ; and the men and women, lay and professional, who have the influence to effect change.

The monograph was distributed widely by NFTB to every rabbi, cantor, and educator of our Movement, and I was subsequently invited to speak on the topic with congregational leaders, lay and professional, at national and regional URJ conventions, Central Conference of American Rabbis (CCAR) regional meetings, Hebrew Union College–Jewish Institute of Religion (HUC-JIR) study forums, as well as individual congregations. With rare exception, my findings that our Movement faces an increasing disparity between men and women's participation resonated with many, as my listeners had had similar experiences in their home congregations. As time went on, it became increasingly apparent to me that I should spend less time defending the proposition that men were disengaging and spend more time focusing with my audience on the more exciting and challenging task of collaboratively generating new directions and programmatic initiatives that would reverse the disengagement.

While the monograph provided a number of reasons why I felt our Movement had failed to grapple to date with the issue, there was one explanation that many felt was critical: the Movement's misinterpretation and subsequent faulty implementation of the goals of genuine feminism. Specifically, there had been a failure to distinguish between gender stratification and gender differentiation. Rather than focusing, appropriately, on eliminating the uneven distribution of leadership positions, power, and related rewards of prestige, a considerable amount of Movement effort had been misspent on eliminating any and all signs of gender differentiation. This in a sense, made all activities—be it prayer, study, or ritual activity—gender neutral. There had been a refusal to acknowledge that there may be a significant difference in male and female spirituality. Such a refusal was actually at odds with, if not outright anathema to, the original ideals of feminism.

At the same time, I must acknowledge one of my strongly held beliefs. Whether our temple serves as a *beit t'filah*, a *beit midrash*, or a *beit k'neset*, I believe that most of the time it is appropriate for men and women to come together and pray, study, and interact as a single community. That is a given. But for the spiritual and social needs of some men and women to be sufficiently met, it is my belief that the synagogue must also create, at times, gender-exclusive space—namely, women's space and men's space. In the past four decades, the Reform Movement has readily recognized and supported the need for the former; to date, however, many in our Movement still find the suggestion of the latter problematic.

This book is designed to assist all of us in taking the next steps in dealing with this complicated and sensitive issue. It is filled with numerous essays from leaders, both professional and lay, generously sharing their perspective on the issue of male involvement. Some of the essays originally appeared in *Achim* magazine, the national membership magazine of MRJ; some appeared in *Reform Judaism* magazine; but many of the articles were written specifically for this publication.

Readers will quickly discover there is little in the way of agreement either in the causes or in the remedial directions we should undertake. This does not surprise me in the least. From the beginning of this journey, I have asked my colleagues, lay and professional alike, to recognize that we are not dealing with a monolithic group. How men will choose to participate in their congregations, how men will choose to express their spirituality, how men will seek out prayer and worship experiences, and how men will demonstrate their commitment to *tikkun olam* will be varied and diverse.

Based on my experiences working with adult men, we ignore at our peril some obvious elements of diversity. We have men in our Movement who can chant Torah, while there are many others who never learned Hebrew. We have men in our Movement who had strong, multigenerational Jewish role models (male and female) growing up whom they now wish to emulate, while others are recent converts. We have men who have attended our summer camps and were active as teens in our youth groups, while others are stepping into our congregations for the first time only because their oldest child is ready for Hebrew school. Additionally, I am increasingly aware of the significant generational differences that impact upon the attitudes and behaviors of our target audiences. Place men from the civic builders generation (born during the Depression years and grew up during World War II) with baby boomers (1945–1962) or even with members of Generation X (1962–1982) in a room together to discuss their views on Israel, the Holocaust, anti-Semitism, interfaith marriage, the impact of feminism, the increasing use of Hebrew in our liturgies, and the pros and cons of guitar-playing cantors, and watch the sparks fly! No, my brothers are not monolithic!

Even with the stated caveats and at the risk of being accused of perpetuating stereotypes, I will go out on a limb and suggest that when comparing men with women, men as a group, more often than women:

- Tend to be task and problem-solving oriented
- Tend to be risk-taking oriented
- Correlate their self-esteem more with achievement than with relationships
- Are actively engaged in pride protection and go to great lengths to avoid situations of potential intimidation and expressions of vulnerabilities, be they physical health, mental health, or Hebrew literacy competency issues
- Have a tendency to prefer talking in intellectual, abstract terms and are less interested in expressing emotions and strong feelings openly

- Focus more on external subjects (e.g., a task, a text, a sports game, or experience) rather than internalizing or individual socializing.

Do these tendencies or trends assist us in generating congregational programs and activities that will attract more men? For some, maybe, but for others, my suggestions will have little impact. The truth is that complex cultural phenomena cannot be resolved by simplistic answers.

What I am certain of, if we are going to successfully address this crisis—and for me, it is a crisis—is that a collaborative effort is required. At this stage of the cultural change process, the best strategy for the congregations of our Movement is to be receptive to trying a variety of alternative men's programmatic avenues, and to be prepared for some failures as well.

We know that every temple, and in a broader sense, the entire Reform Movement, is best served only when both men and women participate fully in congregational life. The challenge is to find new win-win paradigms for both Jewish men and women interested in ensuring a strong Jewish community in the twenty-first century. Let's begin the conversation to make that happen!

Doug Barden
Executive Director,
Men of Reform Judaism

Introduction to *The Gender Gap*

Carolyn Bricklin and Owen Gottlieb

In February 2006, an article by Debra Nussbaum-Cohen appeared in the *New York Times*. Something radical had happened in the Reform Movement at the Biennial convention of the North American Federation of Temple Youth (NFTY): a prayer service was offered for men only. In a movement that was built from its inception on assumptions of egalitarian prayer service, what could possibly be the cause of such apparent departure from the Movement's imperative? Nussbaum-Cohen explained succinctly, writing of the Movement, "It is losing its young men." This was far from the first article or mention of the subject. Rabbis had given sermons; rabbinical students, camp counselors, and professionals knew there was a serious problem. Nussbaum-Cohen even reported in her article that the Reform Movement had already convened a commission to study the issue. But such a prominent article in the *New York Times* somehow signaled to many that the problem of the loss of men and boys from progressive Judaism had graduated to the status of high priority.

In recent years, the numbers of men and boys participating in many aspects of Jewish life, from synagogues to camps, has been on a marked decline. This "flight of men," as Doug Barden, the executive director of Men of Reform Judaism, has referred to it, is alarming. In some contexts, participation is skewing in the range of 30 percent men to 70 percent women. What would our Jewish world look like if this trend were not stopped and reversed, moving us back toward a gender equity? Would progressive Jewish life be an exclusively female arena? What would this mean for our heritage—that of both our Jewish women and our Jewish men? Why is this occurring, and what should we be doing about it?

The essays in this text serve a number of functions. They observe the trends, they analyze data about learning and styles, they express personal stories and opinions, and in some cases they even offer experiments or possible directions in which to proceed. These essays are not intended to provide absolute solutions or answers. They do not, overall, reflect careful and thorough research (though some do). What they are intended to do is provoke thought and conversation. Most of these essays provide a personal, anecdotal perspective, rather than objective data. The essays that were written specifically for this volume are each based on a hypothesis or assumption that may or may not in fact turn out to be true or valid. You may disagree with a hypothesis, an opinion, an approach, or an analysis. But this is particularly the point. This text is a resource guide to jump-start conversation on the gender gap. From the springboard of that debate, we hope you will be inspired to move to action to make our institutions welcoming to men and boys and to move to action with an eye toward the goals of gender equity in our synagogues, camps, schools, and institutions.

Background

The mitzvot that defined a daily Jewish life were once a male responsibility. Women were not required to take on that same responsibility. Women were not counted for a minyan, were not required to say *Kaddish* for their parents, could not be ordained as rabbis or cantors, and were rarely the leaders of synagogue-affiliated activities other than Sisterhoods. Although women were historically responsible for maintaining a Jewish home and were often active in the secular public sphere such as the marketplace, they were excluded from almost all public Jewish roles. The sphere of public Jewish practice was exclusively male. But this kind of Judaism has slowly disappeared from the liberal movements since the early 1970s.[1]

The cry for the equality of women in the liberal synagogue gained widespread legitimacy and recognition in the 1960s and 1970s.[2] Women began taking official congregational leadership roles with the ordination of Sally Priesand in 1972. In 1980, *Keeping Posted*, a Reform Movement youth magazine, declared, "We are in the midst of a social revolution that has changed the course of Jewish life in America. It started about ten years ago when Jewish women began to reexamine and to challenge religious laws and communal practices that relegated them to second-class status."[3] A significant change had begun in the Jewish community. No longer was the face of the congregation a sea of men. Women's and men's voices counted equally. Women stepped into the world that had excluded them for millennia and began to demand that Judaism meet their needs equally in addition to the needs of the male congregants.

Today

Rabbis in congregations, NFTY youth group leaders, teachers in Hebrew schools, camp directors, and lay leaders each have their own anecdotes of their creative attempts to meet the needs of Reform Jews. They face the reality that in today's world every Jew is a Jew-by-choice. As a result, these leaders are charged with the task of creating meaningful and satisfying Jewish experiences so that Jews will continue to choose to actively participate in the Jewish community. Anecdotal reports as well as formal studies reflect the emergence of an alarming trend. Our leaders tell us that in the population of Jews actively engaged in their Judaism, women now outnumber men. Women and girls are disproportionately represented in every activity of Jewish life after the age of bar or bat mitzvah. It seems as though we have moved from being a male-dominated religion toward becoming a female-dominated religion.

Despite the current attention this issue has received, the trend itself is not sudden. Doug Barden brought this long-overlooked problem to the attention of the Reform Movement with the publication of his monograph *Wrestling with Jacob and Esau: Fighting the Flight of Men; A Modern Day Crisis for the Reform Movement*. His goal was "to convince the professional and lay leadership of the Reform Movement to be sufficiently interested in the male-flight crisis to utilize a men's gender resource guide and commit the required time, energy and resources to promote such a program."[4] Barden encouraged the leadership of the Reform Movement to address a growing reality: the disengagement of boys and men with Reform Judaism. His book treats the politically sensitive issue of how to celebrate the presence of women in their newfound roles as Jewish leaders while working toward a Judaism that enables both men and women to be spiritually fulfilled by their religious experiences.

The Fall 2006 edition of *Reform Judaism* magazine's Focus section was dedicated to the topic of "Re-engaging Men." Articles with anecdotal evidence supporting Barden's assertion that men are less religiously involved filled the magazine. Contributing authors from different walks of life examined their personal perspective on why boys and men feel less connected to Jewish life. The authors also offered their own suggestions and ideas on how to bring men back to Judaism. These pieces were thoughtful and provocative, written by those who already attempted to create Jewish opportunities and experiences that meet the needs of men in different ways.

The Men of Reform Judaism (MRJ, formerly North American Federation of Temple Brotherhoods [NFTB]) is dedicated to serving Jewish men, Reform Judaism, and local Reform congregations. MRJ affiliates give local Brotherhood members the opportunity to explore and celebrate their male Jewish spirit. Because the MRJ believes that the loss of men is part of a systemic problem within Reform Judaism, they chose to support the creation of this book for the larger Reform community. This work has been crafted to continue the conversation initiated by earlier Movement publications.

Research

A brief overview of the statistical evidence regarding the numbers of men participating in Jewish life will explain the parameters of the current reality. The statistics reinforce what has been anecdotally noted in previous publications: there are fewer men participating in Jewish religious life in the Reform Movement. Though this research is only the beginning and there is much more we still need to learn, it at least gives us a place to start.

Steven M. Cohen's and Arnold M. Eisen's 2000 study[5] of the Jewish community researched factors that led individuals to participate in more intense Jewish activity and discovered trends that appear related to the gender imbalance. They write that "more and more, the meaning of Judaism in America transpires within the self. American Jews have drawn the activity and significance of their group identity into the subjectivity of the individual, the activities of the family, and the few institutions (primarily the synagogue) which are seen as extensions of this intimate sphere."[6] In other words, they concluded that for the participants in their study, Judaism is valued not because it provides membership in a community but rather because it is a means to self-fulfillment. When an individual chooses to participate in Jewish life, she or he chooses to engage in the existential questions of who they are and what is the purpose of her or his life. For this reason, when Jews participate in Jewish activities, they do so as part of an act of personal identity formation.

Cohen and Eisen go on to assert that Jewish identity is maintained through ritual practice. Ritual practice, such as holiday observance, is now centered in the home and predominantly involves children. Cohen and Eisen note, "To a remarkable degree, the 'action' where Jewish activity among the moderately affiliated is concerned now rests with women."[7] In most households, even with two-career families, women continue to have primary responsibility for child-care activities. With the trend toward a personal Judaism that is mainly practiced in the home, and the continued predominance of women acting as caregivers, women have become the primary enactors in Jewish life.

Cohen and Eisen posit another reason for the increased proportion of women involved in Jewish life. From their interviews they came to believe that women are "generally more open than men"[8] to exploring their spirituality. There is an increased Jewish interest in spirituality overall that mirrors a larger trend in American religious life.[9] Cohen and Eisen further note that all religious life in America has become more privatized.[10] No longer is the public sphere the important arena in which to participate in a religion. Rather, what seems to be a higher priority today is the individual identity that religion can foster in a person. If people are choosing to participate in Jewish activities based on the ability of that activity to help make meaning for the individual, and if more women than men are open to exploring those avenues, then it should not be surprising that more women than men are participating in communal Jewish life.

Cohen and Eisen also found that women are more comfortable participating in "conversations about and experiences of transcendence,"[11] with the accompanying possibility of ambiguity. Based on their research, they posit that these types of experiences may come more naturally to women. Women feel empowered by the visible presence of women rabbis, lay leaders, and communal professionals who are publicly reinterpreting the tradition. Women respondents reported feeling more comfortable struggling to reinterpret the tradition without any end to their search in sight. Women, it seems, are naturally more comfortable with the ambiguities of involving themselves in a search for meaning that has no definite answer. Their analysis, then, may provide useful background for better understanding the phenomenon we seem to be facing today.

Through a study focused on adolescents, researchers at Brandeis University's Cohen Center for Modern Jewish Study confirm Eisen and Cohen's observation regarding the importance of gender in determining participation in Jewish life.[12] The findings of this study indicate that a teenager's negative attitude toward participation in Jewish educational studies cannot be explained away by the idea that teens simply do not like school. In fact, their research suggests that young adolescents enjoyed their schooling and took it quite seriously.[13] It was only to Jewish extracurricular education that the adolescents responded negatively. Complementing Cohen and Eisen's study, the Brandeis study affirmed that "boys rejected their supplementary Jewish education—and, with it, continued involvement in Jewish life—more decisively than did girls. Actual participation in formal Jewish education showed a decline predictable from these attitudes, with the same gender differences persisting."[14]

The Brandeis study provides us with the following statistics to support the claim that boys feel more negatively than do girls about their Jewish education:

> Given the statement, "I have enjoyed my Jewish schooling," 46% of boys disagreed while only 30% agreed. The girls who took a position on the question split evenly between agreement and disagreement. With the statement, "My Bar Mitzvah was basically my graduation from Jewish school," 47% of boys agreed while 43% disagreed; among girls, 34% agreed while 52% disagreed. The statement, "After my Bar Mitzvah, I wanted to get more involved in Jewish life," yielded disagreement from 42% of boys, agreement from only 25%. Among girls, 37% were neutral while the remainder split evenly between agreement and disagreement.[15]

Boys had a more negative experience in their Jewish schooling and were less interested in continuing to participate in Jewish education.

Although boys regarded their Jewish education more negatively than did their female counterparts, they did not reject the goal of finding meaning in their lives. The Brandeis study found that 73 percent of girls and boys expressed a great interest in finding meaning in their lives;[16] only 31 percent of those expected that they would find this meaning through Jewish involvement.[17] It seems that young Jews do not see the synagogue as a place that is conducive to searching for meaning. Although boys and girls responded similarly to these questions, an important hypothesis can be gleaned from this result. Both boys and girls search for meaning, but neither believe the synagogue is a place for that search. Since the statistics show that girls continue to participate at higher levels than boys in Jewish activities (discussed below), we can infer that girls are getting something more out of their participation in Jewish activities than boys are, even if they do not understand the synagogue as a place to search for meaning.

The Reform Movement has begun tracking the participation of young men in order to ascertain whether the statistics found above were reflected in the reality of the Reform Movement. The Young Men's Project[18] was established in 2005 by the NFTB in cooperation with the URJ Youth Division. The Project had a threefold purpose: First, to collect and analyze data on male participation within URJ Youth Division programs. Second, to research possible causes for the trends and their short- and long-term implications for the Reform Jewish community. Third, to develop potential programs and resources for URJ camps, NFTY, and Reform Movement congregations.

The Young Men's Project gathered statistics on male and female participation in their programs. Data was gathered from URJ camps, NFTY regions, NFTY conventions, NFTY in Israel summer trips, Eisendrath International Exchange (EIE) High School Semester in Israel, Mitzvah Corps programs, the Meitav Youth Fellowship, Religious Action Center (RAC) L'Taken Seminars, and KESHER programs. Though a formal and thorough analysis of the data has not yet been undertaken, the initial data is revealing. The research conducted uncovered a significant imbalance between male and female participation in almost all programs through young adulthood. The gap in participation grew as age increased so that by the time of college KESHER activities, it was likely that female to male participation had a ratio of two to one.[19] The report states "that there is, in fact, a disparity between the number of girls and the number of boys participating in our programs. This was thought to be the case prior to beginning this project, but our research proves that the imbalance is consistently wide-reaching enough to call for action on the part of our Movement."[20]

Using This Book to Start the Conversation

The Gender Gap is an attempt to launch conversation on the issue of male involvement in Reform Jewish life. The initial statistics available at this time support what our clergy, educators, and laypeople have been noticing for years: we are not adequately engaging boys and men in Jewish communal life. When the NFTB originally brought this possibility to the Movement's attention, some people may have wondered if it was a temporary shift, or even just the long anticipated equalization between men's and women's participation. But the numbers show us otherwise. Women outnumber men. We are left to ask ourselves: What is it about our current programming that does not speak to men? What successful programming exists for men? What do the people at the forefront of this field think is necessary for Reform Judaism to become part of men's lives again? What do *you,* your family, your friends, and your fellow congregants think?

Rather than a prescription or set of answers, this book is a conversation starter. Much the way the pages of *Mikraot G'dolot,* The Commentators Bible, can be read as a discussion between the sages of different eras on the same topic, so too do we make room in our book for differing ideas regarding the same issue. Judaism is a tradition that has always valued, validated, and retained the minority opinion. Here too, in this book, we have some challenging pieces that will contribute additional dimensions to the conversation.

With the idea of conversation in mind, this book is split up into seven different sections. Each section begins with a synopsis of what is covered as well as a suggestion of the major themes that emerge when the section is read as a whole. Each section also includes a series of questions specific to the topic of that section. These questions can be used as part of a discussion between colleagues about how to meet the needs of their constituents. They can also be used among congregants to help clarify their own needs. The questions are also helpful in comparing articles with different points of view. You as the reader have the option to choose to read only the pieces you feel would be most helpful to you. They may stand on their own as sources of information. That being said, we highly recommend reading entire sections of the book. Many of the pieces we have provided offer divergent views as to the needs of men and how best to reach them. When taken as a unit, the individual pieces in a section can blend together into a thought-provoking discussion. You are invited to participate in this discussion by answering the questions for yourself, by taking the suggestions made by our authors and trying them in your own setting, or by choosing to disagree and chart a new path by which you can reach out to Jewish men.

Finally, we have provided you with a bibliography for further reading, which we hope this book will inspire. Ours is one set of ideas among a wide array. Many of our authors have written on this topic elsewhere; many authors who have already written elsewhere are not among the contributors to this book. The goal of this book is to help you consider and respond to your male congregants' needs in a thoughtful, thorough, and informed way, while remaining sensitive to the needs and rights of all. To expand the conversation, and to have a chance to hear the men's narratives to which many of the authors in this book allude, we urge you pick up the companion text to this volume: *The Still Small Voice: Reflections on Being a Jewish Man,* edited by Michael Holzman, with a preface by Doug Barden (URJ Press, 2007). These two works, used in tandem, will serve you well as you build a path toward gender equity in your community. The discoveries and reflections of the authors of these works will provide possible templates for action and bases from which to brainstorm. These books will also serve to remind you that you are not alone in the community and synagogue explorations and experiments to come. There is a family of Jewish men and those who care about those men beside you on the same journey, the journey to bringing men and boys back, en masse, to our Jewish communities.

The problem of the gender gap requires all of us to shift out of our comfort zone and consider changes. Change is difficult, but change may be the only way that we can bring men and boys back into organized Jewish life. We may be uncomfortable in making changes, experimenting, trying something new, or trying again. But we can also be excited that there is a new frontier of programs, ideas, and exploration. We have the opportunity to forge a new kind of Reform Judaism in America that provides a challenging and fulfilling Jewish home for men and women alike. We can take this challenge and, in the coming years, use our energy to find a new path and bring a vision of a gender-balanced, gender-equal Reform Judaism to fruition. We can once again have a Reform Judaism in which our women and men stand together—even if it means also exploring and allowing opportunities for single-sex prayer and discussion groups—celebrate together, worship together, learn together, and raise our families together, partnered with our Jewish institutions.

Section I

Notes from the Field

Introduction

Despite the use of statistics in the introduction to *The Gender Gap,* this book is not focused on scientific studies or statistical analyses. In contrast to statistics, this section consists of the reflections of the rabbis who have noticed the changing gender demographic in their congregations and institutions. Present here are the thoughtful comments and ideas of rabbis whose work has already been affected by the decline in the activity of men. These are also the rabbis who have thought deeply about why that change has occurred and what would be needed at the synagogue level to change it.

In her High Holy Day sermon "Jewish Men on My Mind," Rabbi Mindy Portnoy explores the history of male role modeling in Jewish history. She examines the model of the quiet scholar created by the Rabbis after the destruction of the Temple, the strong man of the Zionist movement, and the "true" American man who blends seamlessly into the American landscape. Portnoy explores the repercussions of each model on the male Jewish psyche and the Jewish community. In doing so, she wonders how Jewishness can add value to the life of the American male and how we can begin to explore this question.

Rabbi Stephen Pearce's sermon "Man Enough" addresses the loss of men to Jewish synagogue life while also making reference to similar problems in churches. He recounts statistics including the rabbinic class admitted to Hebrew Union College in 2005 in which 77 percent of the students were women. He discusses a variety of approaches to bringing men back, including a range of ideas from serious to those he notes are "downright silly," such as church services based on a football theme. In the end, while continuing to try to find a solution with creative programming, Rabbi Pearce admits that he is stumped with regard to long-term retention of men. How can men find the synagogue to be a way to explore their spirituality? How can we ensure that our children have active mentors in their Jewish fathers and elders? Rabbi Pearce invites his congregation and the wider Jewish audience to work together to help generate viable programs and outlets for men and to find viable, thoughtful solutions to the problem of bringing men back to the world of Jewish community life.

Rabbi Michael Holzman believes that synagogues have to change radically to meet the needs of men. In "Connecting Men to Judaism: The Need for Comprehensive Cultural Shift," he asks congregations to recognize that men's roles in our communities and larger society are no longer clear. Instead they exist in a world of shifting and uncertain expectations. Rabbi Holzman charges the synagogue to create a culture that invites men to explore masculinity through personal experience and to provide a safe space to express those personal experiences as male narratives. Rabbi Holzman calls for focusing creativity on solutions, as the Jewish people have never lacked creativity. He also asks for the development of a new men's ethics, appropriate for today's world—an approach that is mindful of the abuse of power and sensitive to the great strides made in gender equity over the years. He puts forth self-examination as a critical part of this new Jewish men's exploration.

In "Where Do We Go from Here? One Woman's Perspective . . . ," Rabbi Elyse Goldstein begins with the long-term repercussions of gender considerations within the Jewish community.

She argues that such considerations originally began as a women's liberation movement, a movement of transformation that worked toward equality between men and women. Rabbi Goldstein notes that the movement has moved beyond its initial search for equality toward an understanding of the distinctions between womanhood and manhood. She notes that while much has been gained for women in the synagogue, much has been lost for the men. As men and women search for their Jewish identity and meaning in religious community, Rabbi Goldstein notes that Judaism must meet men's needs as well as women's needs.

We conclude this section with Debra Nussbaum-Cohen's article from the *New York Times*, "Reform Jews Examining Ways to Retain Their Young Men." Bringing the loss of young men in the Reform Movement to national attention, Nussbaum-Cohen illuminates the scope of the flight of boys and young men as it appeared in the winter of 2006. The article includes history of the Movement's stance on egalitarian prayer and opinions from leaders, such as drawing the distinction between creating a space for boys and young men and negating space for women. Nussbaum-Cohen's piece helps give the context and set the stage for the entirety of this book—because her article is about naming the problem and the search for solutions on the ground.

Each of the authors, having noticed that the Jewish world in which they operate has been affected by the loss of men, questions why men have abandoned the institution. Approaching the issue from different points of view, each author suggests different approaches for solutions.

Questions for Discussion

As you read each piece, consider the following questions:

1. Does the reality described in this essay mirror your own observations? How does it reflect or not reflect what you have observed or experienced?
2. Choose an essay or several essays. What assumptions are made in the essay(s) you have chosen? What is unsaid, but implied? How do these assumptions relate to the issues raised?
3. Is the assumption and issue you discussed in question 2 at play in your synagogue? In your life? If so, how? If not, why not?
4. Does the author offer a suggestion as to how to address the need, and if so, what is it? Do you think such a solution might be effective in your community? If not, how might the idea be altered or adapted to better fit your community?
5. Do you believe there is a completely different solution set that would be successful? What would that be? And why do you think it would be successful in your community in particular?

Jewish Men on My Mind

Mindy Portnoy

What's a Jewish world without active Jewish men?

I spent a lot of time this summer thinking about Jewish men. Now, please don't get the wrong idea—these were thoughts of a purely professional nature. I read books by and about Jewish men—from the Bible to Saul Bellow, and Philip Roth. I saw movies about Jewish men, like *Hank Greenberg*, *Keeping the Faith*, and *Sunshine*. I found out only after the fact that the nasty British officer in *The Patriot* was played by a nice Jewish guy. The only non-Jewish fellow I paid any attention to was Harry Potter, and if you think about it long enough, maybe there's something a little Jewish about him, too: an outsider, attends a special kind of yeshiva, and struggles with a dual identity. Okay, enough, I don't want to carry this too far!

So why have I suddenly become so obsessed with Jewish men? Well, actually it's been going on for quite a while, only it crystallized for me when I read a very enthusiastic article in the *Post* this spring about a women's seder being held at one of the local Reform congregations. After a few of our own female congregants began pestering me to do our own, I began to explore my own initially negative reactions to the proposal. Then I began to think about the Jewish men I know. How do they feel about the increasing female presence in the synagogue, and more significantly, about women as the driving force behind much of what counts as Jewish creativity today—spirituality, healing, adult bat mitzvah? Where do men fit in anymore? Do they feel left out? And as Freud didn't say, what do guys really want?

I don't only obsess, but being Jewish, I also worry. More and more often, as we look for Jewish teachers, Torah and Haftarah readers, or adult education students, we look to Jewish women. Not only in our community, but throughout American Jewry. As women enter the mainstream (at least the non-Orthodox variety), we are so excited by the newness of our Jewish equality that we volunteer and study and show up. Cantorial school is dominated by women, rabbinical school is moving right up there. Our youth groups are equally skewed toward female participation. As my colleague, Rabbi Jeffrey Salkin, has written, "Jewish men seem to be fleeing from synagogue life and leadership. For many years, Jewish education has become increasingly feminized, with fewer and fewer men entering that noble and crucial field . . . Jewish adolescent boys report far less of an investment in their Jewish identity than do Jewish girls of the same age. . . . There has been a slow disappearing act on the part of Jewish men." Rabbi Seymour Rosenbloom adds, "The Jewish community . . . has not begun to address what is happening to men."

So I became intrigued and started reading. I read Rabbi Salkin's book, *Searching for My Brothers*, the Berkeley scholar, Daniel Boyarin's book, *Unheroic Conduct*, and the American

Studies' professor Riv-Ellen Prell's book, *Fighting to Become American: Jews, Gender, and the Anxiety of Assimilation*. And as I share with you some of my thoughts on the subject today—what I consider only preliminary speculation—I would in turn love to hear from you on the subject. As a woman, I feel a little chutzpahdik prescribing solutions to this problem; as a rabbi, I am genderless in my anxieties and observations.

As we Jews always do, we must start at the beginning, and where better to look than to the Torah? Genesis, of course, is filled with sibling rivalry and dysfunctional families. And although the Reform movement (mistakenly, I believe) eliminated from the Rosh Hashana service the story in Genesis 21 on the birth of Isaac and the casting away of Ishmael, we need to retrieve it. Who is Ishmael? Sent away from his father, Abraham, he becomes the founder of nations, and of course, a hunter. Philip Roth's quintessential Gentile male stereotype is a man who hunts and eats anything, and therefore is capable of doing anything! And Isaac, on the other hand, the man who stays at home, is almost sacrificed without a complaint. His life is first run by his mother and father, and then by a strong wife, but he eventually becomes the bearer of the covenant. As Rabbi Salkin writes, "Someone once said that there is substantial proof that Isaac really lived: no nation would invent an ancestor like him. No nation, except the Jews." Isaac becomes the model of the passive Jewish man, a victim; a few commentators have even suggested he was disabled in some way, either before the Akedah event or as a result of it. And yet, he is also the first of whom it is said that he loves his wife, a man who makes peace with his neighbors, and eventually reunites with his brother when they bury their father. And unlike Abraham and Jacob, whose names are changed when their covenant with God is affirmed, Yitzchak, Isaac, never changes his name. And Abraham? The same man who argues with God silently prepares to sacrifice his beloved son. Over the years, we've all heard the multiple, disparate interpretations of the Akedah story (most created to make us feel better about a difficult text); but who is Abraham really? This seemingly very tough and courageous guy is nevertheless very distressed at the thought of sending away Ishmael (until God reassures him), and cries at the death of his beloved wife, Sarah. He is no stick figure, purely unemotional, a myopic fanatic.

Such cases run throughout the Bible. Our male heroes are multi-dimensional: Think Joseph, Moses, Saul, David. Our sacred literature, though filled with wars and violence, rarely glorifies the warrior-hero; David's legacy resides more in the ascription of psalms to his pen than to his crafty military finesse. In the Bible, when power becomes too centralized and glorified, things begin falling apart, like after the death of King Solomon. And yet, certain biblical figures, if read directly from the biblical text, can still surprise us at times with their toughness, their virility, their raw power. Think Joshua, Samson, Gideon, most of the Judges. No wimps need apply here.

Yet for most of the past 2,000 years of Jewish history, we have read the Bible with the eyes of the rabbis of the Talmudic period. And the rabbis were Isaac people, forced by historical circumstances, and prodded by their own understanding of covenant, to mold a new male image. In doing so, they created an alternative male model that may yet be of value today. As Rabbi Salkin writes, "what became of the ideal Jewish male virtues? Virtues that the rest of the world might regard as being unmanly—restraint, renunciation, resignation, reconciliation, patience, and forbearance." The wise son, the student of the Torah, became the ideal; Moses was turned into a rabbi, Solomon into a sage, David into "the sweet singer of Israel." Warriors need not apply—words were to replace swords, particularly the words and teachings of the Torah. The Maccabees, for example, got short shrift from the rabbis. Why glorify men when God was the real hero? Massada, home and burial place of the Zealots, lost the place of honor to Yavneh, seat of rabbinic Judaism.

And yet, later representations of the rabbis as asexual, feminized, pale little fellows are also a distortion. The rabbis were still all male (in both senses of that term). And yet they created from their texts and their history an alternative male. Think for a moment of your own mental image of a 2nd century rabbi discussing Jewish law. How close is it to what the scholar Miriam Peskowitz describes?

> In the imagination of my students, the rabbis of . . . Palestine and Babylonia are "little old Jewish guys," "nice, sweet," "kind of grandfatherly." They are "bearded" and "balding." . . . Rabbis are imagined as "sitting," "studying," "hunched over," and "slight of frame." They "would have worn glasses, had they been invented." . . . Invariably, my students think ancient "rabbis" are "very unattractive," if their bodies can be imagined at all.

But according to Daniel Boyarin:

> Such a man is interpreted as anything but sexless within rabbinic texts; indeed, he is represented as the paramount object of female desire. . . . though hardly feminist, rabbinic Jewish culture . . . refuse(d) prevailing modes through which the surrounding culture represent maleness as active spirit, femaleness as passive matter, a representation that has dominated much of European cultural imagination and practice. Maleness is every bit as corporeal as femaleness in this patriarchal culture.

This is not to say that this image was the only available model. Sephardic Jewish culture, for example, picked up on different cultural models—the most famous example being the great poet and communal leader, Shmuel Ha-Nagid, who led the armies of Granada in the early 11th century.

But for us, predominantly descendants of Ashkenazic culture, male antecedents are those of the rabbinic imagination. Scholars, fathers, rabbis, peddlers, soft men, so to speak—paragons of virtue at their best, their highest appellation being a mensch, a nearly untranslatable word. Power and wealth are not disparaged in the rabbinic world-view, but neither are they the ultimate objects of desire. As Boyarin writes, "the study of Torah is the quintessential performance of rabbinic Jewish maleness." Tevye, our pop-culture shtetl man, views wealth as simply a means to enable him to pray and study full-time. As a 17th-century Jewish woman wrote in her memoirs:

> However much my husband toiled, and truly the whole day he ran about his business, still he never failed to set aside a fixed time to study his Torah. . . . So good and true a father one seldom finds, and he loved his wife and children beyond all measure. His modesty had no like, throughout his life he never once gave thought to holding public office . . . in brief, he was the perfect pattern of a pious Jew, as were his fathers and brothers.

This, Dr. Boyarin notes, "the very qualifications that would render a young man fit to be a monk within European Christian culture—scholarliness, quietism, modesty, and a spiritual aptitude—are those that qualified him to be a husband in this Jewish culture."

But as Jews became westernized, modernized, enlightened, Americanized, and Zionized, male images began to change as well.

Zionism, most particularly, tossed the traditional Jewish masculine image overboard. Theodore Herzl had been a member of a dueling fraternity at the University of Vienna, and he saw dueling as a way of overcoming the image of "the cowardly Jew." Those of you who saw the movie *Sunshine* think of the image of Adam Sors, the Hungarian fencer. Falling prey to anti-Jewish stereotypes in the general culture, and seeking to replace them, many early Zionists rejected what they viewed as weak, effeminate Diaspora Jewish men in favor of the new, virile Zionist pioneer.

They even had a term for the new persona: "muscular Judaism." As Michael Berkowitz writes, in the Zionist literature of the 1920s, it was the traditional Jews of Jerusalem "not the Arabs, whom the Zionists presented as the most burdensome obstacle to the flowering of their plan, and whom they treated to their harshest invective."

Underneath and alongside the other Zionist motivations, then, sexual politics, and a re-ordering of gender also played a significant role. Once again, as in the time of the Judges, no wimps need apply.

During the past 100 years, the image of the sabra has evolved into the attractive, tough, Hebrew-speaking, gun-toting secular Israeli—in contrast to the traditional, Yiddish-speaking yeshiva bocher, soft, studious, and pale. And Hollywood certainly nurtured the image as well, most famously in the movie *Exodus*. What young Jewish boy wouldn't prefer to grow up to be Ari Ben-Canaan played by the half-Jewish Paul Newman, rather than the rabbi, let's say, in *Fiddler on the Roof*?

And what about the men here in America? Our ancestors here sought most of all—if not for themselves then for their children and grandchildren—to be real Americans. And that came to mean, for most Jews, speaking English well, learning how to play and appreciate sports, achieving security of person and of possessions. In the most famous novel about a male immigrant, Abraham Cahan's *The Rise of David Levinsky*, the protagonist is able to amass a fortune only by abandoning Jewish tradition. Caught between the Old World and the New, Levinsky replaces traditional Judaism with capitalism, but is left loveless and longing for the world he abandoned.

The traditional high value placed on Torah—on study—was transformed into the high value placed on secular education. And that value would be, and has been, our ticket to success—but also in many ways our ticket out of a life deeply immersed in Judaism, particularly Jewish literacy. Jewish men can now do and be anything—and that may be both our blessing and our curse.

One of my favorite immigration generation stories is about football, believe or not, rather than baseball. Sid Luckman, of Columbia University and Chicago Bears' fame in the 1930s and 1940s, had a father who was—what else?—a tailor in New York. He rarely got to see his quarterback son play football, but one Sunday the Bears were in New York playing the Giants at the Polo Grounds. Luckman arranged for his parents to have seats on the 50-yard line. For most of the first quarter, things went smoothly. But then on one play, the Bears' pass protection broke down.

Giant defenders rushed in, and Luckman had to scramble, to dodge the tacklers before they could get to him. As he was running back and forth, trying to avoid these great, big linemen, his father's voice suddenly called out from the sidelines, "Sidney, let them have the ball. I'll buy you another one."

Jewish fathers are still buying the balls, but today they too know the rules. With little left to prove on the Americanization front, what are Jewish men to do about their Jewishness? Many Jewish women, newly empowered, are ready to take on all roles. But what's a Jewish world without active Jewish men?

Can images of Jewish men be helpful in some way? Some recent images may be instructive. The Hank Greenberg documentary has succeeded beyond expectations—who can't love a Jewish sports hero, especially one so talented, and one forced to counter anti-Semitism? Even our latest Jewish sports hero from the Olympics, Lenny Krayzelburg, interests us primarily because he emigrated from the Ukraine, and states clearly that his family left to escape anti-Semitism. But where are other contemporary American Jewish sports or other heroes for our sons? Surely they're out there, but their Jewishness is often closeted. That's why the movie *Keeping the Faith* was so right on target, and so frustrating. Here was a perfectly cool, totally American Jewish male who cared about his Judaism, even became a rabbi. But here was a movie that—while it got that part right—still felt obliged to downplay sexual responsibility and deprecate Jewish women. This is also one of the reasons why, partisan politics aside, Jews were excited this summer about Senator Lieberman's candidacy. He was a normal, successful politician who was clearly Jewish, and not embarrassed about being so, who embodied professional success while observing Shabbat. A male Jewish role-model—not someone who is simply Jewish by origin, whose Judaism is barely breathing. And we need many more such role-models—for our sons and our daughters—and not only of the Modern Orthodox variety. We Reform Jews too have a legacy to leave our children.

If Judaism is still to matter (for mere survival is not really the issue, but rather whether being Jewish matters in any significant way is what's at stake), then Jewish men must build on the multiplicity of traditions they inherit. They inherit the love of scholarship embodied and encouraged by the rabbis, and the ideal of *menschlichkeit*—the belief that values such as integrity, decency, and kindness are what we really want to teach and model for our children. They inherit the self-confidence and pride of the early (and even later) Zionists, their Hebraic literacy, their connections to our land and our people, combined with physical strength. Adult men must be found in the synagogue and within the religious school, serving as teachers and role models for Jewish boys. We should continue to recognize that even, and maybe especially, in today's world, Judaism has something unique to say about what it means to live a good life, what it means to make a better world, and what it means to be a man. As my friend Rabbi Gary Schoenberg has written about the movie *Sunshine*, "Jewish men must celebrate who they are in order to find manhood."

Jewish men and Jewish women must work together to build our Jewish future. Inclusiveness means not only bringing women into the inner circles, but also keeping men there as well. We Jewish women are not replacements or substitutes; we don't want to be the bullpen coming in to save the game the starting pitcher has failed. We're all on the same team. This is one of the reasons why, unlike some other rabbis, I will never make my bat/bar mitzvah class gender-exclusive —and why perhaps we need to create an additional program called "Adult Confirmation" or "post bar-mitzvah" for you guys out there who long ago became a bar mitzvah.

In our Jewish world, we have finally learned, thank God, to restore Sarah, at least through midrash, to the Akedah story. And the matriarchs have been added in the amidah, and lots of women become b'not mitzvah at a later age. But like God and the Jewish people, both men and women are partners in the covenant. Leaving patriarchal inequality behind should not require leaving men behind. God prevented Abraham from sacrificing Isaac long ago. Because Isaac was necessary, because Isaac was important, because Isaac was the future. Each child, male or female, is precious. That is our lesson, too—and our challenge.

Man Enough

Stephen S. Pearce

God is a woman! At least that is what comedian Carlos Mencia suggests. After all, when you look at the world around you—the beautiful flowers, puffy clouds, colorful tropical fish, cuddly animals, painted gossamer butterfly wings, and brightly colored seashells—you find the imprint of a feminine creator. Not withstanding the pain of creation, women still create and nurture; and all they ask for is to be considered "mother earth." Conversely, if God were a man, the world would be entirely populated by sharks, ferocious tigers, porcupines, violent storms, and then all men would look to win special effects awards.

Although I do not believe that God has gender or human shape, nevertheless a strong case can be made for a female God because, in addition to a feminine hand in creation, women relate better to matters of faith and the spirit and are often more engaged by religious life than men are. This bleak view of men is exacerbated by those who devalue bygone eras when men's religious participation and leadership were preeminent. For example, I recently attended a lecture on biblical personalities given by a feminist author. I was quite taken aback by her portrayal of biblical males as easily beguiled, hapless milquetoasts, enticed by strong, determined, action-oriented women who used their wily ways to get what they wanted in order to preserve and transmit Israelite religion. The lecturer even praised the patently shameful behavior of Delilah, a hired gun who seduced and betrayed Samson; Bathsheba, who became pregnant by King David and then did not object when David arranged for the murder of her husband Uriah; and Jezebel, who engineered the murder of Naboth to allow her husband, King Ahad, to take possession of Naboth's coveted vineyard.

I was appalled. Nothing in the speaker's approach could be further from the truth, because biblical religion is androcentric. In general, women mentioned in the Bible are not portrayed in a favorable light. Only occasionally does a Rebecca, a Deborah, or an Esther appear on center stage. Men, on the other hand, are the movers and shakers—they think grand thoughts, pronounce and transmit the truisms they construct; they philosophize, command, care for the clan, instruct sons in the ritual, rite, and sacrament, keep the communal history and cult secrets, influence public opinion, dominate and oppress challengers, fight the battles, and build cities. Women, in this culture, are tangential and silent.

The Binding of Isaac in the Rosh HaShanah Torah reading can easily be interpreted as a nomadic father indoctrinating his son in cultic secrets. Men of bygone eras instructed their sons in manliness—how to be men, how to offer sacrifices and connect with the deity, how to influence the forces of nature to ensure that rains arrive on schedule and crops mature in due season. Men were visible and present; men were mentors who taught boys about being men.

It has taken millennia for women to achieve parity with men. However, whether you consider patriarchal society to be a positive or a negative, the role that men play today in fathering, religion, and civic responsibility raises some serious concerns. There is recognition that the absence of a significant male often results in a search for manliness. Insufficient fathering can result in amateur males who fake masculinity, doing whatever it takes to look and feel like a man, but never quite knowing how. The craving of masculinity carried to extreme becomes "machismo," a word derived from the Greek word for "battle." Macho men are always trying to feel man enough, but invariably sense that something is missing. It is a vicious cycle. Deficiency of fathering makes it difficult for men who have not had adequate models to provide their own sons with instructions on how to achieve hard-earned manliness, leaving the next generation of sons ill-prepared for male roles. Pat Conroy's classic film *Prince of Tides* exposes the secret shame, loneliness, and despair that "men feel when they have not been anointed by their fathers, when they don't find heroism inside themselves, when they can't reveal to one another how inadequate they feel, and when they are dependent upon women who don't understand their secret inadequacies."[1]

The Iowa Fox tribe of Native Americans considers being a real man to be "The Big Impossible." And, of course, no man who sets out to achieve the big impossible, total masculinity, can ever be man enough.[2] Thus it is no wonder that men who struggle with their own masculinity are ambivalent about being present in their own families and being there for their sons. They are also hesitant to play any significant role in both religious and secular life. This is particularly noticeable in lower socioeconomic groups. But in all social strata, men today absent themselves from participation not only in their families, but in many social and religious configurations. Furthermore, we have witnessed the decline of the male breadwinner as the primary wage earner as a generation of women floods the paid workforce, resulting in the concomitant decrease in discretionary time for outside of home and work activities. Furthermore, the overloading of home by entertainment, communication, and workplace technology—cable television, faxes, PlayStations, DVDs, the Internet, and cell phones—has rendered ineffective what was once a haven from a heartless world. Civic and religious disengagement, particularly by men, are symptomatic of this new reality.

A recent publication, *Wrestling With Jacob and Esau: Fighting The Flight of Men; A Modern Day Crisis for the Reform Movement*, discusses disengagement and disappearance of male teenagers and adult worshippers, learners, Torah students, and religious education instructors.[3] Temple youth groups are increasingly filled with females who wonder where their male counterparts are. Religion has increasingly come to be perceived by many men and boys as being a female province that favors the needs and interests of women. This is especially puzzling because this phenomenon is absent in traditional male-dominated Orthodox congregations, where men continue to play important roles.

The disengagement and disappearance of men are also noted in many churches. David Murrow, author of *Why Men Hate Going to Church*, suggests that the trappings of contemporary culture are "driving men away"[4] from organized worship. "Church is sweet and sentimental, nurturing and nice. Women thrive in this environment."[5] Men do not, he writes. Everything, from the compulsion to participate in singing to the pastel tones and frilly accoutrements of the modern sanctuary, spells trouble keeping men in the fold. Murrow calls churches "spiritual sorority houses." Even more stinging is his assessment that these institutions have become a hostile environment to men, particularly "masculine men" who are uncomfortable in the feminized atmosphere of the typical church designed to appeal to their greatest constituency—women. Though the top leadership is often male, women constitute the backbone of most churches, representing an ever-increasing percentage of the membership and even more of the volunteer force. The claim is that men want an authentic faith experience but find matriarchal church services to be boring and irrelevant. They want to be challenged, but they're only challenged to be good husbands and fathers.

Murrow's Web site *churchformen.com* offers a number of compelling statistics:

- The typical U.S. congregation draws an adult crowd that's 61 percent female, 39 percent male across all age categories.
- On any given Sunday almost 25 percent of married, churchgoing women will worship without their husbands.
- Midweek activities often draw 70 to 80 percent female participants. [At Temple Emanu-El of San Francisco, nineteen women and two men attended our recent Elul retreat.]
- The majority of church employees are women.
- As many as 90 percent of the boys who are being raised in church will, by their twentieth birthday, abandon it, never to return.
- More than 90 percent of American men believe in God, but only two out of six attend church on a given Sunday. Those who do attend do so to keep their wives, mothers, or girlfriends happy, or simply out of habit.
- The majority of men who attend church are largely unaffected by what they hear and do nothing during the week to grow their faith.
- Relatively few churches are able to establish or maintain a vibrant men's ministry.

Murrow suggests a list of no-nos that make men flee. He recommends not:

- Asking people to hold hands or hug one another.
- Trotting out children to sing or perform, because it reinforces the notion that church is for kids.
- Encouraging emotional displays.
- Asking people to stand up and introduce themselves.
- Beating up on men for being lousy husbands and fathers.
- Using "churchy" language that does not conform to regular men's language.

Liberal Jews are witnessing these same winds of change that Protestant denominations are experiencing. When I was ordained by the Hebrew Union College, the first woman rabbi was a member of my class. Over the years, the ratio of women-to-men candidates has grown as increasing numbers of women have entered the rabbinate. For many years, we wondered when women rabbinical students would outnumber the men. That tipping point finally occurred in 2005 when 71 percent of the newly admitted students were female. In the same year, 66 percent of the new students at the Conservative Jewish Theological Seminary were women. The cantorate has already become an almost exclusively female calling. The ratio is not any different in other constituencies of the Reform Movement. For example, in 2005, 88 percent of the ninth grade teenagers who participated in the Union for Reform Judaism's Youth Leadership Camp program were female. The numbers are similar at the URJ summer camps for children, where girls vastly outnumber boys.

Is there any hope for men and boys, or are they doomed to disappear from the religious landscape? Male bonding may be seen as some kind of primitive cultic ritual, but the truth is that men need to be reengaged in order to enrich religious life and to foster connections between men and their maleness. It is not a simple task, as Margaret Mead once observed: "Motherhood comes naturally, but fatherhood must be learned."

The era of the temple Brotherhoods and men's club bowling leagues is long gone, but there must be a way to bring men back, not only into the religious landscape but also into family life and civic discourse. It will not be an easy task because it forces reexamination of basic assumptions about feminism, male education, and why contemporary institutions, including synagogues, fail to attract men. Furthermore, it is difficult to address men's issues without making it seem as if women should be sidelined. As my colleague Rabbi Jeffrey Salkin, author of *Searching for My Brothers: Jewish Men in a Gentile World*, notes, "We haven't figured out how to reenfranchise (men) without disenfranchising (women)."[6] If we hope to foster a healthy society, then we need to find a way to invite boys and men back into the mainstream. If men's spiritual needs are being ignored, then we need to find out what they are and what we need to do to meet them. Our national movement is experimenting with male-only worship, in spite of the discomfort male-only ritually related activities create. At Temple Emanu-El, we have held very successful annual retreats for men, but the success of the follow-through provided by additional programs during the rest of the year has been modest. I admit that I am stumped.

Some of the suggestions to reengage men are downright silly. *Churchformen.com* suggests a "Big Iron Sunday" with a Harley parked in the church lobby or a "God for the Guys Sunday," or a "Men's Huddle." An Essex, New Jersey, church held a football service with women playing cheerleaders and the pastor, who prefers the title "head coach" to "senior pastor," dressed in a numbered jersey.

There are a number of questions we need to answer in order to engage men in Jewish life. How do we help fathers and sons talk about God, faith, and Torah as easily as they do about football or golf? How do we get the message across that men who are drawn to faith are not sissies? How come fathers are present at soccer games but not at temple? How do we put an end to fathers' drive-by-Judaism—dropping children off and then going for a run, tennis, bike ride, or breakfast?

I would like to convene a community of strong, institutionally-savvy men who could sit down together and brainstorm innovative solutions to this problem, but I do not know if anyone would come. I am aware that there are some long-running private men's groups that focus on relationships and not programs, where men can speak freely and frankly about emotional and spiritual issues that are unique to men. I would like to learn why they work and what formula for success we could utilize from them.

I am not prepared to give up on men, and that is why I am appealing to you to help figure out what to do. At this sacred time of the year, the question of how to empower men to step back in is in the forefront of my mind, perhaps because tomorrow we will walk with Abraham and Isaac. *Va-yeilchu sh'neihem yachdav*—"The two of them walked together" (Genesis 22:8). Even though the beginning of the narrative has them starting off together, at the end of the narrative each returns alone. The only way that a son can reach maturity and individuality in order to go off on his own and take his rightful place in society is to begin walking to the mountain summit hand-in-hand with his father; a contemporary man cannot bypass the synagogue to get there. On Rosh HaShanah, we listen to this narrative, mindful of the disappearance of Jewish men. I wonder what would have happened if Abraham had dropped Isaac off at Mount Moriah and then went off to play tennis. In this New Year, let us consider how to strengthen the powerful bonds like the one that linked Abraham and Isaac, links that can once again connect men—fathers and sons in a community of faith.

Connecting Men to Judaism: The Need for a Comprehensive Cultural Shift

Michael Holzman

When we talk about "connecting men to Judaism," what is our goal? I mean the big goal. If we simply aim to increase numbers in order to equalize proportions, we hollow out our Judaism, reducing our heritage to a series of measurements and statistics. So, what is the real goal? We want to connect Jews—men and women—with the all possibilities for reflection, expression, action, and transformation that can be found in the breadth of Jewish tradition. We want our synagogues to be places that facilitate those connections. At synagogues, connections happen in the context of expectations, behaviors, language, symbols, jokes, and power structures. For the purpose of this article, I will call these factors the "culture" of the synagogue, though I'm sure an anthropologist would take issue with my use of the word. For some reason, in many synagogues, or at least parts of those synagogues, the culture does not seem to be facilitating male connections as well as female connections. I propose that in addition to all of the other factors synagogue leaders consider in their decision making—the balance between classical, traditional, new age, and contemporary styles; the use of Hebrew; economics; diversity of class, race, and sexual orientation; generational trends; and ethical imperatives—we add the issue of men. In a women's Rosh Chodesh group, such connection, obviously, is not a concern, because for a Rosh Chodesh group, the goal is explicitly to connect women and only women. But at services, meetings, Torah study, and other activities, the culture needs to connect everyone. If it does not, then a change must occur.

Women added themselves to the list of communal priorities over a generation ago. What is interesting is that for women the issue was hardly limited to participation and access. Of course, for most of Jewish history, women were excluded from public leadership in the synagogue, but when most of American Jewry broke away from the Orthodoxy of the cities and moved to the suburbs, our trajectory followed the same path as that of other American religious groups: women began to fill the pews. As the primary caregivers for a baby boom of religious school students, women filled synagogues. By the 1960s and 1970s, women were also demanding greater access to leadership. While feminism grew out of this demand, it quickly came to include a drive for the consideration of women's perspectives and experiences in how we think about theology, practice liturgy, create community, and engage in study and action. Not only did the women want into the boardroom, but they wanted to change the culture of what happened there. While sexism, ignorance, restriction, and exclusion still exist throughout much of the American Jewish landscape, feminism has succeeded. It has changed the culture.

In contrast, thousands of years of male public leadership and power obviate the need for a similar drive for inclusion. Since men had been inserting their perspectives into texts, liturgy, and law for generations, the assumption was that Judaism spoke to male needs. For millennia men were the *subjects* of Jewish text. But as feminism has shifted expectations, comfort levels, cultural norms, and methods, many men wind up confused. Manhood today is mired in a bog of unpredictable expectations, unreliable measures of self-worth, tangled social norms, and muddied concepts of appropriate behavior. Each week brings another popular article about how men (and the women who want to love them) try to navigate their way through this new and challenging terrain. Today men are only partly the subject, as they are also now objects tossed about in this world of newly questioned expectations. The old texts do not speak adequately to today's men. And since we have had power for so long, the idea of special consideration seems counterintuitive to many.

In order for synagogues to create a culture that successfully connects men to Judaism, both communal leaders and the men they serve need to rethink outdated notions of male centrality in our tradition. We can no longer assume that generations of male domination will speak to contemporary conditions. We can no longer assume that male leadership of the past will enable male participation in the present.

At the same time, this kind of cultural shift requires that men also change the way they see themselves. Many men may feel the sense of disorientation in society, but few have a compass or GPS to confirm and explain the emotion. Those (missing) tools would be the products of a gender consciousness, but, unlike women, whose exclusion was a constant reminder of gender's power, men often lack an awareness of gender. They do not realize how this important aspect of identity sets social expectations and boundaries. To really reach men, we need to raise consciousness about gender's importance to men, just as the feminists of a generation ago raised consciousness about gender's oppression of women.

If fifty years ago I was to have asked a group of men "What does it mean to be a man?" I would have likely received quizzical stares. Then, the expectations of manhood were assumed and understood. Men did not think about being men because most had little incentive to imagine any other form of existence. Because men have historically benefited from the privileges of their gender, they could afford to ignore its existence. Groups in power generally do not recognize the factors that grant the power. For example, in surveys about racism, white people have much more positive attitudes about race relations than African Americans. Because whites enjoy the advantage of race, they often fail to see differences in race.[1] I argue that men did not see masculinity, and therefore they could not describe how it affected their actions, choices, perspectives, relationships, and beliefs. When men begin to see how being men affects their lives, they will look for resources that help them make sense of their manhood. If synagogue culture has adequately evolved to address these questions, men will find the connection to spirit and soul that synagogues offer. This kind of communal change depends on a few initial steps.

First, for men to describe and understand masculinity, they will have to tap into the authenticity of personal experience. Men have been denying this authority for most of human history. As men encountered an experience worthy of note, they have used their power to externalize that note. When an issue arises, men have been trained to move it outside, study it academically, profit from it economically, analyze it psychologically (on others—or on women even, à la Freud), or pontificate upon it politically. In Judaism, male desires and concerns have been expressed through public rituals and texts. If a man could not generalize the personal in this way, then he knew to hide it in the realm of the private. If individual experience could not apply to all men, then it did not deserve mention. The middle ground, the sharing of experiences amongst men, the reliance upon the personal experience, was either squelched by the individual or co-opted by the community. The two realms were mutually exclusive; the private realm was not shared, and the public realm was not seen as personal. To ask men to share experience is to validate a new source of authority—the private self—that most men have been trained to distrust in their quest for public authority. The feminist movement has taught us that the authority of experience can lead to a rich and deep spiritual existence. Therefore once we see masculine experience, we need to learn how to talk about it. All of the remnants of external masculinity of the past can serve as catalysts for an internal reaction in the future.

Second, we need to create a safe environment in which to express the narrative of masculinity. We need to develop the language and the markers and the communal norms that advertise our openness to a healthy focus on men. And we need to eliminate the norms (be they political correctness, egotism, sexism, stereotyping, or plain insensitivity) that defeat a man's attempt at openness. We need not fear the labeling of a subject, text, prayer, or issue, as a derivation or reaction to a male experience. Why not describe Jacob and Esau as brothers—not just siblings, but brothers—whose ambition can ultimately lead to betrayal? Does this exclude women? To some extent, yes. That is why we read the Torah every week and every year. Next year we can talk generically or talk about sisters. And even when we focus on men, we often include women in the focusing group. We hear their perspective on watching their brothers, fathers, uncles, and sons. A focus on men need not exclude women entirely.

Unless, of course, it does. Unless we need to create that all-male space, that group or gathering dedicated to men only. Should this be the norm? Absolutely not (more on that later). But for some men, comfort will be most effectively achieved only with other men. And comfort will lead to security, introspection, opening, revelation, and ultimately to meaning. And that is our goal. So the all-male space is a tool we should not be afraid to call upon.

Third, the welcoming of Jewish men ought to inspire new forms of creativity. Every cultural change inspires new texts. Zionism helped us see the Maccabees differently. The *Shoah* gave new meaning to Lamentations. The civil rights struggle transformed our celebration of the seder. Feminism resuscitated Dina, the literally raped and figuratively suffocated child of Israel. These are just tiny examples of how historic and social changes have inspired Jewish creativity; and a new focus on men, a new men's narrative, should cause us to do the same.

Fourth, all of this talk of a focus on men requires a new men's ethics. Let's be honest. We Jews have a three-thousand-year tradition of excluding women from all forms of public power in Jewish life. This demands male awareness of our tendency toward any recurrence of female exclusion. We cannot assume a particular aspect of Judaism speaks only to men unless we name it as such. For example, I recently heard an extremely prominent scholar of Judaism expound upon the *Sh'ma* before a group of rabbis. He spoke from an entirely male perspective even to the extent of discussing male sexual experience. The use of masculine experience to explain the *Sh'ma* is not a problem, but when the scholar assumes he speaks for everyone he crosses the line. Since he did not specify that he was speaking only about male experience, his assumptions put only men at the center and marginalized women in the room. So as we propose a new focus on masculinity, we do so with a new ethics of specificity. This leaves the norm as neutral or balanced and allows us to claim as ours what is particularly male.

In addition, ethics demands that we discover those parts of male desire and experience that nurture *and* those that destroy. Writers like Robert Bly and Sam Keen have lamented the rise of the "soft" man, advocating a return to manliness, ferocity, strength, and toughness. Those qualities may be helpful and they may nurture men's souls, but we also know that they have the power to abuse. Since our history is riddled with men who have abused that power, as we reconsider masculinity, ethics demands that we anticipate masculinity's potential for excess. The trick is to embrace, promote, and utilize those male traits that will empower and welcome our community members, but as leaders we must always be ready to nip the bud of negative male behavior.

Finally, the best way to avert the historic propensity to male destructive behavior is to examine it. Things like the exclusion of, prejudice against, objectification of, and the abuse of women are historic male behaviors. We should ask ourselves why. For example, Riv Ellen Prell's masterful analysis of the history of Jewish stereotyping between men and women shows how we projected upon the opposite sex the exact images we feared non-Jews projected upon us. For example, as non-Jews criticized rising immigrant Jewish success and wealth, Jewish men focused that criticism on women by labeling them overly materialistic. Eventually this critique became the stereotype of the JAP. When we examine this blame shifting, we learn about men's own insecurities and desires for acceptance. By teaching men to deconstruct their own bad behavior, we discover the deeper struggles of self-image and understanding. These are the angels with whom we struggle in the night, but they are also the angels that offer blessings upon daybreak.

This road to culture change is no small task for any segment of the Jewish community. The examination of Jewish masculinity has been tiny and narrow in comparison to the attention and resources devoted to other major topics of Jewish life. I had more educational sessions in rabbinical school on transgenderism (not that there's anything wrong with that) than I did on men! As we create a culture that considers masculinity in its planning, the above steps—the use of male experience, the careful creation of safe male spaces, the rise of Jewish male creativity, and the application of a new male ethics—should facilitate men's connection to the treasure and meaning that is Judaism.

As our communities develop this changed culture, some easy tools will be the occasional use of stereotypical male activities—softball games, sukkah building—and the development of all-male spaces—Brotherhood, Men's Club, *Kiddush Lavanah* (blessing of the new moon) groups. These are stepping stones, useful ones that communities and individuals will always need in order to explore and express changing masculinities. We may use them, but we should not forget the goal—the big goal. The goal we all share, of creating a culture that enables all of us—men and women alike—to enhance our lives and our souls to the richness and meaning of Jewish tradition and creativity, and thus to become vehicles for the betterment of the world. How can we be serious about that goal—or any goal of the soul—without a culture that notices the gender of half the population? We can't.

Where Do We Go from Here? One Woman's Perspective . . .

Elyse Goldstein

There is no doubt that the proliferation of women's study groups, Rosh Chodesh groups, and resources for those exploring the issues of gender and Judaism attests to the explosion not only of interest in the subject, but to the extent of seriousness in pursuing it. Twenty years ago, "women and Judaism" courses were a fad, a nod to the populist culture, and an appeasement to "uppity" Sisterhood ladies questioning their traditional role in the synagogue.

Today, there is hardly a congregation, school, youth group, or women's organization without some scholarly or rabbinic investigation of this topic in its regular curriculum.

Now that we have "women and Judaism" courses, we can see that we have been studying "men and Judaism" all along, mistakenly believing we had been learning "just Judaism." We have assumed that what we received was a neutral form of Judaism. There is no such thing as "neutral" or "just Judaism," because by hearing the same stories retold by women, by being at the same events led by women, by simply sitting in the pews and looking up to see women in front of us, we have grown to understand that the Judaism we inherited was filtered through men and the male experience.

In the early years of the new studies in "women and Judaism," the questions centered around equality and equal access, and the early cry of "Jewish women's lib" was for the same opportunities, responsibilities, and access to resources as men. The issue seemed simple enough; the biological differences between men and women should not translate themselves into social barriers. Although men and women differ biologically, they are essentially the same. Thus both proponents and opponents of early "women's lib" defined equality as sameness.

Today's "women and Judaism" has entered a second phase. We no longer believe that to be equal to men religiously and spiritually we have to be like men. Indeed the question has come from its original roots in equal access. We now ask if it is possible to *specialize* as women while we *equalize* as women. We want to know if there is a unique "women's way" of seeing and hearing the text, of practicing the traditions, of living the rituals, that might be different from what we have received. We are no longer so completely convinced that women and men are essentially the same. Do we see and experience the world differently than men do because we are women? Does being female so influence our perceptions of ourselves that it also colors the way we perceive the rest of life and everything around us? If so, how does gender affect our religious life?

Do not assume that "women and Judaism" is no longer an issue, is over and done with, in the egalitarian movements. Though the Reform Movement began ordaining women in the 1970s, with the Reconstructionist and Conservative Movements following suit, the "women and Judaism" question has not gone away with the advent of equal access. For egalitarianism does not insist upon women's voices as *women* being heard, women's perspectives *as women* being sought, women's experiences *as women* being recorded. It assumes a spiritual equality, a halachic equality, even a ritual equality, but it has not yet dealt with the question of *difference*. . . .

Men, Sexuality, and Integration

The Issues

So much has changed for women in the Jewish world over the last decades that it is tempting to say the "women's question" is over. Women are rabbis in the Reform, Conservative, and Reconstructionist denominations and present in the leadership of Orthodoxy. Women serve as congregational presidents and as director of national organizations. Jewish education for girls is practically a universal given now in the entire Jewish world. So where do we go from here?

Three areas remain critical challenges for the new generation of female Jewish leadership. One is the challenge of male reaction and male inclusion into the growing network of "women's spirituality" and the advances of women into Jewish life. The second is the area of Judaism and sexuality and, with the increasing visibility of gays and lesbians in the Jewish world, a growing awareness of their spiritual needs and particular experiences and inclusions, as well. And the third is the ultimate task of integrating our female selves with our Jewish selves.

Jewish Masculinity

For many years the Jewish community has held a unique definition of masculinity. While others favored brawn, we valued brains. Our national and historical heroes are rabbis and learned men, statesmen, holy men, and miracle workers. Jews never idolized men of physical power, aggression, warfare, or cruelty. Why?

There is a logical historical reason. For so long Jewish men were powerless vis-à-vis the general society, and there was no way to "compete" with the masculine norms of the non-Jewish world. Stripped of their rights to bear arms in a violent society, deprived of voting rights until Emancipation, constrained in their choice of careers and professions, how were Jewish men, noncitizens, non-landed, non-gentry, to define themselves if not in opposition to the prevailing ideas of masculinity in their time? Aviva Cantor writes:

> On the one hand, there was a necessity for Jewish men to compensate for having been deprived of power vis-à-vis the men of the general society. Exile deprived them of the ability to engage in physical aggression and of using it to defend women and children and the community from attack. Exile reduced men to the powerlessness associated with women. . . . The rabbis ingeniously resolved this conflict by changing the concept of what constituted male power, and even more fundamentally (since power is part of the definition of manhood) what constituted masculinity. They stripped male power of the glorification and practice of violence, of rugged individualism, rapacious exploitation, machismo, rampant cruelty, conquest, military prowess, physical heroism, and the abuse of women. They

redefined manhood itself in terms of commitment to and achievement in learning Torah. Thus they replaced the classic patriarchal definition of masculinity, of man-as-macho fighter, with the alternative definition of man-as-scholar.[1]

Man-as-scholar became the Jewish form of machismo, and so it essentially remains to this day. But this redefinition was not without its price. To retain some sense of elitism, to be sure the learning of Torah was utterly attractive as a central element of self-definition for men, it also served as a bonding experience for men. The yeshivahs thus became places where men would go to "retreat" from the world at large, and also from the world of women. The synagogue, not the battlefield, became the place where men could prove their mettle. This was not possible if women were accorded the same privileges and opportunities there.

Today, many other definitions of masculinity are open to men. The synagogue is no longer a proving ground for masculinity. Because of that, it has also suffered. Many have noticed the "flight" of men from egalitarian synagogues as more and more women [take on] leadership roles. What is this flight about? Is it about the last male bastion being stormed, or about the feeling of not being "needed" anymore, or about a male devaluation of something as soon as it becomes open to women, or about a genuine frustration with the "feminization" of today's Judaism? These are questions that must be answered by the men who take their Judaism seriously and who wish the next generation of boys to do so as well.

MEYERS LIBRARY
REFORM CONG. KENESETH ISRAEL
OLD YORK RD. & TOWNSHIP LINE
ELKINS PARK, PA 19027

Reform Jews Examining Ways to Retain Their Young Men

Debra Nussbaum-Cohen

There was a new option among the dozen kinds of worship services available last winter at the biennial convention of the North American Federation of Temple Youth, which attracted about 1,400 young Reform Jews to Los Angeles.

As always at the conventions, there were lots of choices: one service was totally in Hebrew, for example, another used meditation and another was tailored to gay men and lesbians.

But one service, offered for the first time, seemed a throwback to a different time. It was for men only.

Male-only services could be considered a paradox in the Reform movement, a denomination established in the United States in the 1870's with sexual equality at its core. It broke from tradition by introducing mixed seating, bringing women down from balconies and from behind the partitions that had separated the sexes in synagogue sanctuaries.

The Reform movement, now American Judaism's largest denomination, with some 1.5 million members, was also the first to ordain women as rabbis, in 1972.

But it is losing its young men.

That is enough of a concern that the Reform movement's major organizations recently formed a commission to study the matter, and the director of admissions at the movement's rabbinical seminary is leading the panel.

The class of 39 people that began rabbinical studies at the Hebrew Union College–Jewish Institute of Religion last fall has twice as many women as men. Still, of 1,888 members of the Reform movement's Central Conference of American Rabbis, only 432 are women.

Rabbi Michael Friedman, director of junior and senior high school programs at the Union for Reform Judaism, which serves its congregations, recently surveyed all of the movement's youth groups, leadership training, camping and Israel programs for teenagers and young adults.

Attendance records since 2003 showed that girls accounted for 57 percent to 78 percent of participants in each activity.

Rabbi Friedman said there had been a major cultural change in the past 25 years.

"The change has been not only who the leaders are but also in their leadership style," he said. "Before, it was always a man high up on a bimah wearing a big robe in a deep voice, a model of leadership that was male-only and top-down."

"With growing egalitarianism, which I totally support, we've seen a major cultural change," Rabbi Friedman said. "Those synagogues now have everybody sitting in a circle with someone playing a guitar sharing feelings. It's much more participatory. These are all good things, but they are styles that women may be more comfortable with than men."

"I don't think boys have a problem with it, but they don't necessarily see themselves there."

Peter LaRosa is one of those boys. A 16-year-old 11th grader in Brooklyn, he attended Hebrew school at a Reform temple, starting in third grade. But the day after his bar mitzvah, "he announced he was never setting foot in temple again," said his mother, Susan LaRosa. "He's kept to his word."

A lot of his friends continued going to the synagogue, Peter said, but "I decided to focus more on baseball and snowboarding than Judaism."

Like many other young people in the Reform movement today, Peter has one Jewish parent and one Christian. Each year his family celebrates both Christmas and Hanukkah, and Peter said he felt that "we're never fully Jewish," adding, "I never understand things at temple, so it didn't strike me as an interesting place to keep going."

Interfaith families account for a significant minority of members in some Reform synagogues and a majority of them in others. Those numbers amplify the challenges congregations face in reaching adolescent boys and young men, which are rooted in a complex set of issues, one expert said.

In liberal Judaism, "we have to find something that relates to the reality of what boys go through," said William Pollock, a psychologist on the faculty of Harvard Medical School and the author of *Real Boys: Rescuing Our Sons From the Myths of Boyhood*.

"They are struggling with who they are, with what masculinity means and what being a Jewish male means in American society," Mr. Pollock said.

"The denominational youth movements haven't tapped into things from that gendered perspective," said Mr. Pollock, who has been hired by an independent feminist Jewish organization, Moving Traditions, to explore the issue.

The problem does not seem to exist in Orthodoxy, whose public religious rituals are led exclusively by men, which allows boys to see an obvious place for themselves.

In 2002, Moving Traditions started a program of monthly celebrations for teenage girls called "Rosh Hodesh: It's a Girl Thing!" There are now 175 Rosh Hodesh groups around the country, whose activities are intended to foster self-esteem and Jewish identity.

"Many of us, because of the women's movement, had a sense of what girls want and need," said Deborah Meyer, executive director of Moving Traditions. "Ironically, now there's less known about adolescent boys. We wonder what do guys want?"

"We get asked all the time by our partner organizations with Rosh Hodesh groups for something for boys," Ms. Meyer said. "It's really an unmet need."

Moving Traditions recently started its own study of boys' needs and may develop some regular activity with both social and religious components just for them.

The Reform movement's initiative is approaching the problem in several ways. It is coming up with programming suggestions for its congregations to use at what it identified as six major entry points in synagogue life, including Hebrew school, bar mitzvah and holidays.

It also plans to help congregational educators learn how to distinguish between girls' learning needs and boys', and how to help the boys, Rabbi Friedman said. The initiative will also recommend that synagogues create mentoring programs pairing teenagers with boys preparing for their bar mitzvahs.

More male-only worship services may also be held in Reform settings, he said.

"We can't have a healthy, vibrant Reform Jewish community without men or without women," Rabbi Friedman said. "This is not about pushing women out and men retaking the high ground, but about creating space" for boys and young men.

When that happens it is a powerful thing, said Andrew Shoenig, who attended the men-only service at the Temple Youth convention.

"It was packed," said Mr. Shoenig, a freshman at Emory University and president of the youth group, which has about 10,000 members.

In ordinary services, "guys may not sing or chant as loudly" as girls do, he said. "The guys are just sitting there in many cases. So when we stuck 40 or 50 guys in a room, how was it that we became the loudest service there? The room was bursting with testosterone and energy."

"Maybe it's because guys didn't have to sing up an octave with a female song leader," Mr. Shoenig said. The setting "allowed us to just be comfortable and not have to worry about anything on the outside."

Section II

Young Men and Their Needs

Introduction

This section addresses a wide range of issues relating to boys and Reform Judaism. Topics of the section include: exploring the specific learning needs of boys and how Hebrew schools can meet their needs; two radically different ideas on what should be taught to boys as they become bar mitzvah; two pieces in which the authors offer their own insight into the difference between the needs of teenage boys and girls; an essay focused on the Jewish camping system and how it must strategically plan to meet the needs of boys; and finally a list of suggestions for programming that will meet the needs of young men.

Evie Rotstein's "Jewish Learning and Multiple Intelligences" addresses the issues that boys face while they are in formal Jewish educational settings. She explores the research available on multiple intelligences and the implications this has for the traditional models of teaching used in Hebrew school settings. She offers specific suggestions for Jewish education settings, suggestions to help young students of all kinds achieve the highest level of learning possible.

Dana Jennings's "A Letter to My Sons" was originally published in *Reform Judaism* magazine. His piece is written from the personal perspective of a Jewish father to his sons. For Jennings, "real men pray and sing and study and walk humbly with their God." Jennings challenges the idea that men's needs are not being met in the synagogue; instead, he asserts the counterthesis that men, in order to be fulfilled, must stretch themselves to participate in these activities, and only then will they be fulfilled.

In his piece "Bar Mitzvah with a Side Order of Testosterone," Rabbi Jeffrey Salkin asserts that the bar mitzvah is part of a process of becoming. He believes that the ritual needs to be reinvigorated and infused with activities that enforce the masculinity with which the boy is beginning to struggle. He understands that for a rite of passage to be successful, "adolescents need mentors, ordeals, tests, rituals, and community celebrations." Accordingly, he offers six suggestions for revamping the bar mitzvah.

Leonard Saxe and Shaul Kelner articulate what most parents of teenagers know intuitively. Their article "Teenage Boys and Girls: A Jewish World Apart" addresses the different orientations of adolescent boys and girls. They also explore the difference in levels of involvement between boys and girls vis-à-vis the Jewish community. Saxe and Kelner offer suggestions for how to best support teenagers within the Jewish community including the seldom considered solution of providing well-paying meaningful employment for teens in the Jewish community.

Melissa Zalkin Stollman's essay "Change It Up!—Creating an Appealing Youth Program for Your Male Teens" suggests the possibility of programming changes in NFTY and other organizations that could excite and interest teen boys, providing gender-specific as well as developmentally specific approaches. In addition, Zalkin Stollman argues that through early education we can also change the mindset of our teens and develop at an early age an appreciation and taste for Jewish learning. Identifying a number of key discoveries through experimentation in programming, the author provides both programming ideas and trends regarding retention of male teens.

In "Teen Brotherhood," Jason Freedman and Bobby Harris recount their experience creating successful programming for boys in youth groups and camp settings. These programs allow boys to express their emotions and to tell their personal stories to each other in a single-sex setting. In sharing their stories, the young men create a depth of bond otherwise unexplored. For those who believe that boys don't respond to such activities, this article provides a powerful counter-argument, grounded in real-world programming experience and participants reporting life-changing results.

In "A Look at Jewish Camping," Rabbi Daniel Zemel demands that camping needs to provide more activities for boys that promote and reward "maleness." His approach to maleness here is active and skill-driven: more camping in the sense of actually learning to pitch a tent or cook a meal, more active in terms of physically challenging activities. Rabbi Zemel ties this need for addressing "maleness" with activity and skills to the wider application of such skills. If our young men are to be able to truly contribute in *tikkun olam* activities such as rebuilding after Hurricane Katrina or building houses for the poor, they will need real tangible skills—from roofing to drywalling. He notes that a NFTY trip to Israel would be even more meaningful for our youth if they could use such skills to make a tangible contribution during their visit.

Each of these pieces in this section conveys ways in which we are not meeting the needs of our young men. It is clear that changes need to be systemic and widespread. Our authors may disagree regarding what steps should be taken, yet they agree that meeting the needs of our boys and young men is a top priority if we want to have healthy Jewish communities in which both men and women are involved and invested.

Questions for Discussion

As you read each piece, consider the following questions:

1. Compare the pieces that appear to disagree in this chapter. In what ways do they agree, and where do they disagree? What aspects do you accept or agree with?
2. What are the assumptions in the essay(s) that you have read? Where do those assumptions differ from your own understanding?
3. What do you believe your young men need? What experiences or observations have led you to this conclusion?
4. What programs would you like to see created that would meet our young men where they are and push them to grow?

Jewish Learning and Multiple Intelligences

Evie Rotstein

Eighty years after Alfred Binet developed a means of determining an objective measure of intelligence with the IQ test, Howard Gardner, a Harvard psychologist challenged this concept with his theory of multiple intelligences (MI theory). Gardner introduced a new approach to the conceptualization and assessment of human intelligence and broadened our understanding of human capacities and how people learn. In his book *Frames of Mind* (1983), Gardner suggests that intelligence is not necessarily numerically quantifiable, but rather is exhibited during a performance or problem-solving process and that intelligence should not be measured in isolation but rather in context/real-life situations.

According to Gardner's theory, each human being is capable of eight relatively independent forms of information processing, with individuals differing from one another in the specific profile of intelligences that they exhibit. Gardner determined the following eight intelligences:

- **Verbal-Linguistic Intelligence**: The capacity to use words both orally and in writing including the ability to manipulate syntax, semantics, and rhetoric.
- **Logical-Mathematical Intelligence:** The capacity to use numbers including sensitivity to logical patterns, categorization, classification, and hypothesis testing.
- **Spatial Intelligence:** The capacity to visualize, to graphically represent visual or spatial ideas involving a sensitivity to color, line, shape, form, and space.
- **Bodily-Kinesthetic Intelligence:** The ability to use physical skills such as coordination, balance, dexterity, strength, flexibility, and speed.
- **Musical Intelligence**: The capacity to perceive and produce melody, rhythm, and tone and analyze musical forms.
- **Interpersonal Intelligence**: The ability to perceive and distinguish the moods, intentions, motivations, and feelings of other people.
- **Intrapersonal Intelligence:** The capacity to be self-aware, to gain access to one's own feelings and emotional states.
- **Naturalist Intelligence**: Having the ability to be highly attuned to the natural world of animals, plants, and natural objects.

Gender and Multiple Intelligences

Research on learning has shown that students learn differently and that they process and represent knowledge in different ways. Studies indicate that there are significant differences between males' and females' preferences of intelligences. In the studies, males preferred learning activities involving logical and mathematical intelligences, whereas females preferred learning activities involving intrapersonal intelligence (Honigsfeld and Dunn 2003). The growing work in brain research has identified more than one hundred structural differences between male and female brains. The differences are both genetic and socialized. Following are some of the findings in which gender learning is affected by the structural and chemical differences in the brain.

- **Verbal/spatial differences**: Male brains have more cortical areas associated with spatial-mechanical functioning, and female brains have greater cortical emphasis on verbal-emotive processing. Females tend to think more verbally (Blum 1997).
- **Frontal lobe development**: The prefrontal cortex, which controls the decision-making areas of the brain, is more active and develops at an earlier age in females, allowing females to sit still, read, and write at an earlier age and be better at literacy in general (Rich 2000).
- **Chemical differences**: Neurological and chemical differences influence the tendency for females to be less competitive in their learning style, while males tend to be more impulsive and aggressive (Taylor 2002).

As Jewish educators we need to acknowledge that these scientific differences must be incorporated into the ways we design learning specifically for boys.

Religious Education and Gender Differences

In the recent study about American Jewish teenagers, sociologists Kadushin, Kelner, and Saxe (2000) reveal what many of us involved in Jewish education have observed for years. Their study of 1,300 students from ages 13–17 from the Boston area indicate that boys tend to be less interested in Jewish learning and Jewish activities such as youth groups, Jewish camping, and even Israel trips. In response to the question, "I have enjoyed my Jewish schooling," 30 percent of boys agreed while 39 percent of the girls agreed. The question posed about wanting to become more involved in Jewish life indicated that 25 percent of the boys agreed and 32 percent of the girls agreed.

The lack of participation by boys in such programs is consistent with the findings of teenagers from other religious affiliations. According to "Monitoring the Future," a large national survey of over 30,000 teenagers from grades 8-12 measuring religious service attendance and youth group participation, American adolescent girls are more involved than boys in religious activities. According to the data fully "14 percent more 12th grade boys than girls have never participated in a religious youth group" (Smith, Denton, Faris, and Regnerus 2002, p. 605). This difference mirrors a similar pattern of religious variation among adult men and women in the United States and other countries as well.

The question we must ask is how gender learning and multiple intelligence theory can inform both the effectiveness of our Jewish educational settings and other various informal Jewish activities.

Implications for Jewish learning

Our Jewish classrooms are generally a better fit for the verbal-linguistic, sit-still, take-notes, listen-carefully female student. There are a number of ways to design rich learning experiences that offer students the opportunity to perceive themselves as potentially smart on many levels. Based on their research, Saxe and Kelner (2001) ascertain that girls are more oriented to social activities and boys toward individual activities. Taking these findings into consideration, here are a few learning strategies that can make a difference for male students:

- Offer task-oriented discussions and interactions.
- Provide activities that include physical movement.
- Utilize spatial-visual aids to reinforce learning.
- Engage students in project-oriented learning tasks.
- Present many different topic choices within a unit of study.

Finally and perhaps the most salient suggestion for Jewish learning, which holds true for both girls and boys, is that our schools need to establish authentic purpose and meaningful, real-life connections to all that we teach.

I suggest that Jewish learning needs to be personally meaningful. Personal meaning-making is learning that connects an individual to Judaism and Judaism to the individual. Each learner must have the opportunity to make Jewish learning a Jewish living experience (Aron 2000; Kress and Elias 1998).

Conclusion

With the expanded understanding of human intelligence provided by Howard Gardner's MI theory and the evolving scientific knowledge about the brain, we are in a position to change the way we engage our male students in Jewish learning. This new awareness can assist us in providing new opportunities and fresh challenges for our schools and congregations.

References

Aron, I. 2000. *Becoming a congregation of learners.* Woodstock, VT: Jewish Lights Publishing.
Armstrong, T. 2000. *Multiple intelligences in the classroom.* Alexandria, VA: ASCD.
Blum, D. 1997. *Sex on the brain: The biological difference between men and women.* New York: Viking.
Honigsfeld, A., and R. Dunn. 2003. High school male and female learning-style similarities and differences in diverse nations. *Journal of Educational Research* 96 (4): 1-12.
Gardner, H. 1983. *Frames of mind.* New York: Basic Books.
Gardner, H., and T. Hatch. 1989. Educational implications of the theory of multiple intelligences. *Educational Researcher* 18 (8): 4-10.
Gurian, M., P. Henley, and T. Trueman. 2001. *Boys and girls learn differently: A guide for teachers and parents.* San Francisco: Jossey-Bass.
Kadushin, C., S. Kelner, and L. Saxe. 2000. *Being a Jewish teenager in America: Trying to make it.* Cohen Center for Modern Jewish Studies, Brandeis University. www.brandeis.edu/ije.
King, K., and M. Gurian. 2006. With boys in mind: Teaching to the minds of boys. *Educational Leadership* 64 (1): 56-61.

Kress, J. S., and M. J. Elias. 1998. It takes a kehilla to make a mensch: Building Jewish identity as part of overall identity. *Jewish Education News* 19 (2): 20-22.

Rich, B., ed. 2000. *The Dana brain daybook*. New York: The Charles A. Dana Foundation.

Saxe, L. 2005. *Why gender matters*. New York: Doubleday.

Saxe, L., and S. Kelner. 2001. "Teenage boys and girls: A Jewish world apart." *Sh'ma*, May.

Silver, H. F., R. W. Strong, and M. J. Perini. 2000. *So each may learn: Integrating learning styles and multiple intelligences*. Alexandria, VA: ASCD.

Smith, C., M. L. Denton, R. Faris, and M. Regnerus. 2002. Mapping American adolescent religious participation. *Journal for the Scientific Study of Religion* 41 (4): 597-612.

Smith, C., R. Faris, M. L. Denton, and M. Regnerus. 2003. Mapping American adolescent subjective religiosity and attitudes of alienation toward religion: A research report. *Sociology of Religion* 64 (1): 111-123.

Taylor, S. 2002. *The tending instinct*. New York: Times Books.

A Letter to My Sons

Dana Jennings

Dear Drew and Owen:

In today's culture, we like to think we have shattered most taboos. We talk to our children about sex, about drugs, about mental illness. Still, strangely, I don't hear much talk between fathers and sons about God, about faith, about Torah, about what it means to be a Jewish man. As the two of you stand proudly at the brink of full adulthood, I want to start that conversation.

As a Jew-by-choice, I feel like the man who falls in love with a brilliant and beautiful woman who is taken for granted by those who have known her for a long time—think Cinderella with a *kipah*. I don't want either of you to ever take Judaism for granted. Though you may not understand it as such now, being a Jew is a gift. *An absolute gift*.

But it's a gift that too often is abandoned in the back of the spiritual attic. We're struggling through a time when Jewish men are vanishing of their own volition from our communities. It saddens me to watch them shun their birthright, letting it rot and grow brittle like the leather on their grandfathers' *tefillin*, treating Judaism as if it were an ethnic accessory to be shrugged on and off at will . . . as just another entrée in the cultural buffet, rather than what it truly is: a profound covenant with the God of Abraham, Isaac, and Jacob.

We are trapped in a culture that sends the message that men of faith are sissies; the man who prays with heart and soul is somehow suspect. Well, boys, I'm here to tell you that real men *pray* and *sing* and *study* and *walk humbly* with their God.

As a man who has been stunned wide awake by Judaism, by Torah, I want the two of you to know soul-deep that real Judaism can suffuse each moment of each day—if you let it. You need to understand that some mornings when I pray I feel barely tethered to this earth. You need to understand that when I read that 20th-century prophet Abraham Joshua Heschel, he almost always carries me back with him to Sinai. You need to understand that when I look at the Hebrew script of Torah, I don't see mere letters; I see the ancient, transcendent tents of Jacob billow and snap.

Sure, it can be frustrating to be a man of faith in this culture of hollow desire. It is easier to obsess over how the Knicks and Lakers are going to do this season. To ooh-and-aah over the latest sleek idols made by BMW and Porsche. To admire your very expensive pecs in the mirror. To buy your season tickets to the local synagogue, and only show up for the big games—you know, Yom Kippur and Rosh Hashanah, and maybe the occasional bar or bat mitzvah. I don't want you to become men who think that Sunday morning softball and dropping the kids off at Hebrew school—drive-by Judaism—is what makes a Jew.

We are slaves to the culture of the self. To get ahead, we are told to brag, to polish our images into a kind of Golden Calf. But, boys, we were not made to praise ourselves. We were made to praise Adonai, made to praise all Creation. We have to let Torah—that holy turpentine—strip the varnish of falseness from our souls. We have to admit—and this is hard—that our mewling, pathetic self is not why the universe exists. Only in humility can we be open to the awe that the Holy Breath should inspire. In the same way that the Eternal contracted to make room for Man, so Man must contract his ego to make room for the Eternal.

There are so many ways to avoid the big questions, to shun God, to lead a Teflon life. Drew and Owen, don't become one of those men who spurn our tradition to chase wind: the candy-apple-red Hummer, the third home in Aspen, the trophy wife. The goal is to be the opposite of wanting. It's your souls that matter in the Economy of Holiness.

Our people survived slavery in Egypt, the razing of the Temple, pogroms and persecutions beyond reckoning, the Holocaust. But I put this question to you, my sweet Jewish sons: Can we survive a future of Jewish fathers who buy a new suit, sheepishly show up as strangers on bar or bat mitzvah day, awkwardly pass the Torah on to a still-unformed 13-year-old—and then never come back?

That very real image nearly makes me weep. I know some would write my deep feelings off as the zeal of a convert. But, boys, there's one last thing you need to understand: In this day and age, we're all Jews-by-choice.

Bar Mitzvah with a Side Order of Testosterone

Jeffrey K. Salkin

As Dennis Miller would say, I don't want to get off on a rant here, but my particular Jewish bugaboo is how we've added "ed" to certain terms. Like "Reform*ed*." Or, maybe even worse, "bar mitzvah*ed*." It is way too passive. Years of working with young people have taught me that bar and bat mitzvah is not only a noun signifying a status. In order to be a true rite of passage, it must be a process of becoming.

How can we re-invigorate bar mitzvah as a rite of passage, with particular emphasis on the maleness of the ritual?

A basic philosophy of rites of passage is that adolescents need mentors, ordeals, tests, rituals, and community celebrations.

First, the boy should discard his old life in some way, in order to symbolize his rebirth. Our bnei mitzvah candidates might give away their old toys or sell them in a garage sale, using the proceeds for a charitable cause.

Moreover, the bar mitzvah could discard some of the more childish versions of Judaism which he has learned. Jewish teenagers want a grown-up Judaism. They are ready for bigger truths. They are old enough to learn the "real" story of Hanukah, as opposed to the "jar of oil" story. Bar mitzvah might also be a time when kids give some of their old and usable religious textbooks to younger children in the religious school. We could invent a ritual for it at a worship service.

Second, the boy could create a set of questions that he wants the elders of his community to answer. A friend once said to me: "We are missing the wisdom of old men in the Jewish community." Have we become too professionalized? Can we restore a sense of tribal wisdom to Jewish life? Older laymen (not just rabbis, cantors, and educators) could teach Hebrew, Torah, and synagogue skills to younger boys in the community. More than that: the community could honor the elder-tutor at the bar mitzvah ceremony.

Third, the boy could take a solo trip in which he accepts that his boyhood is dying and that his manhood is emerging. Throughout religious history, the journey has been symbolic of maturation and change. Abraham journeys through the desert to come to the land of Israel. Moses journeys through the desert in order to begin his mission to save his people. The Israelites journey through the wilderness to get to the land of Israel.

A journey story: When I was nine years old, my parents permitted me to go with some "older boys" (all of eleven years old) on the train and subway to the old Polo Grounds to see the Mets.

True, it was not exactly a solo journey. And upper Manhattan is not exactly the desert. But I remember it as being a true rite of passage. I remember the day that my father let me drive on the expressway for the first time. As the dial moved up on the speedometer, my father sighed. At that moment he not only sensed my growing up; he could feel his own aging.

Our boys could take solo trips to local Jewish museums, restaurants, and other places of Jewish interest. (They should also take their cell phones, just in case . . .)

Fourth, the boy should experience the fullness of the life cycle. Years ago, a close relative of my great-uncle Harry died. One evening during the *shiva* mourning period, a boy in his early teens came to lead the *minyan* service. He went over to my great-uncle Harry and said to him: "May God console you on your loss." He then distributed prayer books to the mourners in the living room and began to lead the evening service. After the service was over, the boy went into the dining room, wrapped some *rugelach* in a napkin, shoved the little bundle in his pocket, returned to my great-uncle's side and shook the old man's hand, and left. I turned to my great-uncle and asked, "Who was that boy?" Uncle Harry shrugged his shoulders and answered, "A kid from the *shul*." That was how Harry identified the boy; as part of his religious community. The boy had truly become bar mitzvah; old enough to do mitzvot.

Fifth, there should be a physical challenge in some way. By and large, bar mitzvah is about intellectual preparation. Should there be physical adventures as part of bar mitzvah? For example, might bar mitzvah training include Jewish "Outward Bound" camping programs for bar mitzvah candidates? Could there be organized father-son outings, such as camping trips, rock climbing or bicycle trips as part of the bar mitzvah process? They could ask themselves: "How do we overcome obstacles and fears?"

The Jewish people has been disembodied in the Diaspora and it has looked to Israel for embodiment; for examples of Jews who use their bodies to build the Jewish people. The active, physical body must return to Jewish life.

Sixth, there should be a communal celebration; which is to say there should be a community. As Michael Gurian wrote in *A Fine Young Man*, "If a boy has no real clan in place before he enters adolescence, he's very likely to go out and find one that consumes him, tribalizes him, redirects him, even brainwashes him—a formal gang, a peer group that disaffects him, a cult, a media obsession."

America has depended on the myth of the rugged individual. To quote Bogart's character Rick in *Casablanca*: "I stick my neck out for nobody." But the rugged individual is a broken myth. We need other people. Boys in particular need to know that they need others and that they may express emotions. Boys need to hear the sages' advice: "Do not separate yourself from the community."

There is something here in the great folk love of bar mitzvah. The bar and bat mitzvah experience feels like a trial. A young person is growing up. The child struggles with learning Torah and then has to present it to a community.

It should not be irredeemably politically incorrect to say that boys and girls are different, especially in their approach to bar and bat mitzvah. Boys tend to parrot the folklore that bar mitzvah is "when I become a man." I have never heard a pre-bat mitzvah girl say that it's "when I become a woman." Perhaps girls are more in touch with the physical and emotional process of approaching womanhood. Moreover, boys view maturity as the onset of more privileges. Girls view their growth as the onset of more responsibility.

We don't have to entirely restore the cliché that bar mitzvah is when Jewish boys become men. An uncritical acceptance of the myth is not necessary. The very concept of manhood in American life today has become increasingly vague.

But there is massive potential in taking that transition from boyhood to manhood seriously. A re-imagined bar mitzvah process could be just what the doctor ordered.

Teenage Boys and Girls: A Jewish World Apart

Leonard Saxe and Shaul Kelner

Today's American Jewish teenagers are the first to grow up in an era when gender equality is both the law of the land and a principle of non-Orthodox Judaism. Just as our society has removed barriers to women taking leadership positions, so too have non-Orthodox Jewish movements removed barriers to women becoming rabbis and communal leaders. In the world of federations and Jewish philanthropies, gender neutrality is accepted at least in principle if not always in practice. The increasing prominence of women in visible public roles, however, has masked another important shift in the gendered experience of American Jewish life, one that is playing itself out among Jewish adolescents: teenage Jewish boys are rapidly exiting the playing field, leaving the girls to hold the ball.

Although young people in North America are perhaps the most studied and tested group of individuals who have ever lived, there is a surprising lack of systematic data about Jewish teenagers. We tried to redress the lack of information by surveying nearly 1,500 Jewish adolescents and their parents, asking about their lives, activities, and attitudes about school, religion, and family. Our goal was to understand how teens make sense of their Jewish and secular worlds and to examine how this changes over the course of adolescence. One of the most striking findings was that boys and girls often see their world in quite different ways. Consistently, we found that girls were more likely than boys to be active members of their Jewish communities, to espouse Jewish values, and to enjoy participation in the community; boys more readily bid farewell to Jewish involvement.

Affective versus Instrumental Orientations

Although both boys and girls were highly motivated to be successful, girls were more oriented to social activities and boys toward individual activities. These different orientations have been called affective versus instrumental orientation and reflect traditional views of women as nurturers and men as producers. Girls, in contrast to boys, place greater value on things such as family, finding meaning in life, working to correct social injustice, and being Jewish. Girls were also more likely to be involved in volunteer work. They were also more favorably disposed to school, less often bored and less likely to blow off either their assignments or entire days of school.

Involvement in Judaism/Jewish Community

Boys expressed consistently less interest in things Jewish, held more negative opinions about past Jewish experience, and generally considered Judaism more peripheral to their lives in comparison to girls. Boys were twice as likely to say that they saw their bar mitzvah as their graduation from their Jewish schooling. Judging by their participation in post-bar/bat mitzvah Jewish education, youth groups, and Israel experience programs, it does not appear that they are merely more negative in expressing their views. Indeed, boys participate less and, even when they do participate, enjoy it less and find it less meaningful.

Overall, we found that by the end of high school, nearly half of those who had become bar or bat mitzvah had little involvement in the Jewish community. They neither participated in formal Jewish education, nor informal programs such as youth groups, Jewish camps, or Israel trips. Although this trend applies to both boys and girls, it is more pronounced among boys and is accompanied by more negative attitudes. This should be a cause for concern.

Supporting Teenagers in the Jewish Community

This disproportionate withdrawal of teenage boys stems from a basic mismatch between their instrumental orientations and the Jewish community's affective presentation of self. Not everyone is looking for a Jewish identity-building experience, nor should one have to, in order to find an open door to Jewish life. Instead of demanding that teens first conform to a normative vision of Jewish involvement as an end in itself, the Jewish community can engage them by identifying and serving their needs.

The teenagers we studied, both boys and girls, live stressful lives; school, work, and social pressures are not trivial. Jewish organizations can help young people cope with the pressures of adolescence—providing physical outlets like sports and intellectual support like preparation for SATs. Some of these programs, like competitive sports, may attract more boys than girls and fill gaps in engagement that currently leave boys on the outside. Work contributes to teen pressures, as many teens are forced to choose between the jobs they love and the jobs that pay. The Jewish community can offer a better alternative: well-paying, meaningful employment within the Jewish community.

The disaffection of boys from Jewish life opens a window into a central fact of American Judaism: Except for a minority who make it their full-time profession, Jewish life in North America is primarily a voluntary activity, and meets affective rather than instrumental goals. In a society that defines itself by work, and judges success by material gains, Judaism is treated as something to be done in one's spare time, if at all. Boys are more likely than girls to take this as a cue to exit, but the problem transcends gender. It calls out for a response.

Change It Up!—Creating an Appealing Youth Program for Your Male Teens

Melissa Zalkin Stollman

Based on studies regarding multiple intelligences, as well as anecdotal evidence, youth workers have learned that typical Jewish youth programming is not appealing to male teens. Girls outnumber boys in most areas of participation in camping, local youth groups, regional NFTY programs, and summer travel programs. In most cases the split is about 58 percent female to 42 percent male. Female participation in these kinds of programming increases with age while that of males decreases; males make up only 35 percent of the population in Reform Jewish college programming. Even fewer young men participate in young adult programming after college. The Reform Movement must quickly change its mindset about teen programming and focus its energy on engaging young males before this ratio of female to male participation by teens and young adults widens even further.

In many congregations youth group participation starts as early as the seventh and eighth grades. The opportunity to join NFTY-based programming begins in the ninth grade. However, instead of signing up, boys are dropping out of religious life. Where are they going? Charles Kadushin, Shaul Kelner, and Leonard Saxe conducted a study published in December 2000 entitled "Being a Jewish Teenager in America: Trying to Make It," which looks at the kind of activities in which teens participate during their adolescent years. They found that boys engage in a range of activities during this time, but for most they are not Jewish activities. Teen males pursue activities in areas prioritized by the greater society such as athletics, academics, and work experience. While the Jewish community can serve as a place for teens to build their résumés with regards to work and leadership experience, males are less interested in signing up for these activities.

In addition, values expressed by Reform organizations like congregations, youth groups, and NFTY often do not appeal to male teens in the same way that they may appeal to females. NFTY's stated values are: Jewish education, worship, religious action, leadership development, Reform Jewish community, personal growth and ethics, the Jewish people, and the Land and State of Israel. The choice for NFTY to list these universal Reform Jewish values implies a youth event filled only with Jewish learning and religious programming. Such values do not correspond with the general culture of America's males, which typically puts an emphasis on goals and outcomes rather than process and personal growth. Jewish activities often lack elements of competition or a clear-cut message. Since many male teens do not receive these Jewish values listed above outside of the home—if they are receiving any at all—the male teens may not feel competent when thrust into a youth group situation with their peers. Jewish males are less likely to participate in Jewish discussion-based activities if they feel uncomfortable, especially when the purpose of the activity relies on process and not clear-cut results (i.e., the activity is mostly about the discussion itself rather than the discussion concluding with a specific result to be implemented in the future).

While leadership is an important social norm for male teens, leadership roles do not encourage them to participate within the Reform framework. Specialized leadership programs have significantly higher female participation than male. The URJ Kutz Campus, which offers an excellent leadership development program for high school students during the summer, has a ratio of two females to every male. This number has increased over the past few years when only 28 percent of attendants were male, but there is still a significant imbalance. NFTY's EIE High School Semester in Israel, as well as the Meitav Fellowship (for highly engaged Reform teen leaders), on average have only 41 percent male participation.

Over the past three years, leadership positions within NFTY regions have predominantly been held by females. While the 2007–2008 NFTY North American Board is all male, as was the board of the prior year, on average, 42 percent of the regional board presidents have been male. For the upcoming 2007–2008 school year, 75 percent of all regional board members are female, and for 2006–2007 it was 53 percent. This resulted in several articles and letters to the professional staff of the Union for Reform Judaism after the election of a second all-male board that argued that this single-gendered leadership did not encourage females to take on more active roles in leading their peers. The articles stated that females may not feel comfortable representing NFTY, and this was the message the professional leadership were sending. I would argue just the opposite. Females thrive in this environment. So much so that when they finish their tenure within the region, they state their intention to move on to the college experience. Boys, who generally mature at a slower rate than girls, may not feel as comfortable starting over on a college campus. Being a freshman in a college environment is reminiscent of when they started with NFTY as the "small fish in the big pond." It is difficult and uncomfortable. Instead, NFTY allows them to become the "big fish" by providing these graduating males with the opportunity to lead an organization within which they have grown, that has fostered their development, and where they feel comfortable. However, while NFTY does well at grooming leaders, this current situation is still not helping to bring in more boys at the ninth-grade level. This is ultimately one of NFTY's greatest challenges.

Opportunities for Change

The shortage of teen males in our programs leaves the Jewish community with an important choice to make regarding how to keep young Jewish males involved in Jewish life after bar mitzvah age. Given the statistics, we are faced with two options. The first is to help socialize and acculturate boys, especially those beginning high school, to successfully manage typical youth programming so that they feel comfortable within this setting and start to enjoy it. This can be done by offering more opportunities starting at a younger age, like within the seventh grade, for boys to participate in retreats and discussions for shorter periods of time, so that they become accustomed to this model of youth program. We need to teach them the language and norms while encouraging them to develop friendships within this setting to motivate them to return.

The second option is to change our programming. Rather than giving a one-size-fits-all model that we expect to appeal to a ninth-grade male and twelfth-grade female at the same time, we should be dividing our programming based on developmental needs and gender. This means that instead of offering a time for mingling or unstructured free time at programs, there should be structured activities to help alleviate anxiety for all the teens present, both male and female. Social times come with pressure to find someone to talk to or to approach a love interest, which is typically an uncomfortable activity for shy teens. Structured free-time activities will allow the teens to interact with one another without having to initiate a conversation. Such activities can be as simple as leaving out some decks of cards on tables so that when teens attend an event they can play with one another or by themselves. At retreats, structured free time could include outdoor activities like basketball or Frisbee. By introducing activities within the uncomfortable setting, boys will more likely participate and therefore get to know one another so that they will want to return again to see their new friends.

As professionals and lay leaders who work with youth, it is incumbent upon us to act on both options. Starting boys in informal youth programming at a younger age is more likely to keep them engaged after bar mitzvah age and help them to enjoy the benefits of being with their peers in a more independent setting. Also, by altering programming at these events, males will have the opportunity to feel more competent as they participate in activities that are more comfortable for them. These activities should include independent activities and movement rather than sitting in a circle and having a discussion.

Both at summer camp and on retreats, there is a built-in single-gender environment—the housing or bunk. These single-gender places provide a great opportunity for males to be with adult male mentors. Also, older males could serve as peer mentors for younger, newer members of the group. Programming within this setting can provide valuable, meaningful experiences. From playing games indoors to going on hikes, male mentoring allows for a unique bonding situation.

As the Regional Advisor for NFTY's New York Area Region, I have had a lot of time over the past few years to observe male and female teens, ages 14 to 18, interact with one another within the informal Jewish educational setting. While I only see the teens who have already opted in, I am able to experiment with programming focused on retaining participants over time. Here are some ideas I have discovered through my work:

- The number of male staff members makes a difference, as does their "coolness" factor. Male teens tend to bond better with male staffers and want to come back to see them again.
- Male teens consistently choose to participate in structured free-time activities. They most often will choose high energy, active ones, such as hiking, basketball, and drumming.
- Male teens will choose to participate in what society may deem as feminine activities if the program is active. This includes making scrapbooks, song leading, yoga, and drama.
- Older teen males who participate in NFTY become so accustomed to the programmatic model of sitting in a circle and having a discussion that when they plan activities they cannot creatively think of other ways to teach their peers.
- Ninth-grade boys have the hardest time integrating into the larger group unless they have an older sibling, friend from home, or youth advisor who helps them with this process.
- While there are always a smaller number of males at NFTY events, a greater percentage of males than females run for leadership positions.
- Male teens in leadership positions have a more difficult time successfully completing their job responsibilities than female teens. While both are pulled in multiple directions due to

their participation in a variety of other extracurricular activities, more often it seems that boys and their parents place a greater emphasis on the victorious achievement of these activities such as school athletic teams, drama, Boy Scouts, or work.

Program Ideas

Listed below are some programmatic ideas to help increase male participation within a youth group and congregational setting:

1. **Staffing.** Provide resources for staff to help them understand the differences in learning between teen males and females so that they can create programming to best fit the teens' developmental needs. Hire males to serve as mentors to the teen boys.
2. **Develop leaders.** Help boys to obtain leadership skills so that they feel comfortable running activities, meetings, and youth groups. Assign roles within holiday celebrations. Ask them to serve as teachers' assistants or mentors to younger children, or to be responsible for bringing something to a meeting. Most importantly, give them opportunities for them to succeed and feel competent.
3. **Create active programming.** Programming needs to be energetic and dynamic. Think of activities in fifteen-minute blocks of time. Even though a program may be scheduled for an hour, change the activity every fifteen minutes so that students will have to change their physical positions. Use multimedia resources within the program.
4. **Structure free time.** Unstructured free time is a daunting activity for many young male teens. By making small activities available, or having a space for sports, boys can engage in doing something that is less stressful. It helps them bond.
5. **Mentors and role models.** Never underestimate the power of one individual to make a difference in a young male's life. Whether a young teen is serving as a mentor to a younger child or has a mentor who is an older high school student, this helps to create a meaningful relationship with another male. Even matching teen boys with adult professional males who work in a field of interest to the teen allows that teen to see a successful adult Jewish male outside of the home.
6. **Celebrate rites of passage.** The bar mitzvah is a special time, but not the only time a boy can be celebrated within the Jewish community. Celebrating a boy at holiday celebrations by allowing him to help lead a seder or say the *Kiddush* are additional ways for him to participate in Jewish religious activities. Having intergenerational retreats for male teens when they reach confirmation is another way for them to bond with their fathers.

I can recall as a teen member of Temple Beth Am in Miami, Florida, how I loved going to the synagogue. It was my community center and home away from home. My brother, only two years younger than me, as well as my boyfriend at the time, felt the same way. While youth group programming still looks the same today as it did then, our synagogue was creative in many other ways to gain teen involvement. For example, we had our own lounge. Participation in the Hebrew high school earned us college credits through a partnership with the local community college. Teens were allowed to work and earn money as teachers' assistants. On the nights I went to participate in my singing group (which had about ten females and only one male), my boyfriend played on one of the teams within the congregation's own basketball league. I realize that not every synagogue can afford an indoor gymnasium like this one, but how many congregations offer at least one of these activities beyond youth group for its teens? What about offering shorter-term activities such as college preparatory courses or a college or job fair? These activities were seen as less daunting entrees for participation for both the males and females. They were also a way of meshing synagogue life with secular values. Just getting the teens to participate in something offered by the synagogue, even if the activity is conducted in someone's home, would give them a chance to see it as a safe place where they feel comfortable and have some friends.

We are facing a critical time in the Jewish community where the pendulum is swinging in the opposite direction. The Reform community, which now embraces its female leadership and egalitarian worship, has begun to alienate the young Jewish male. In the nontraditional community, Jewish males are not praised for dedicating their life to religious study and are encouraged at an early age, by both American culture and their families, to gain the skills necessary to survive in the secular world. By thinking critically about the types of programming you offer male teens, you can help shape the next generation of successful Jewish males who are just as savvy at leading holiday celebrations as they are at closing a deal at work. Give these teens a chance to experience and enjoy Jewish life in a language they understand so that they will continue to transmit Jewish values for the next generation.

Teen Brotherhood

Jason Freedman and Bobby Harris

Twelve high school Jewish guys gather in a room at a NFTY (North American Federation of Temple Youth) conclave and talk about their fears, regrets, and aspirations. One teen speaks about his struggles to stay in school and how badly he wants to lead a normal life. Another reveals his secret—he's shy and desperately wants to fit in. Another talks about how much he misses his brother who passed away a few years before. Many of them have never even met each other before. Yet they're staring deeply into each other's eyes, unafraid of judgment and eager to support one another.

Eighty male camp staffers arrive at camp for a week of orientation. Twenty-four hours later they're having a discussion around the campfire: "When did I first start to feel like I was becoming a man?" Four peer leaders start the conversation, "stepping up" to share their personal stories—the only other sound is the crackling of the fire. The eighty young men then break out into smaller groups, where everyone can share his own story—and by the time the groups rejoin, the counselors have their arms round each other—connected male energy. They no longer care about being "cool." In fact, they've redefined "cool" in terms of "brotherhood"—the overwhelming sense of men's acceptance and community.

Having run the young male bonding program at temple youth group conclaves and Reform camps six times as part of a "separate gender" program, we now know that it *is* possible to create an environment that enables young men to express what's really going on in their lives. In our American culture, confiding our inner thoughts may be perceived as unmasculine, but our camps and youth groups can become places where young men feel safe enough to talk about their troubles, apprehensions, and regrets, sometimes for the first time. They perceive their overworked and overstressed parents as too immersed in their own concerns, and fear that sharing their vulnerabilities with friends might result in a backlash of ridicule.

Given this reluctance, the key to successful young adult discussion programming is establishing a social climate in which it's okay for teens to reveal their doubts and personal weaknesses. To create the environment, we enlist peer leaders who have the maturity, charisma, and credibility to demonstrate to the group how to be real, open, and vulnerable. They join us in a pre-program discussion based on Jewish texts. Sometimes we use the biblical story of how King David acted immorally by impregnating Bath-sheba—a married woman—and then conspiring to have her husband killed in battle. In the end, David is punished for his sin. This affords us the opportunity to discuss the most distressing regrets in our own lives, and what we'd do differently if given another chance. Other times we use the Hillel quote in *Pirke Avot*—"In a place where there are no men, try to be one"—to examine such questions as: "Where am I on my path toward becoming a man?" and "What was my defining moment when I realized where I was on my path?" We also talk with the peer leaders about how difficult it is for guys to be open with each other, and explain that they'll play a special part in the program because they're perceived by others as role models. After the orientation, we say, just as you've been able to be open, supportive, and trusting of one another in this small group, you'll be able to model openness, support, and trust in the large group.

It's program time. We choose the King David story. The large group is asked the questions previously asked of their peer leaders. Everyone is silent. All of a sudden one of the peer leaders stands up to answer. He's been preparing himself since our pre-program discussion, but he's still visibly nervous. In emotional tones he tells the group about the time he cheated on his best friend and how much he regrets it. There's no preaching about cheating, morality, etc.—he just ends by saying what he would do if his friend gives him a second chance. The other group leaders follow, sharing equally powerful stories.

Just a few minutes ago the teens were hanging out and playing ultimate Frisbee, but now there's a new energy in the room. The young men are amazed by the raw honesty, impressed by the risk their peers have taken in sharing their stories.

The larger group is now divided into smaller group sessions where each person can share his story. The emotional floodgates open. Two hours fly by as they speak candidly about their lives with unprecedented intensity.

Afterwards we regroup and finish the King David story. We talk about how David repented and all the great things he did with his second chance—and what it means to leave a legacy. King David left us his passion for music and prayer. The psalm we sing before the *Amidah* is David's way of saying that he wants to overcome his own selfish needs and trusts God to "open up his lips in praise." We talk about Gandhi's quote, "Be the change you want to see in the world," and how it applies to us. And we acknowledge how different and good it feels to overcome inhibitions and "be real" with others. We suggest that everyone continue to look beyond his inhibitions and join us in song.

Slowly we join in a friendship circle and sing *"A na na na na . . . Adonai. . . ."* The awareness is palpable—we're in the midst of a life-altering experience.

Later, one camp counselor reveals that this program has "changed the way I live my life. I realize that . . . put[ting] people down [to] get a laugh . . . I don't have to do it anymore . . . the laugh that I get is not worth the hurt that I could cause to that person: . . . I [am now] more sensitive to that. It's weird, even talking about it now and hearing me say that that one program really changed me . . . but I can't deny it, it's true . . . it really did!"

Our young men may not show it, but they're asking to be engaged in Jewish life. They deserve safe Jewish environments where they can be themselves. And when they experience the joy of being themselves, they will always want to return.

A Look at Jewish Camping

Daniel G. Zemel

When I was a young man, the girls in my extended family went to Jewish summer camps while the boys went to a camp where we could play fast pitch baseball. My parents would have it no other way. In the forty years since I stopped being a secular camper, I have become an active participant in Jewish camping, as a Hebrew Union College student, a staff member at Jewish camps, later as an assistant rabbi at a congregation that owned a summer camp, and finally as rabbinic faculty at a URJ camp. Though I cherish my involvement in Jewish camping, I believe that Jewish summer camps need to learn to foster more male-friendly environments. As they operate today, Jewish summer camps do not do enough to reach the essential "maleness" in boys.

"Maleness" in boys manifests itself in many different ways. Whereas girls keep pencil boxes and orderly school supplies, boys tend to keep "stuff" in disheveled backpacks and find no problem in writing with pencil stubs that look as if they have just been run over. Girls socialize in small groups after school, waiting to board school buses or walk home, while boys wrestle in the dirt and go exploring for hidden treasures in the woods, eschewing the manicured lawns and hedges of school yards. Boys think the purpose of the new family refrigerator is to turn the box it came in into a fort.

"Camp Judaism" as it is currently constituted is centered around lessons, discussions, role playing, and worship. There is, to be sure, some hiking and climbing thrown in, but not nearly enough. This is, after all, camp. There needs to be a strong infusion of sports and games of every kind from team sports like soccer and baseball to individual sports like wrestling and archery. Is there a Jewish camp that even offers both baseball and softball? We need more challenging canoeing, camping out, and physical exertion. Our most potentially pro-boy environment has in many ways been stripped of its "maleness" and rendered gender-neutral. We have to recognize that girls, as a generalization, like sharing their feelings, while boys like throwing, kicking, and wrestling. When was the last time someone at a Jewish camp learned how to pitch a tent? Our "Camp Judaism" needs to broaden its focus. Just consider arts and crafts. Why should it not include wood and machine shop—or, as one colleague put it to me, "fewer talent shows, more wrestling." Another astute observer of our camp scene has mentioned to me that more competitive sports might be just the right outlet to mitigate the bullying problem that can be prevalent with young adolescents. They need to get "it" out of their systems, and bunk discussions won't do it for everyone. Boys could benefit from more competitive sports, more physically challenging activities, more baseball, archery, and actual camping. Bunk discussions and role-playing exercises are great, but so are batting cages and canoe trips.

Our youth groups and NFTY should do the same. We should learn from Outward Bound. All of these activities are for boys and girls. How much can we expect our young people to sit in discussion groups about topics remote from their lives? When we offer relevance, they see right through it as if the adult programmers are trying to be cool in order to relate to the young. We should refrain from offering mini-courses on "Jews and Rock and Roll," "What Makes a Movie Jewish," "Sensitivity Training through Guided Imagery," or "A Jewish View of Body Piercing and Tattoos." Let's put all that behind us. Let's try something totally different—how about skill building and the companion lessons in trust, teamwork, and being a responsible, contributing member of society and community?

The Zionist youth groups of Europe in the 1930s were physically and intellectually challenging, relevant to their everyday lives, and taught skills such as farming and carpentry. Why can't we teach our kids how to change the motor oil of a car or repair a lawn mower? What about how to cook a meal, bake bread, hang drywall, or repair a toilet? What can be more Jewish than contributing in a meaningful way to the life of your family or your community? If we, as a matter of course, taught these sorts of skills, our high schoolers would be naturals for everything we claim to believe in, from Hurricane Katrina relief to Habitat for Humanity. It would even serve to make a NFTY in Israel trip an even more meaningful experience for our kids if they had some real skills to offer when they arrived and could leave something meaningful behind. If we want to do more than pay lip service to building our movement in Israel, our NFTY kids could play a real part if we prepared them for it. When they do become involved in work projects, our kids are all too often given routine, boring, even meaningless jobs because they never learned how to cook over an open fire, use a food processor, electric mixer, or hammer, let alone a drill or saw.

It is hard to see what life skills Jewish youth movements currently offer teenagers. What is the end of these sentences? "In youth group I learned . . . At camp I learned to . . ." The answer list for most kids is shockingly short. Make Jewish friends, yes—but make friends through challenging experiences and the learning of useful skills. Jewish life need not be a disembodied spiritual experience. The Jewish life of the spirit is not divorced from the reality or tasks of everyday living. The spiritual can be found both in sunsets as well as fields planted, houses rebuilt, bread baked, and cars repaired. We can not only teach Jewish values, we can offer the requisite tools to put them into action. Our camps and youth groups can be places of greater *tikkun*—not only for the world, but for our youth who can leave us ready to face the world not only with a Jewish religious commitment of the heart, but a sense of self and a skill set to match.

Ten Suggestions for Reaching Young Men

Michael Holzman

1. **Trust:** An essential quality for working with any teenage population, this is the litmus test for boys. They are already willing to check out after bar mitzvah, and they are torn between American ideals of manhood versus the feminization and intellectualism of Judaism. Show them an honest, trustworthy adult role model and they will respond.
2. **Goals:** Boys need to see the purpose of the program. Do not invite marginal guys to a "hang-out" social program. Consider inviting them to a hands-on social action project or a sports program with clear goals. Give them a sense of accomplishment by the time they leave.
3. **Translation:** So much of NFTY programming involves "inside knowledge" of regions, positions, conventions, jokes, camps, rituals, songs . . . try to minimize the amount of time a newcomer spends feeling lost. Assign an older guy to take a younger one "under his wing." Be careful when inviting young men to regional programs where inside info will be most common.
4. **Smaller Groups:** Try breaking away from the large group activities which force a newcomer to fend for himself. Try programs that create small groups where a boy's lack of knowledge or inexperience might not be so scary. Also, the teamwork created in a small group engaged in a common task might form valuable friendships.
5. **Get a Man:** If the advisor is female, try asking local college students or male friends to help staff programs. If your synagogue can afford it, pay these people and try to get a consistent "assistant advisor." Or perhaps a younger member will volunteer to consistently staff programs. This volunteer or assistant can serve as a male role model.
6. **Try Multigenerational:** Tap into the positive role models that grandfathers and fathers present to young men. Most male Jewish teens do not see their fathers as involved Jewish men; therefore they do not have an immediate goal for Jewish male adulthood. The same positive effects can work for young women as well. Possibly contact your local Brotherhood or Sisterhood to have a joint program.
7. **Single Gender:** Create all-male and all-female spaces within your programming. On programs about sex, romance, body image, and sexuality, separate-gender discussions make sense. But boys and girls will also see issues like prayer, success, academics, and sports differently. Try single-gender break-out groups and then come back together for discussion. Or try single-gender prayer, single-gender teams, or entire single-gender programs. Removing

the romance pressure (for the heterosexual teens) will lower inhibitions and make newcomers more comfortable.

8. **Strike a Balance:** Encourage advisors and leaders to mix programming. Often temple youth groups get in the "talking" rut, where every program is either a discussion or a "hang-out." Get youth to use their bodies, music, food, and creativity. Different learners will appreciate the opportunity to give their minds a rest.
9. **Validate Struggle:** Because identity forms during adolescence, teens are looking for help defining their selves. Show them that having questions, being unsure, and seeking answers are acceptable positions. Boys tend to look more definite than they actually feel. Communicate your own struggles and encourage them to keep struggling.
10. **Be Aware of Success:** In surveys boys show more interest in professional and long-range goals. This drives male teens to take more restrictive jobs and internships. Try to design synagogue programs or regional programs where teens are paired with Jewish mentors in internships or teens receive SAT training. Acknowledge the male drive for success and incorporate that into programming.

Section III

L'Dor vaDor: From Generation to Generation

Introduction

Studies show that as women have taken over the majority of the childrearing and Jewish activities in a family, even those activities that take place outside of the home, children are often left without a Jewish male role model. This chapter explores the reality of the loss of Jewish male role models and with what can be done to address the problem—both as a family unit and as a society. The essays included here look at the complex relationships that do, or should, exist between Jewish boys and their mentors.

Jerry Kaye's piece "Remedy for an 'Absent' Father" speaks about the relationships that sustained him despite his father's absence. A senior member of the synagogue who took a special interest in a fatherless child, a Boy Scout leader, a rabbi, and a Hebrew school teacher all left lasting and distinct impressions on Kaye's childhood. Having personally experienced the importance of Jewish role modeling, Kaye now leads a *kallah* for fathers and sons. He believes that boys need more time with adult men who will permanently affect their lives in positive ways.

"Torah for a Jewish Father" by Rabbi Michael Holzman explores the biblical relationships between fathers and sons. Rabbi Holzman asserts that the Bible knows the importance of the father-son relationship, placing it even on the same level as our relationship with God. He encourages synagogues to re-recognize the truth of this claim and to begin creating rituals, programming, liturgy, and texts that enhance these relationships.

Rabbi Allan Tuffs's "The Gift of Fierce Father Love" demands the return of an element of "fierceness" in a father's love for his child. Tuffs believes that men are suppressing this natural aspect of their love and that children suffer as a result. He draws on traditional Jewish sources as well as gender theory to assert that there needs to be a reintroduction of a particular kind of male love in a child's life.

Rabbi Joel Soffin recognizes the many roles a man in today's world must fulfill. "The Real Man" challenges the idea that it is the roles of pillar of the family, financial provider, and protector that fulfill a man's existence. He believes that men fulfill these roles not realizing that they often do so at the expense of their true selves. Soffin challenges Jewish men to move beyond these roles into greater fulfillment.

In "Journeying Together: Reflections on the Obligations of the Jewish Father," Michael Geller uses Morris Rosenfeld's Yiddish poem "*Meyn Yingele*—My Little One" (1887) to address the loss men feel when they are not involved in their children's lives. Geller compares and contrasts contemporary times with those of Rosenfeld and discusses a number of ways for a father to teach a son. Geller considers the Talmud requirement of a father to teach a son "to swim," interpreting the phrase metaphorically to refer to the various life lessons a father teaches a son that fall neither in the realm of prayer nor trade nor text study. He stresses that fathers have essential lessons to teach about honesty, tolerance, *tzedakah*, and support for Israel. Such lessons, he writes, are a way to teach our sons to "swim."

From a retreat that allows fathers and their sons to reconnect, to the reclaiming of "fierceness" as part of a father's love, Jewish men are exploring the role of mentoring/fathering. How will the next generation's mentors maintain, shift, or reinvent what it means to be a father, what it means to mentor a young man? How will your community support and encourage and explore the possibilities of the mentoring of the next generation of Jewish men?

Questions for Discussion

As you read each piece, consider the following questions:

1. What assumptions underlie the essay(s) that you have read? Which assumptions do you think are fair? Which do you question? Which, if any, concern you?
2. What is unique about a male mentor for a young man? What aspects of male mentoring do not fall into our stereotypes?
3. What aspects of mentoring were important in your own life? Who were your living sages? How can we carry ahead the best traditions of Jewish mentoring?
4. How can we alter and bolster the current systems of fathering and mentoring?
5. How can we initiate mentoring in parts of our communities that are yet to experience mentors?
6. How can we all become better mentors?

Remedy for an "Absent" Father

Jerry Kaye

It may be simply because I never knew my own father that the dwindling away of men and boys from synagogue life weighs so heavily on my mind. At my childhood synagogue, Lawn Manor Hebrew Congregation on the southwest side of Chicago, everyone had a dad . . . everyone except me. Other kids always talked about "Dad" and looked on with pride as their fathers took positions of leadership and moved about the *bimah*. I derived a certain sense of inclusion by proxy, but of course it was not the same as having your own father present.

As I prepared for my bar mitzvah, I attended what was known as the Tefillin Club, a weekly ritual in which the twelve-year-old boys of our traditional congregation came every Sunday to learn how to put on *tefillin* and master the elements of the adult worship service. No more Junior Congregation for us; after all, we were about to be pronounced MEN.

In those formative years I had four Jewish male mentors. At the Tefillin Club, Harry Schlitten, one of the senior members of the synagogue, would come over to each of us individually, put his arm on our shoulders, and share his wisdom. I have no idea what he did for a living, but to this day I can still see the diamond-encrusted pin he proudly wore on his lapel, his symbol of being a 33rd-degree Mason. What that meant we didn't know, except that it was a sign of exceeding accomplishment. He regularly told us so. He also seemed to know the details of my life and, with a caring hand on my shoulder, would tell me: "The most important thing is to be a *mensch*."

During my Tefillin Club days, I learned there is a benefit to boys learning to become men from adult males who are *not* their fathers. Other men can support what dads may say and thus reinforce the father's message without personal dynamics playing a role.

The second of my mentors was my Boy Scout leader Harold Robbins (not to be confused with the bestselling author). He and the other men he brought together to take charge of our synagogue's Troop 635 knew they had the awesome task of teaching us responsibility. Preparing for the annual Scout Jamboree, held every June in Marquette Park, was one of those times when responsibility counted. If you accepted the responsibility to bring the equipment up from the synagogue basement storage room, you were doing the right thing. If you accepted the responsibility of leading the annual service at the Jamboree—usually my job—you were again doing right. If you shirked the tough jobs, Mr. Robbins would simply ignore you. I well remember his line-marked face reflected in the myriad campfires as he let each of us know individually that being a Boy Scout was a key step on the road to becoming a man, that fun should follow work, and that the "jobs" had to be done right. We were the only Jewish troop among scores of others. Mr. Robbins taught us that we had to be at least as good as the best of them—that our tents, our equipment, should always be in top condition and "look smart." Jews needed to behave that way.

And then there was my Orthodox rabbi, Mordecai Schultz. Right after I became a bar mitzvah he would call me regularly, telling me that I was needed to fill out a *minyan*—would I come? My bar mitzvah counted. I was *needed*. Imagine that! I have been in the Reform Movement for nearly forty years now, and no one has ever needed me for a ritual function that could be fulfilled only by a male.

The fourth seminal male figure in my life was my Hebrew school teacher, David Fox. He used to drive to the school building in his plumber's truck and arrive about fifteen minutes before class to toss around a football with us. What a way to reinforce the message that our synagogue really cared about us.

One summer, while I rested in my bunk at Camp Moshavah, some 250 miles away, the door parted and David Fox's face appeared! I was ecstatic. There was no doubt in my mind that he had come all the way out to camp just to see me. I learned later that he had made the long trip to central Wisconsin to see a friend, but, as an eleven-year-old, you never could have persuaded me of that. He was like a father to me, representing all that was important and right . . . just because he was willing to toss a ball for a few minutes before religious school.

These experiences influenced my decision many years later, as director of URJ Olin-Sang-Ruby Union Institute in Oconomowoc, Wisconsin, to create a *kallah* for fathers and sons. For one weekend a year just before Passover, men and their sons between the ages of six and bar mitzvah could come to camp to celebrate Shabbat and *Havdalah*, go on a hayride, sit around the campfire, participate in sports, and take walks together. We'd pepper this with music and time for dads and lads to be together unencumbered by the pressing schedules and agendas of daily life.

One Friday in April 2002, at around 4:00 PM, fourteen families began arriving. They settled into their rooms, took a short walk around camp, began meeting and greeting one another. In the dining hall, the tables set with white cloths, challah, and grape juice, people talked. Services followed; then the dads put their sons to bed. Afterwards, most fathers returned to the common room to talk about the day's experience and reminisce about the important men in their lives. The word "absentee" came up frequently. Men had learned early in their married lives that being a good provider was equated with being a good father and spouse. They found professions and businesses they enjoyed and companionship with colleagues and friends. Unfortunately, many of the fathers could never emulate these positive experiences when they were with their own boys.

It also became clear that the men felt Jewishly incompetent. Turning religious life over to their wives had left many of them unfamiliar with Jewish ritual.

During the *kallah*'s Friday night candle-lighting and *Kiddush*, the men, supported by the group, began to refamiliarize themselves with words that for years had not passed their lips. At Shabbat morning services, creased prayer shawls came out of *tallit* bags that had long been zippered shut. Men turned to those next to them for help in keeping up with the service, and a kind of *minyan* pride emerged as people stood together and lent their voices to melodies they remembered from an age past. Some really knew them; others clearly wanted to be in the know.

Each subsequent *kallah* has grown. Nearly a third of the participants return. The schedule remains more or less constant. In addition to the sports, music, and celebrations, there are joint projects such as designing a *tallit* or *afikomen* bag for Pesach where boys interact with their dads and other adult males. The activities are only the sweetener which provides the framework for men and boys to engage in genuine conversation about their relationships. If there is a pivotal moment in this event, it is the time set aside for dads to take an evening walk with their sons along the camp's tree-lined paths and cabins, then put their sons to bed in the rooms they share.

Mothers heard about the event from their husbands and sons, and soon there was a groundswell of requests for a similar mother/daughter event. Our first such *kallah* took place last fall, run by camp associate director Susan Alexander.

The imprint of Harry and Harold and Mordecai and David and so many others has lasted all these years. And it is my hope that these boys who are sharing a rich Jewish bonding experience with their dads at our camp will treasure it as much as I did growing up at Lawn Manor Hebrew Congregation.

Torah for a Jewish Father

Michael Holzman

> Then Isaac said to his father Abraham, "My father," and he answered, "I am here, my son."
> (Genesis 22:7)

In our earliest stories we place the relationship between parent and child—and particularly father and son—on the same level with our relationship with God. Within the story of the *Akedah*, we hear Isaac call to his father, and Abraham responds to his son in the same way he answered God: "*Hineini*"—I am here. In the Talmud (*Berakhot* 30b), we learn that one should honor, revere and speak to parents in the same way that one speaks to God. Why, the rabbis ask? Because the three of them are partners in creating the child.

Since this relationship plays a special role in our ancient and rabbinic texts, we expect it to feature prominently in synagogue life. With the recent proliferation of family education initiatives and professionals, more attention has been paid to the Jewish implications on parent-child relations. But what have we taught/learned about the particulars of the male half of this equation? Do we have lessons to learn about the particular experiences of Jewish fathers or Jewish sons? Ought we not write rituals, programs, liturgy and texts that appeal to fathers and sons?

So far, this type of focus has been largely absent from our communities. While we see the value of family programming and intergenerational community, we largely ignore the specifics of the father-son relationship. The reason is largely logistical. Many families contain no sons. Should these men be excluded? Should we ignore the father-daughter relationship? Should we heap more pain on those in our community struggling to bear children? In addition, many sons in our community do not live with their fathers. Again, should we highlight the difficulty of divorce, or the pain of losing a parent? And what if the father is not Jewish? Or if the sons are not being raised Jewish? Should we exclude these individuals from our programs or our rituals? By focusing on the more general, gender non-specific, relationship of parent and child, rather than father and son, we avoid these emotional and logistical difficulties presented by the millennial Jewish family.

But the fact remains that all men are sons, and all men with children—children of either sex—are fathers. If we want to speak to the souls of Jewish men in our congregations, certainly this central part of our male identities should be considered. It should be studied, taught, discussed, shared, celebrated, mourned, and sanctified. These are Jewish ways of living, and the experience of a father or of a son can be interpreted through a Jewish lens. We should acknowledge the diversity of the Jewish family in the new millennium, but we should also acknowledge the particular experiences of Jewish fathers and sons today.

Abraham and Isaac: Where We Come From

The experience of today's Jewish fathers and sons springs from a rich history. In the Torah we find stories and laws that describe the relations between men and their sons. In particular, the laws of the rebellious son, the *ben sorer u'moreh*, shed light on what happens when this relationship goes awry. The father of such a son could, with his wife's permission, indict his son before the elders of the town, who would then execute the son by stoning in order to set an example (Deuteronomy 21:18–21). Why so harsh a penalty? In ancient Israel, the entire community depended upon strict inheritance rules between fathers and sons. Moses and Joshua had granted each tribe a limited amount of land. If a rebellious son left his father's house, he could take tribal land with him. Such a threat required prevention. Thus the Bible displays strict father-son relations. In their male roles fathers passed the responsibility for family, economic, and political leadership to their sons.

This type of bond that existed within the father-son dynamic eventually dissipated. As Jews were exiled from Israel, first by Assyrians, then by Babylonians and later Romans, a crucial element of the father-son relationship—land and tribal inheritance—gradually disappeared. Authority over tribal land became irrelevant when there was no tribal land. In its place rose authority over communal law: rabbinic authority. If ancient authority rested upon the land inherited from father to son, rabbinic authority rested upon knowledge inherited from teacher to student.

While this new relationship could not completely replace the father/son experience in ancient Israel, it certainly competed. The *Mishnah* (*Baba Mezia* 2:11) teaches that when a man finds objects lost by both his father and his teacher, the teacher takes priority; his father brought him into this world *(ha-olam hazzeh)*, but his teacher is bringing him into the world to come *(ha-olam habbah)* through the study of Torah. This was the paradigm of male inheritance throughout the Middle Ages as well. The rabbinic authority so greatly outweighed family authority that the dominant sphere of male relationships became the academy and synagogue, and not the home.

But as we entered the modern period, most rabbis lost power to the state. Just as the expulsion from Israel ended land inheritance between generations of men, so the Emancipation from the ghetto ended most models of rabbinic inheritance from teacher to student. As Jews moved to the United States, for instance, they enjoyed even greater freedom from the hand of rabbis. While some families became quite close through the immigration experience, the pull of American individualism prevented the reemergence of strong father-son relationships. In fact, the story of the twentieth century is one of strife between parents and children, especially for the Baby Boom generation. As the most educated, professionally successful, and wealthiest generation of Jews in ages began to come to represent the American dream, work often pulled families apart. Extended families stretched across North America, and nuclear families sometimes sank in the rising tide of divorce. In such an environment, and with professionals—usually men—frequently tied to their desks, father-son relations diffused even more.

A Jew coming of age in post-war America lacked the tribal structure of ancient Israel, the rabbinic structure of the Middle Ages, and even the nuclear family structure of the early modern period. In our lifetimes, the take-care-of-number-one ethos saturated North American culture and alienated members of the family. For many Jewish families *kabeid et avicha v'et eemecha* (honor your father and your mother) became limited to superficial interactions over TV dinners. The synagogue usually exacerbated this by putting parents into the role of enforcing often onerous religious school attendance and Bar Mitzvah preparation.

Calling Out: Then Isaac Said to His Father Abraham, "My Father."

While Jewish history illustrates how the tribal, rabbinic and nuclear father/son relations deteriorated, practical Jewish experience demonstrates the communal effects of this decay. Anecdotally, men have absented themselves from large swaths of synagogue life. Women fill the seats on Friday nights, often without their partners. Men often abandon committee membership, serving only on the temple's executive board if they serve at all. This trend begins at the youth level, where national youth programming regularly attracts twice or three times as many girls as boys. Upon hearing this statistic, many people joke that if the boys only knew the odds, they would show up. But when asked in individual interviews and focus groups, teenage guys say such a ratio hardly attracts them. "I can meet girls anywhere," they often say. "But why should I sit through something Jewish?"

In contrast, when these same boys are asked what they long for, the same answers return, almost incessantly. When asked about what makes a discussion or program work, the teens answer, "A good role model." These teens seem to feel the lack of structure inherited by Jewish history. Without tribe, rabbinic community, or nuclear family, they long for meaningful relationships across generations. But when asked to name examples of this male Jewish role model, the boys named three groups: teen advisors, rabbis, and grandfathers. Few mentioned their father. Yet they long for men with whom they can discuss their lives. As women fill more and more advisor and rabbi positions, and grandfathers age and pass, our young Jewish men will find fewer and fewer male role models. We should not wonder about why they absent themselves from Jewish life.

If adolescence is the time when a boy discovers his identity as a man, and if Judaism is the language of identity and meaning, surely we want our sons to learn about adulthood in a Jewish environment, from Jewish men. If Jewish text exists to inform the deepest parts of our lives, and if Jewish ritual exists to celebrate, mourn and mark the most intense moments of life, then should not our young Jewish men understand how these texts and rituals speak to them as a man? Should they not learn these lessons from other adult Jewish men? Older Jewish men?

Our teens long for this experience. As part of my rabbinic internship with NFTB and NFTY (North American Federation of Temple Youth) I recently attended two experiences that exemplify this longing. First I staffed an all-male youth retreat at Camp Coleman in Georgia. There a group of NFTY men met, discussed, studied, ate, sang, prayed and competed in "ultimate Frisbee" for three days. The subject of this retreat—being a Jewish man. When asked what made the weekend work, the guys repeatedly said that talking to Jewish guys a generation ahead of them made the difference. Hearing from an adult man how a Jew ought to compete with others, see himself, make friends, and find romance brought the texts, the rituals, and the weekend to life. These teens enjoyed connecting with adult Jewish men, including the men who are not their fathers. This opens the door for intergenerational, father-son programming even when not every son has a Jewish father at the synagogue, and not every father has a Jewish son. The teens want to hear from older, wiser, adult Jewish men, father-figures, and mentors.

Lest you think the teens only want to learn from a young rabbinic student and not their fathers! My second experience came when I taught at a New York synagogue's father-son retreat weekend to New Orleans for Jazz Festival. On the first night the adults all thought the teens (mostly seniors in high school) would abandon their fathers and head to Bourbon Street. But they returned well before curfew and informed their fathers that they came to be with Dad. The teens spent the rest of the weekend listening to music with their fathers, eating Big Easy delicacies (read: shellfish) with their fathers, and studying Torah with their fathers. Imagine a group of high school seniors, sunburned from Jazz Fest, sitting in a hotel just off of Bourbon Street, and studying the Talmud's dictates on caring for a father in his old age.

Hearing the Call: And He Answered, "*Hineini*, My Son."

Now imagine that group of forty-something fathers studying text with their sons. Some of these men knew synagogue life (the president of the congregation was there), but some hardly stepped foot in the building. The population of adults largely mirrored that of the youth. They ranged from the very to marginally involved. However, they all came because they knew other fathers and sons making the trip, they wanted to spend time with each other, and they wanted to hear good jazz. In such an environment they felt enthusiastic, motivated, and, above all, safe.

Jewish life requires a high degree of knowledge. Synagogue aficionados speak a language of their own. They describe committees, board positions, names, services, organizations, and religious concepts that might be unfamiliar to a newcomer. They speak of Jewish geography and inside jokes gathered from years of work in the community. On top of all of this, much of synagogue vocabulary is spoken in Hebrew. This can be daunting for a newcomer, and that is particularly true for men. The old joke about the Israelites wandering because Moses would not stop to ask for directions rings true to male psychology. In the new synagogue environment women are more likely to seek help and guidance. Men are more likely to check out.

In this, fathers and sons share a common bond. Sadly, that bond is alienation from Judaism, from the language of meaning that could bring them together. When I asked male teen focus groups to describe their inactive male friends, they commonly spoke of people who came once, felt uncomfortable in an unfamiliar environment, and left. When I asked teenage girls the same question, they described relying upon their friends, coming in groups, and learning together.

The New Orleans group worked because they all shared a common tongue: jazz, crawfish, fatherhood and sonhood. The group worked because Rabbi Tom Wiener devoted time, money, and energy to the project. The group worked because in a small, safe, all-male environment they felt comfortable sharing their embarrassment over low Jewish education levels. The group worked because we studied texts about sons honoring their fathers, and fathers teaching their sons. By specifying that a group of men can gather and discuss the most important male relationship in their lives, we did honor to fathers and sons.

When Jewish men gather, they are always sons, and some are also fathers. Regardless of how much Torah we have learned, or how much Hebrew we speak, what songs we sing, or what services we *daven,* we can speak the common language of manhood and share our experiences in this crucial relationship. We can learn from each other. Abraham Joshua Heschel once said in reference to Jewish education, "What we need more than anything is not textbooks but text people." When we study our own lives as Jewish men, we open ourselves as text people.

As I write this article, my wife and I are expecting our first child. With God's help I will become a father before Rosh Hashanah. I am a rabbinical student, exposed to Torah and prayer almost every day. Yet the text for which I long, the Torah I want to study comes from the mouths of those men older and younger than I, who can share their experiences going through birth, fatherhood, grandfatherhood, and even sonhood. As a soon-to-be Jewish father, I have inherited the traditions of fathers and teachers stretching back to the Torah. As I learn and teach from the Biblical and Talmudic words written in our Jewish father tradition, I also long for the modern and contemporary words spoken in our Jewish father community. This is the Torah that will connect me to my child, to the Jewish world, and, ultimately, to God.

The Gift of Fierce Father Love

Allan C. Tuffs

> Your old grandmother says,
> "Maybe you shouldn't go to school,
> You look a little pale."
>
> Run when you hear that.
> A father's stern slaps are better.
>
> Your bodily soul wants comforting.
> The severe father wants spiritual clarity.
>
> He scolds, but eventually
> leads you into the open.
>
> Pray for a tough instructor
> To hear and act and stay within you.
>
> We have been busy accumulating solace.
> Make us afraid of how we were.
> —*Rumi*, translated by Coleman Barks

Where have the fierce fathers gone? Where have the instructors who demanded spiritual clarity gone? At the turn of the twenty-first century, they seem to dwell in the same spiritual exile as all things patriarchal. In bygone eras, a father was praised for being fierce, resolute, and demanding. In modern times we no longer praise such a father; instead we opt for the father who is soft, compassionate, and accepting. While the qualities of the soft, nurturing father are wonderful in many ways, some wonder if fathers should possess an element of fierceness in their love for their children.

By fierceness, I do not mean anger that leads to abusive behavior; I define fierceness as that strong, decisive, and passionate concern men are capable of expressing for the people and causes they love. Carl Gustave Jung alluded to that kind of masculine spirit energy when he wrote, "It is difficult to say to anybody, you should . . . become acquainted with your animal (fierceness), because people think it is a sort of lunatic asylum, they think the animal is jumping over walls and raising hell all over town. Yet, the animal . . . is pious, it follows the path with great regularity. . . . Only man is extravagant."

When men suppress their fierceness they cut themselves off from the wellspring of their masculinity. When men are too soft, their vision is dulled, their ability to experience and express deep emotion is diminished, and their decisiveness is curtailed. Furthermore, when men ignore their fierceness they lose the ability to discipline and set limits for their children, elements of good parenting missing in many modern families.

This is the epoch of feminine spiritual energy, the era of New Age ideas, a time in which we deny the rewards of discipline, struggle, and rebuke. This is an era that does not esteem the steady firm guidance of fathers who love their children fiercely and passionately. Yet, children need both the tender and nurturing love that flows from the feminine spirit and the fierce demanding love that springs from the masculine soul. Every child needs the mother who says, "Maybe you shouldn't go to school. You look a little pale," and the father who says, "How long will you lie there, lazybones . . . bit more hugging yourself in bed and poverty will be calling on you" (Prov. 6:6). When Rumi says that a "father's stern slaps are better," he is not speaking of corporal punishment but of father love which challenges children to expect great things of themselves and not to give in too readily to the easy pleasures. Children who lack either the maternal or paternal love dimension of parental love will be spiritually impoverished.

Many observers of gender differences remark that women tend to seek consensus in group situations, whereas men tend to be hierarchical, seeking a leader to set the tone. This difference is reflected in parenting styles of men and women. A mother is likely to bargain and reason with a young child when met with resistance, whereas a father will be tempted to resort to the old demand, "Do it because I'm your father, that's why." Both approaches are appropriate and necessary in different situations. The problem is, most fathers feel they are doing something wrong when they "lay down the law" to their children. The very idea of a fierce father has come to be identified with the sins of the patriarchal past. Men worry that their natural parenting style might be too harsh or worse, abusive. Consequently, most dads have adopted a more conciliatory and feminine style of parenting. Yet kids still need the firm boundary-setting approach that fathers have traditionally provided.

The kabbalistic tradition speaks of a balance between masculine and feminine energy. It speaks of *Chesed*, the feminine quality of unconditional love and *Gevurah*, the masculine quality of restraint and discipline. A delicate balance of these energies is needed for spiritually sound parenting. When, as in earlier generations, men fail to honor the feminine side of their souls they tend to be severe, unapproachable, and sometimes abusive fathers. Conversely, when men are cut off from *Gevurah*, they tend to be ineffectual, over-lenient, and overindulgent fathers. Perhaps the time has come for us to reclaim fierce father love and to redress the imbalance between feminine and masculine energy in our parenting styles.

If we think of those who helped us the most to grow up, undoubtedly, we will remember a teacher, a boss, or a coach who was hard on us. Nice teachers were just that, nice. We loved them because they made us feel good about ourselves. The demanding teacher, on the other hand, the teacher who taught with father energy probably was not so nice and accepting. We may have even hated him or her for a time. Yet, it was that teacher who taught us the most. By demanding that we master the material we were studying, rather than watering it down or not requiring it at all, they changed our lives. They taught us to expect more of ourselves. With a symbolic "slap on the face," they awakened us to our true potential.

Liberal Judaism does not always honor father energy. Our gender sensitive prayer books have been purged of the word "Father" in favor of the more generic term "parent," suggesting that there is little distinction between fathers and mothers and the way they love their children. The challenge facing contemporary Jewish fathers is to find sources in our tradition that affirm the unique quality of father energy and to suggest positive modes in which to express it.

The Torah suggests that it is not the duty of a father to comfort his children but to strengthen their character. In the Book of Deuteronomy, chapter 8 we read, "Remember the long way that the Eternal One, your God, has made you travel in the wilderness these past forty years, that He might test you by hardships to learn what is in your hearts. . . . He subjected you to the hardship of hunger and then gave you *manna* to eat . . . in order to teach you that man does not live by bread alone, but that man may live on anything that the Eternal decrees . . . bear in mind that the Eternal One disciplines you just as a man disciplines his son." A child finds solace and unconditional love in his mother's presence, but from his father, a child learns how to remain ethical and moral in a broader world, which can be harsh and unloving.

Rabbinic literature speaks of *yisurin shel ahavah* or "chastisements of love." Gunther Plaut explains, "By chastisements of love, as tradition came to call them, a loving Father educates and purifies His children. In doing so, He may be said to experience suffering, to weep over the bitter effects of the afflictions He himself has brought about. . . ." The implication is that fathers teach their children not by giving them all the toys they could want, not by making life as easy as possible, and not by protecting them from the consequences of their actions. A father's job is to strengthen his children's character by demanding that they uphold the high moral and ethical standards of the Torah, even when it is difficult and inconvenient.

Psalm 94:12–13 suggests that chastisements of love give a person the strength of character to survive difficult times of life. "Happy is the man whom You discipline, O Eternal One . . . To give him tranquility in time of misfortune." How differently fathers see their role today. Many contemporary fathers understand their job as avoiding value judgments and not imposing their own cultural and moral "hang-ups" on their children. Fathers today feel that it is more important to be loved by their children than to discipline them. Robert Bly suggests that this lack of masculine energy, the lack of fierce father love, has created what he calls a "Sibling Society" in which fathers are more like big brothers than parents to their children. Fierce father love may be what is needed for contemporary men to be better parents. It may be what is needed to create a safer and saner environment for our children to grow up in.

How might fierce father love express itself in the type of middle class community where most American Jews live? It could be expressed in a variety of ways, but one image that comes to my mind is of a large group of fathers standing in the doorway of the high school. Each father is checking his son's or daughter's book bag for drugs and weapons. Some are embarrassed, some may even be yelling at their dads. A few of them are protesting that their rights are being violated. However, the few students whose fathers are not there know in their hearts that it is their right that is being violated: the right to powerful and passionate father love.

The time has come for us to recognize the beautiful and unique quality of a father's love not only in its nurturing aspect, but in its fierce aspect as well.

The Real Man

Joel Soffin

You may find this hard to believe, but the very first superhero was Jewish—both parts of him.

Who was this first superhero? It was none other than Superman. And how do we know that he was Jewish—both he and his alter-ego Clark Kent? Simple: his fathers, Jerry Siegel and Joe Shuster, were both Jewish.

It seems strange to think of Superman as being Jewish, doesn't it?

Now Clark Kent—that's a different story altogether. We might imagine him as a member of the Jewish community. He's a writer who wears glasses. He's *a nebbish*—an often frightened, incompetent, and powerless man who bumbles along in a non-threatening and reasonably sweet way.

Why would Superman's creators have divided his character into the mighty and the meek? Siegel and Shuster were living out their own ambivalence about being Jewish men in America, following the biblical tradition of separating Ishmael from Isaac and Esau from Jacob: the real men from the Momma's boys. Maybe they were struggling with the American definition of what it means to be a real man and saw themselves as not measuring up to the standard in some way.

A red-blooded American man is a protector, a provider, and a pillar. He defends his family and his community in any way necessary. He provides a good standard of living. He is independent and invulnerable. Big boys don't cry. No pain, no gain. Winning isn't everything: it's the only thing. Stand up like a man.

You can almost hear Abraham speaking these very words to Isaac. In the Torah portion Abraham wakes up his son early in the morning; he's taking him away from home. Isaac is not permitted to ask any questions. His father is strong and powerful, and when he has his mind set on something, it's best not to challenge him in any way. So for three days they walk along in absolute silence, two men being the way men are—strong and silent.

Then it is time to bind Isaac on the altar and to sacrifice him. Some say that Isaac was thirty-seven years old when this happened, so he had to go along with his father's plan of his own free will. Why didn't he protest? He was trying to be a real man. Why didn't he cry? Big boys don't cry.

Our wrestling with images of what it means to be real Jewish men goes back to the very beginning of our history. And the wrestling continues to this day.

A man is a protector. He is strong and brave enough to defend everyone around him, especially his parents, his wife, his sisters, and his children. He is all-powerful and even aggressive and violent if the need arises. All of this is done without evidence of any fear or anxiety.

This description of a real man haunted me for a long time. When I was a young boy, walking home from religious school at the temple that was two blocks from my house was a terrifying experience. Bullies would chase me home; I would barely escape them as I raced through the door to my house.

My younger brother was the fighter in the family. At times, it was he who protected me.

And then there were my early trips to Manhattan just after I got married. I felt an enormous burden as I imagined taking on the role of defending my wife if we encountered any threatening situations away from home. Now I could no longer run away, as Jacob used to do. I had to stand up like a man and face whatever dangers there might be. To be honest, the mere possibility gave me nightmares.

I never played football when I was growing up. Jewish boys just didn't engage in physical contact sports—we might get hurt. When my sons were learning to be more aggressive on the soccer field, I wasn't so sure that was such a good thing. Being so violent didn't seem to be the Jewish way.

How did we become a people who talked and reasoned without resorting to physical violence—whose heroes were not Samson the wrestler, but Hillel, the man of patience and kindness?

The beginnings of an answer can be found in this true story told by Sigmund Freud. One day, as he and his father were taking a walk together, his father said, "When I was a young man, I went for a walk one Saturday. I was well-dressed and had a new fur cap on my head. Someone came up to me and with a single blow knocked off my cap into the mud and shouted: 'Jew! Get off the pavement!'"

"And what did you do?" asked young Freud.

"I went into the roadway and picked up my cap," was his father's quiet reply.

This interchange had a dramatic impact on Freud. To feel like a man, he would have to identify with someone other than his own father.

And yet, his father was acting in the way that he had learned from his own father. This had become the Jewish way to respond to such acts of aggression. Why? Because it was vital to the very survival of the Jewish community.

The rabbis realized as far back as two thousand years ago that our people were too small in numbers and too weak to take on the powers that ruled over us. Each time we tried to do so—against the Romans at Masada or Betar—the consequences were catastrophic. Our people were nearly wiped out.

As Aviva Cantor has explained, during the Middle Ages, when we lived in separate, tightly knit communities, the rabbis developed a new understanding of what it means to be a real Jewish man. Violence was prohibited under virtually any conditions. Even if we might have won a battle or two, the powers-that-be would take revenge on our community as a whole and the suffering would be unbearable. No violence was accepted within the Jewish community either, lest it spill over onto our behavior outside.

And so the rabbis taught: *Aizeh hu Gibor?* Who is strong and a hero? He who is able to control his passions and not yield to the temptation to strike back. Who is the real Jewish man? The *talmid chacham*, the one who studies the Torah and the Talmud. Through his studies, the spiritual hero will save the Jewish people from destruction.

This is the same attitude expressed by the ultra-Orthodox in Israel today who seek exemptions from military service, claiming that they are defending the country by being part of God's army in the yeshivah.

But we don't live in such isolated communities anymore. We live in the aftermath of the Holocaust, with the words "Never Again" ringing in our ears. So it is time we take back more of the protector role. Think carefully: have you ever risked your life and your well-being to save someone else? Have you ever put your life in danger for another person?

There was one time I did so. In April of 1987 I visited refuseniks in the former Soviet Union. I didn't know whether it was safe to violate Soviet laws and bring them medicine and record their stories, but my wife and I and one other couple went anyway. I had nightmares of never returning to my sons, but the trip had to be made regardless. Never again would our people suffer if we could defend them.

Returning to the U.S., I felt heroic, sensing for the first time what it meant to be a real Jewish man. I had taken back my power as protector in a Jewish way.

Men are also taught to play the role of provider. We Jews often define ourselves in terms of the work we do. When we meet new people, we quickly inquire about their career or occupation. When we speak with our children about what they want to be when they grow up, the conversation centers on job choices, not on Jewish sources of self-worth and self-esteem. We do not ask if they seek to become a *tzaddik*. We ask whether they will become a doctor or lawyer or accountant.

This breadwinner role narrows our identity as whole human beings and sometimes transforms the workplace into a battleground. Our co-workers become our competitors rather than our teammates. We have to look out for number one and keep our own upward progress ever in mind.

Worst of all, this makes us vulnerable.

The truth is that we have little control over our lives as breadwinners. There is nothing we can do to offset the fluctuations of the economy or the changes in economic policy introduced in Washington. We have all the responsibility and so little of the power. And worst of all, we can't talk about it openly to each other.

Have you been laid off, this year or last year? Are you afraid your job is in jeopardy? As Frank Pittman has written: "When we lose our work, we lose our dignity, our network, our purpose, our structure, and we live in a state of shame. It's nice if our family loves us anyway, but we [feel] that we haven't earned it and don't deserve it"—that we have failed as men.

In the days of the *shtetl*, this problem was much less intense. If a person lost his job, even for an extended period, he did not lose his identity or his manhood, for that depended primarily on whether he was a *talmid chacham*, a man who knew Torah, or a *chasid*, a pious man who shared his overflow with the community.

And, finally, there is the man's role as pillar. "Real men" keep their emotions and feelings deeply suppressed, don't open up to anyone about their inner lives, and resent the questions asked by spouses and children. "Real men" are never unsure of themselves. We don't say: I don't know—not just about directions, but about anything. We fear being ridiculed as weak, or rejected as wimpy. Interestingly, keeping quiet is a kind of power. It draws everyone else to us as they struggle to discover what we're really thinking and feeling, and erects a wall between us and our families. We remain isolated and alone.

Once again, in the *shtetl* it was easier for men to express their feelings. In those days, according to Aviva Cantor, "most Eastern European Jews believed emotions were made to be expressed, whether in words or in tears, both to achieve communication and as a catharsis. . . . Boys were never told to be brave or to be a man. They were expected to cry when [they were] hurt or unhappy."

Holding our feelings in so tightly also harms our physical health. The life span of men is seven or eight years shorter than it is for women, partly, I believe, because of this suppression of feelings. It is thus vital for us Jewish men to open ourselves up to one another, to share our real thoughts and feelings, to find some company on the common journey of Jewish manhood.

Centuries ago, Hillel taught: "*B'makom she-ain anashim* . . . in a place where there are no real men, *hishtadayl l'hiyot ish* . . . you, you strive to be a man." I would offer this version of Hillel's teaching: In a time and in a place where some think that to be a man is to be strong, silent, invincible, and invulnerable, we need to think differently. We need to remember that to be a real Jewish man we must be strong enough to conquer the temptation to run away and hide behind our roles as protector, provider, and pillar. We must be strong enough to share our feelings, to ask for help and support, and to find our real self.

Journeying Together: Obligations of the Jewish Father

Michael Geller

**Meyn Yingele—
My Little One**

I have a son, a little son,
A boy completely fine.
When I see him it seems to me
That all the world is mine.

But seldom, seldom do I see
My child awake and bright;
I only see him when he sleeps;
I'm only home at night.

It's early when I leave for work;
When I return, it's late.
Unknown to me is my own flesh,
Unknown is my child's face.

When I come home so wearily
In the darkness after day.
My pale wife exclaims to me:
"You should have seen our child play.

"He sweetly spoke; he smartly asked,
'Oh, mama, answer me;
When will papa come and bring
A penny, just for me?'"

I have her speak, I rush within
Oh, yes, yes it must be:
My father love is flaring up,
My child must look at me.

I stand besides his little bed,
I look and try to hear.

> In his dream he moves his lips:
> "Why isn't Papa here?"
>
> I bend and kiss his pale blue eyes
> I see them open then;
> They look at me; they look at me!
> Then they quickly close again.
>
> Your papa's standing very close,
> With a penny for my dear.
> In his dream he moves his lips:
> "Why isn't Papa here?"
>
> I stand depressed and all my thoughts
> Are bitter and heart-sore:
> "One day, when you wake, my child,
> You'll not see me anymore."
>
> —Morris Rosenfeld

When Morris Rosenfeld penned this immortal Yiddish classic in 1887, lamenting the lack of participation in his son's life because of his work as a garment worker, he'd no idea his words would reflect on the lives of many Jewish fathers today.

To be a Jewish father, after all, requires time. And although the Jewish tradition historically provided outlets for fathers to spend time with their children, serve as examples to them, the secular responsibilities placed on Jewish men today cancel out the communal obligations and the ability to be present in their children's lives.

What then, in the face of modern time constraints, long working days, soccer schedules, is the Jewish father? Is he a man of faith, connected to the Jewish community, the synagogue, and lifecycle events? Is he a jack-of-all-trades, a person able to balance all responsibilities placed on him? Is he an imparter of values, ethics, and morals? Is he the quiet man in the corner, nodding and smiling, with no opinion at all?

Jewish tradition offers many examples of what the Jewish father must be. In twenty-first century America, in a Jewish community defined not by traditional communal standards, but by synagogue affiliation, secular Jewish and popular culture, how does one find the time necessary to be a Jewish father when the Jewish calendar and daily rituals are lost, unknown, or unable to be performed?

The roles a Jewish father can play—as educator, mentor, guide, or role model—can begin to provide some idea. The Talmud instructs that a father is obligated to provide his son "with Torah, a trade, and some say, teach him how to swim" (*Kiddushin* 29).

Torah is clearly the most simple to explain. The mindset of those rabbis who converse within the Talmud was directed toward Jewish education and the importance of Torah within that framework. So certainly a Jewish father must provide his son with the cornerstone of Jewish life and learning. This responsibility is not taken lightly at all; for if a Jewish father himself could not teach his son, it was his responsibility to find his son a teacher to perform the task.

A trade? That is even far more applicable to our lives today. The ability to support oneself, make a living, continue building, has often been an element stressed in Jewish fathering. This is about more than money in the bank—it is about legacy, tradition, about knowing the value of things earned and their value in years to come.

Teaching him to swim? This concept is perhaps the most important of all because it rests on survival and, in turn, the ability to carry out the other tasks deemed essential in the rabbinic concept. One learns how to swim so one will not drown; how apropos that the rabbis would adjoin this small, and somewhat minor, task to the Jewish father. To swim, or survive, so to speak, means to be present, active, and responsible. Survival enables one to continue to learn Torah and build up both one's family and community.

Although the roles a Jewish father can play vary, the essential element that was missing from Rosenfeld's life was time. How can a father properly introduce his children to Torah, a trade, etc., if he is not around, having to spend too many hours doing other important things? This may be an instance in which the "swimming" aspect earns its place. "Swimming" seems to represent the column of activities that are essential for life every day.

If a father can show his child those activities, engage his child in those moments, then he fulfills that obligation. Chaim Waxman, a sociologist of the Jewish community, explains that a Jewish father was not only to educate his children, but was "expected to socialize his children into the life of the . . . community." Such a charge falls directly in line with the Talmudic dictate about swimming. Even the simplest task, when done with child in tow, can reap invaluable experience.

Leading by example, being a trainer for life, is easily done in a world of busy schedules. The interaction between father and child during those times provides a lesson in living. It is during these moments when Torah can be passed along. It is also during these moments where a child can learn about what it means to be a father, who his/her father is, and what priorities have been set in life. It is very possible that during these moments the Jewish father is at his best, continuing a historic practice in which he presents to his children a set of beliefs, values, and behaviors that will be beneficial to their development. The Jewish father essentially leads by example; he commits to Torah, work, and life through his moments with his children.

When I was sixteen, my father, a man who very rarely spoke to me, came into my bedroom and handed me Theodor Herzl's *The Jewish State*. He said, "This is what it's all about." And then he walked out. That moment, combined with years of silently watching him do business, interact with people, taught me something about being a man, about being a Jewish man.

He taught me to always be proud of the fact that I was Jewish; this meant always standing up for myself when confronted by people who had less than honorable opinions about Jews, supporting Israel against her enemies, and remembering that my people are my greatest connection to history.

He taught me to conduct myself with honesty in business—to be open, tolerant, and provide the best work possible. He taught me *tzedakah*—to always give to those who needed even if they refused to ask.

He even taught me how to hunt, fish, and wash a car. He taught me "how to swim," so to speak. And although the rabbis would not have been too happy with the hunting lessons, I know I benefited.

Though there are no great words of Torah that depart from his lips, there is behavior deemed honorable by the Torah, lessons in life that leave a legacy.

The obligations for a Jewish father go far beyond traditional norms. When Torah is relegated to our rabbis and Hebrew schools, trade delegated to our colleges and other professionals, there is still room in the modern setting for successful Jewish fathering.

Modern Jewish fathering relies heavily on "swimming"; it may require a departure, but not a complete dismissal, of the traditional role. Perhaps it's the simple melding of the two—secular activity that highlights positive Jewish behavior—that is the essence of the modern Jewish father. Perhaps the ability of a father to take his children by the hand and lead them into experiences that will mold, guide, and ultimately change their lives makes all the difference. It may require a father to silently say the *Shehecheyanu* whenever he is with his child—to bless every moment and bring Torah and life together.

Section IV

Involving Men

Introduction

This section explores adult male involvement in the Jewish community. If domestic Judaism is largely the province of females, these authors raise the question about the lack of male involvement in Jewish communal life. They raise questions including: What does it mean to get in touch with my masculine side? Are men really attracted to leadership positions? Do hands-on social action experiences attract more men? Far from playing into stereotypes, many of the answers are surprising and nuanced.

Rabbi Sheldon Zimmerman's address "To Restore the Brother of Brotherhood"—originally given at the 35th NFTB Biennial Convention in Houston, Texas in 1994—stresses the immediacy of the need for the participation of Jewish men in all areas of synagogue life. He suggests that the synagogue has replaced the entirety of what were once nonvoluntary Jewish communities. By nonvoluntary, the author refers to our history when Jewish community meant a Jewish neighborhood in which all the major institutions were Jewish. Given the breadth of the needs of the Jewish community, Rabbi Zimmerman believes that Jewish men, and thus Jewish Brotherhoods, need to step up to help meet many of the community's needs—from increasing Jewish literacy, to serving as active models of mitzvah practice, to making newcomers to the synagogue feel welcome. Rabbi Zimmerman calls for Brotherhoods to take a role in spiritualizing, which he argues is not the sole province of women. The Brotherhoods should also be creating new liturgy, publishing prayer books, and using their creativity for deepening spiritual experience.

Art Grand's "Men's Stories: The Longing for Holiness" tells the stories of the men in his synagogue, their sense of powerlessness, and their belief that their own competency has been slowly eroded. He explains how different men search for connections to God, a sense of holiness in their lives, and a sense of purpose. He writes of men who are so far removed from the search that they forget that holiness is a possibility for their lives, and how having a context in which to meet together as Jewish men can make all the difference.

Rabbi Kenneth Milhander believes that Judaism has always asked men to delve deeper into their masculinity than stereotypes suggest. "Getting In Touch with My Masculine Side" tells the story of Rabbi Milhander's growing up in what he describes as a female-dominated home and work environment, the benefits he received from such an upbringing, and the recent discoveries he has made as part of his synagogue's Men's Club—the pleasures of bonding with men. He writes that joining the NFTB (now the MRJ) is a key step for the men in his community. He hopes that the men of Reform Judaism will find or create ways to form strong bonds to their synagogues It is critical, he argues, that men as well as women have an important role as well as a stake in their synagogue.

Rabbi Shawn Israel Zevit's "*Lech Lecha:* New Pathways for Jewish Men" notes that men's connection to Judaism and to masculinity are in flux. Given this changing state of identity, Rabbi Zevit explores the different relationships men have with their Judaism and the challenge of how to move forward. He explores the possibilities of what forward movement could entail, including redefinitions of some of the most fundamental relationships in the lives of men.

Dale Glasser explores the generally accepted truth that men involved in the synagogue seek positions of "power." His essay "Men and Leadership in Reform Congregations: More Questions Than Answers" posits that the decrease in the number of men in leadership roles is related to larger changes in the synagogue's organization and structure. He believes that synagogues need to create new opportunities and models of leadership in order to attract men. He closes with a list of thought-provoking questions for any synagogue truly trying to redefine its leadership positions and structure.

Rabbi Marla Feldman explores "The Role of Men in the Social Action Arena." She opens with the hypothesis that the social action arena continues to attract a larger percentage of men when compared to other Jewish arenas. Finding statistics that support this idea, she questions what it is about certain social action activities that attract men. She analyzes a program run by the Religious Action Center for insight. Her analysis of what attracts men is provocative and challenges synagogues to create programming opportunities that may be more appealing to men.

Questions for Discussion

As you read each piece, consider the following questions:

1. What are the assumptions of the author(s) of the essay(s) you read? How do you respond to the assumptions?
2. What programs or suggestions are most appealing to you? Which are least appealing to you? How does that differ from what is most appealing to the majority of men in your community?
3. What ideas for increasing men's participation have yet to be explored in these essays?
4. How might a variety or combination of approaches work in your community to involve more men in synagogue life?

To Restore the Brother of Brotherhood

Sheldon Zimmerman

I have a very simple thesis today which I am going to try to expound on with you, and that is that despite the frustrations, anxieties and literally, those who tell us there is no room for Brotherhoods anymore, this Rabbi believes, believes with a firmness of heart, that we need you today, more than we've ever needed you before. I say that to you with full understanding of all the attacks on same-gender organizations, I say that to you with full understanding of the need for us to work together with women and with the fullness of our community and our movement. But if there has ever been a time for Jewish men to *stand* together, to *be* together, to *work* together as men in making a difference in the society and in this movement, now is that time. I am going to try and explain that to you in the few moments that we share this morning.

First of all we have to understand the world we live in. When we talk about the 21st century, that's still a long way off, though it's only five years off. The reality is, it's a long way, five years. The five years somehow already take us into the realm of prophesy.

I can only tell you what's happening today. And what's happening today is that our Jewish community, the people with whom we work, the people with whom we live, the people whom you lead, and live your lives with, that community is under radical transformation and change. You know that, you don't need me to do it with you historically, but just give me a moment to try to trace it out with you.

Historically, Judaism was built around a non-voluntary community structure, in which the community ran everything. It ran the schools, it ran familial life, it ran hospices and hospitals, it ran everything. That community is long gone, it's a memory, it doesn't exist. In America the Jewish community lived in neighborhoods that even when you were no longer even affiliated or literate or understood Jewish festivals, you lived in neighborhoods where everybody else was "Jewing" it around Rosh Hashana, where everybody else was "Jewing" it around Passover, where everybody else was doing the Jewish thing even if you knew nothing, understood nothing. You knew when Rosh Hashana was, you knew when Yom Kippur was, when Passover was.

Those neighborhoods are gone, forget about it. They're memory of a long past that just doesn't exist any longer.

At one time the Jewish home was an altar, a replacement for the ancient temple. In the home we played out all the rituals and traditions and meaningful moments of our faith experience. That home is gone, not because people want it to go, but because the reality is that for most Jews today, they are neither literate enough, nor comfortable enough, nor able to do in their home by themselves what they used to be able to do. You see, what happened historically, and again this would be another whole set of discussions, you had community which ran everything, to which Jews paid taxes and were members of. You had an academy system which trained the Jewish people. You had neighborhoods in which Jews lived. You had the Jewish family teaching and transmitting Jewish values. And a synagogue was only a place where people came to pray, because that's all they came there for. Now we, your Rabbis, have taught you over the years that synagogues were always houses of study and houses of assembly and houses of prayer. It's not true. It's not true historically. The synagogue was always in Jewish history simply a building, run by the community in which Jews came to pray. It was never what it is today. What you and I have today is a radical new institution that never existed before in Jewish history. The American synagogue is so new and so different that when Israelis come to this country, they don't even understand what the synagogue is. You mean there is a synagogue which educates kids, which has day-care and nursery schools, which has Brotherhoods and Sisterhoods and has a plethora of programming? That's not a synagogue, that's what the Jewish community used to do.

And therein lies the radical difference. The synagogue today is the new Jewish community. That old community—the non-voluntary community—ended many years ago. Now that doesn't mean there aren't JCCs, and that JCCs aren't important. JCCs are important. But when Jews look to the community, to the center of their community, not to the community center, but to the center of their community, where they know they will be cared for, where they know their names will be remembered, where they know their children will be educated and they can count on for rabbis and others in sickness and need, there is only one address, there is only one place they come to and they know it and you know it. They come to the synagogue.

The problem is we haven't even thought about what that means in terms of how to take care of all those people. And most of the complaints about synagogues is that people have expectations that we haven't prepared ourselves even to meet.

How can three rabbis serve two thousand families, you figure it out? But what has happened is that people expect their rabbis to visit them in hospitals, teach their children, go on retreat, be there whenever they need them, do the funerals, do the namings, give them counseling, and no one can do that, you know that and I know that. And you know that no synagogue structure today can handle all the expectations, but our people come to us.

And this will end the history lesson: our people come to us because we are the last institution left that can make a difference in their lives. From before birth till after death, there is only one place that can make a difference in Jewish life today, and that's the synagogue.

Now in addition to all these radical changes and in the emergence of a new kind of community, which is voluntary, or don't have to be Jewish, with the diminution of anti-semitism, with the comfort our kids feel in being American, you know and I know that at the same time men are undergoing radical changes, demands and expectations. We're not even sure what we're supposed to be anymore. Are we supposed to be nurturing, are we supposed to be macho, are we supposed to be jocks, are we supposed to be service providers? What is expected of men as parents, as children, as spouses, as people who care for family, for other people. What does it mean? I'm not even sure we understand that anymore. What was expected in the fifties and sixties has changed radically. I'm not even sure how to teach it to my sons, or my daughters. It's something that's happening all about us.

But amidst all of this, there are certain things that I have come to understand about why we need you. Because it seems to me, the Brotherhoods, if you will renew and transform your vision, can make an ultimate difference in the future of American Judaism.

And what I'm calling on you today is to no longer be satisfied with the old role of Brotherhoods. The breakfast-cookers, the ushers at services, all of the wonderful stuff that we have done over the years no longer can be the vision and mission of what we have to be. And I am going to tell you something else. If you project this vision, the people will come, that I believe. If it makes a difference to be a member of the National Federation of Temple Brotherhoods, people will be part of that vision. If being a member of Brotherhood can make a difference in their lives, and through what you do as a Brotherhood member change the lives of those around you, people will come. Because one thing people are looking for today is the capacity to make a difference. In this anonymous, uncaring world in which people think their lives are irrelevant to the grand flow of history, being a member of a Brotherhood ought to mean that you *can* make a difference, somehow.

Let me try to share with you some of the ways I think Brotherhoods can make a radical difference.

First, I think the Brotherhood can be the humanizing force of the synagogue. In other words you and I live in synagogues today that if you're there, no one notices you're there, and if you're not there, people don't even notice you're not there. And what's the complaint you always hear: Rabbi, I wasn't in synagogue for three weeks and nobody called. I was sick, homebound for a month, and nobody showed up. Now you know and I know that they didn't tell us they were sick. You know and I know that we can't keep track of 400 or 600 or 1000 people, shall we say. But the reality is on the most basic human level, people want to count, and to be a member of a synagogue means that when I'm there you care for me, and when I'm not there you miss me, and Brotherhoods can help with that humanizing force.

What does it mean to be an usher? Does it mean to hand out books, or does it mean that when somebody walks in the place there is a face with a name, that somebody cares, and if you're not there, somebody knows you're not there?

Why is it that people say they walk in one of our sanctuaries and it's as if they've never been there? And no one noticed them, no one says hello to them. Now, you and I know no one is malevolent. You see your friends, you haven't seen them in a couple of weeks, you start schmoozing. Other people feel unnoticed, or left out. What I'm suggesting to you is that in the loneliness and anonymity of modern life, you become the humanizing element. You are the connection, the human connection to the synagogue.

Men need to know just as much as somebody else that someone really cares, and you can be that manifestation of caring. Now I'm not going to tell you how to do it, you can program it better than I can. But wouldn't it be wonderful if the men of a congregation, whatever the congregation would be, would resolve to be that humanizing force. That when people are sick, it's not simply a hospital visiting group that is there, but that people care enough to call, to drop a line. And I know many of you do that. But more than that, that when people are in the synagogue, it is your mission to integrate them, to care enough about them to know what's going on in their lives. The Brotherhood can do that. You are not just being out with the guys, you're doing some bonding of an essentially significant nature. And men can connect with each other. Out there in that dog-eat-dog world we connect with each other but it's an often commercial, financial, "what can you do for me" connection! Brotherhood is the only place where you and I can connect together, where I'm not asking for anything. I don't care how much money you make. I am not worried about a commercial connection with you. I am there because we are Jews, and we are Jewish men, who share history, who share destiny, who can make a difference in each other's lives. That I know there is one place in that town where I'm not simply a number, or a phone number, or something that has to be sold to somebody else. The one place in town I count as a person, that when I walk in that door, when I see a Ron, or an Alan, or a Ken, that their embrace of me is not because next week they're going to call me for a donation or next week they're going to call me to see if they're going to sell me something; but rather it's because they actually care about me as a human being. And then I'll be there for them the same way.

It's alright to say we have feelings, it's ok men to say we have feelings too, we have needs. One of the needs is that *I* count, beyond being a father, beyond being a husband, beyond being a provider. I'm a human being, I need to be needed, and I need to be cared for. Brotherhood is the only vehicle which can do that. Nobody else. It is the humanizing. It is the humanizing, caring, bonding that I am talking about. It's that bonding that we need. No, we don't have to sit and beat drums and schwitz in a steam bath, though that was good too. We don't have to move out to a tent somewhere, for all this meshugass that they call men finding out about themselves. But we need a place to cry, we need a place to say we're weak. But can I come to a place where I can tell you I'm hurting, and you give a damn about me? And I'm telling you that men need that, you know that, I don't have to tell you that. We need it desperately. Profoundly! Brotherhood can be the humanizing element to the synagogue.

Secondly, Brotherhood can be the Mitzvah source. Now this is something we've been doing for years. What do we have to teach our kids? That to be a man is to be more than macho. Our kids have all these models of the macho man. We are going to teach our kids by our very being, that to be a Jewish man is to serve others, that's part of what it means to be a Jewish male, we define what it means to be a Jewish man. Now we, Brotherhood, have been doing that for years, but that's not the image we have out there, you know that. If you say Brotherhood to most of the men in your congregation they think, "Ah, it's a group of, you know, schlumpfs over there." That's an honest opinion, because they don't know what you do, and they don't know what we do, because we haven't told them. Our synagogues only say, "Pay your dues," they don't ask anything else. It's about time the Brotherhood said: You want to be a member of Brotherhood? You've got to do a Mitzvah project every year. Now you will lose some people, believe me, there'll be people out there who are going to say, "I don't want to do that; you can't tell me what to do." Typical Reform nonsense. "No one can tell me what to do." "I'm a Jew, the heck you telling me what to do." But yet to be a member of a Brotherhood, then, is something you aim for. It's a privilege, not a right. You want to serve, you want to be a Jewish man who cares about doing, about serving, about Mitzvah. Then that's what it means to be a member of Brotherhood.

Third. Brotherhood is really the only place where interfaith and interethnic dialogue can take place on a grassroots level. Now what I mean by that is a very simple thing, very simple. We, in the Reform Movement, are well known for glitzy dialogue. ADL does it too, all Jewish organizations do it. You get leaders together and they talk to each other and we think we've done great stuff. Brotherhoods are grassroots. If, in fact we are going to overcome the obstacles and barriers between the African American and Jewish community, between the Hispanic community, whom we really don't know very much about, and the Jewish community, it's going to be done on the grassroots level, men talking to men.

That's one of the key ways in which interfaith dialogue has to take place. It's not going to be done by Rabbi Schindler, although he's accomplished great things, it's not going to be done by the leadership of the Union, it's going to be done right at home, where we build the connections with others. That's why Chautauqua is so important. Don't you know that JCS (Jewish Chautauqua Society) is based upon a profound American belief that if people know us, they'll have a sense of what we're about. They may not like us, because we all know a lot of people and don't necessarily care for them. But JCS is based on the belief that knowledge will lend itself to respect. Tolerance (that's a good word, it's not a bad word) and acceptance of diversity, both are important concepts. Somehow, when you and I create these places, these locales where men can speak to men (of course, women to women as well, and families to families, don't misunderstand me), that will make a difference. Men can do it, because we do have certain languages we speak. If America is going to work, and remember America is an experiment, it's not a reality, if America is going to work, it's going to be the ability of a people of a variety of colors, and beliefs, and ethnicities to work together. That's part of what Brotherhood can be—it can be the force for interfaith and intergroup dialogue.

Let me just do a few more, then we'll stop. Everyone says men are just learning to kiss and hug. I don't know about you, but I had a father who hugged and kissed, I had a grandfather who hugged and kissed. The notion that men can't cry—I saw men, old men cry. And it's not an invention of the Feminist Movement (and I'm all for it, egalitarianism and all the good stuff that has happened from Jewish feminism, so don't misunderstand me); women didn't invent tears. My father hugged and kissed, wept and cried, and held us close.

You can help create that image of maleness, from a Jewish perspective, in all those single-parent families, where there are no fathers around. Do you know how many single-parent families there are in the Jewish community? How many divorces? How many mixed and blended families? When I do a Bar Mitzvah, used to be I could work with two sets of parents, right? Now I have four sets of parents, eight sets of grandparents. And it's no joke, I have become an "on the spot crisis intervention person," because always around Bar Mitzvah, and other lifecycle occasions, things always blow up. "You didn't invite this one to the party," "what do you mean you don't want my significant other whom I've lived with for seven years to stand with me on the bima?" I had a little boy running out of the study the other day in tears, because his parents were using this opportunity to tear each other apart. We need male models, single-parent families need men around to help, we need big brothers, not just for poor, deprived kids, but for our own deprived kids. There are plenty of Jewish kids out there who are rotting without love. I'm not saying you shouldn't do it for other kids, too, but I'm talking right in our own home. Used to be we don't have those problems, right? Jews don't drink, baloney! Jews don't take drugs, baloney! There's plenty of pain in the Jewish community. There's plenty of dysfunction in the Jewish community. It's about time that we, the National Federation of Temple Brotherhoods, say we will become the nurturing male image. We will become the fathers where there are no fathers. We will enable families to work together, to come together, because we Jewish men have something to say, we've said it for years, and it's time to say it again. We have nurturing to do among our own people.

Two more things. Brotherhood is also a force for literacy, and what I mean by that is this: there are plenty of men out there who are embarrassed that they don't know anything, and they certainly don't want their wives to know that, and they certainly don't want anybody else to know it, especially their kids. But you know in the comfort of Brotherhood, they're willing to admit it. Where there are other men who don't know, I can say, I don't know. It's hard, you're supposed to know it all, right? As a parent, as a rabbi, you're supposed to know it all, it's hard to say I really don't know. Brotherhood becomes a vehicle for literacy, no, not with a glitzy adult education thing, but just a way to get men to learn more. Look, we too played hookey as kids. There used to be a 7-Eleven coffee shop across the street from Emanu-El in Dallas, where most of the leadership in the Brotherhood today spent their youth, during religious school hours. But you know something, we all did it. If you really did it well, you became a rabbi later. My point is a very simple one: we all don't know, you understand that? It's ok to say that. Then we can study together.

See, it's ok not to know yet, it is not ok not to know forever. We have to help our men say it's ok that we don't know yet, but it's not ok to say you don't know forever.

Lastly, Brotherhood to me becomes a spiritualizing force. We too are spiritual beings, we too yearn for God, we too yearn for prayer. We've got this kind of crazy world today which everyone is telling us that only women know about spirituality. You read *Reform Judaism,* the official magazine of the Reform Movement, and it's as if spirituality is something new. We too have spiritual needs, we too need to pray, we too have souls that soar as well as minds that think and hands that do. You're not simply ushers at services, my friends. You, I, *we* are participants. And it is time for our Brotherhoods to become the spiritualizing force of who we are. Why should prayer books only be published by the Sisterhoods? I love "The Covenant of the Heart"—you should use it, prayers written by the Women of Reform Judaism. Don't we have prayers, don't we have something that comes from the souls and spirit of who we are? As fathers, as sons, what it means to be the carriers of a tradition? With all the anxieties and doubts that we have, that's what it means to be a man today. Don't we, too, reach out for God? Aren't we creative? Of course we are, and our Brotherhoods can be that spiritualizing force.

For me, being here with you is a special privilege. When I think of that verse from Psalms, "*Hinei Ma Tov Uma Na-im Shevet Achim Gam Yahad,*" we all gender neuterize it. "How good for *people* to come together." But that's not what it says. It says "How good it is for *brothers* to come together." What I am pleading with you, because only you can do it, is to restore the brother of Brotherhood. How good and how pleasant it is for brothers to dwell together in unity.

Men's Stories: The Longing for Holiness

Art Grand

My stories began over a year ago, when I was asked to deliver the *d'var Torah* for a "Men's Service" at the URJ Biennial in Houston in 2005—a service that would focus specifically on men's spiritual issues. I was honored to be asked, but frankly, I was stumped. I pride myself on avoiding stereotypes. It had never occurred to me that there were men's spiritual issues. So I found myself a teacher. Our temple Men's Club was about to put up the sukkah, so I decided to get their advice. Amidst the hammering and the camaraderie, I explained my dilemma. "I have to give a *d'var Torah* for a group of men just like you, and I don't know what will be meaningful to them. Let me describe the Torah portion for the Biennial, and tell me what strikes you." The Torah portion was *Vayeira*. I described the angels appearing outside Abraham's tent, Abraham's becoming a father, and the binding of Isaac. "I wonder how Isaac felt as his father was about to plunge the knife into him," I said. "That's our story," they told me. "That's what your *d'var Torah* needs to be about."

For those men, life was all about being competent. In their work lives, they are businessmen and professionals. They had struggled to find a leadership role in the congregation. They were proud of their work putting up the sukkah, maintaining the building, and cooking latkes for the school Chanukah party. But there were two men who were going through painful divorces, and a third had a child who was gravely ill. Suddenly, they felt powerless. Their sense of competency was gone. They felt that they were dependent on others: dependent on God and dependent on emotional support from the other men.

I've told this story again and again. It's amazing how much it resonates. These men and I are all fathers, but we are all afraid that we will suddenly become as vulnerable as Isaac. Isaac's sudden sense of powerlessness and incompetence is the story of many Jewish men.

Last summer, I facilitated a retreat for our temple board. The question came up: What is the difference between a synagogue and a Jewish community center? Someone said that the answer was easy. In a synagogue, everything revolves around Torah. I looked around the room and I could see backs straighten. One man, whose connection to the congregation was through the Men's Club, got particularly upset. "My main connection to the community is the Men's Club poker game," he said. "If you say that everything revolves around Torah, you automatically exclude me from the community." I reminded him that he had just gone to a shivah minyan for the wife of a fellow Men's Club member, and that he had done a wonderful job comforting the mourner. "Perhaps," I told him, "the Men's Club poker game is different from every other poker game in the world. Perhaps it's a place where you build connections and create sacred community, and where you learn to do mitzvahs for each other. Perhaps the poker game is Torah after all." The man smiled and relaxed in his seat. "I never thought about it that way," he told me. "My life already revolves around Torah, but I never knew it." At that moment, his sense of his Jewish identity changed completely.

Our congregation has been going through a process modeled vaguely after Synagogue 2000. It's been interesting to see how the men react to Synagogue 2000's notion of a synagogue as spiritual community. Rabbi Lawrence Hoffman, one of the founders of Synagogue 2000, defines spirituality as the sense that everything is connected and that our lives are part of something larger than ourselves. And he defines Jewish spirituality as the sense that things are connected through Jewish rituals and the story of the Jewish people. This turns out to be exactly what the men in our congregation are looking for. After studying these ideas at the Synagogue 2000 meetings, one man put it: "I never regarded myself as a spiritual person. But the spirituality you're talking about is something I've been looking for my entire life."

There are so many names for God. We talk about *Adonai* and the Holy One. But as I listened to the men in our congregation, I realized that Connection and Community can also be names for God. And if you listen carefully enough, you may find that Poker is also a name for God. The *Shima* says it all: listen carefully—listen to people's hopes and yearnings, and you will discover that God is one. So the men talked, and I listened, and we all learned something. I learned their language was really God language, and they learned that they had been doing holy acts all along—that even their poker games were holy. They realized that they had a track record for doing holy things and that they might be able to do more. And so this year at Sukkot, the Men's Club played poker in the sukkah. And our Torah readers for Simchat Torah and Shabbat Sukkot were past presidents of the Men's Club (in fact, they were the two men who went through divorces a year ago). Neither of them had read since their bar mitzvahs.

A few weeks ago, our Torah study group looked at a Chasidic text about the unique holiness in every person. One cantankerous eighty-five-year-old man responded right away. "I've been thinking about this idea of holiness," he told me, "and I've decided that I'm just not a holy person. I've never done anything holy and I probably never will." I reminded him that when I met him fifteen years ago, his son had just died of AIDS. And he took all his pain and all of his anger and used it to goad the congregation into building a building. I held my hands up towards the ceiling and almost cried. "Bernie," I told him, "you built this building. What could be more holy than that? Think of all of the programs and all of the learning that happen here—things that wouldn't happen without our sacred space." But he wouldn't believe me. In his eyes, he was just a curmudgeon. The Torah study group spent the next twenty minutes trying to convince him that he was holy. The people in the Torah study group just wouldn't let up. If Bernie hadn't given in and finally agreed, we'd still be there arguing with him. We were able to see the tragedy of his life story as well as the strength and courage that it must have taken him to turn the pain of his personal tragedy into something good for the community. We knew that that space, that room where we were sitting, had brought so much holiness to our lives and to our study. And it would never have happened without Bernie. One person concluded, "That's why Jews need congregations. None of us can see the holiness in ourselves, but we can each help someone else to see it in themselves."

In the end, we're all looking for the same things: a connection to God, a sense that our lives are holy, and a sense that our lives have meaning. The difference is that some of us are afraid to use those words. There are people in our congregations who feel that they are so Jewishly incompetent that they can't even utter a dream of holiness. It seems to be too much to aspire to holiness. And so they use other words, like "I want to meet Jews at a poker game."

My stories are about Jewish men. But the more I tell these stories, the more I'm convinced that they're not merely "men's stories." They are stories of people who feel that they are incompetent Jews, of people who are longing for holiness but are afraid to use the word.

Nine years ago, I went to a Synagogue 2000 workshop at a Biennial. After the workshop, I told Dr. Ron Wolfson that Synagogue 2000 would do wonders for our congregation, but our members weren't very forward thinking. I was convinced that I couldn't find twenty people to be part of the Synagogue 2000 team. Ron and I talked for a few moments, and he told me, "You sound like a congregation where people are afraid to admit how desperately they need God." Ultimately, that's what my stories are about: people who are afraid to admit how desperately they need God.

Getting in Touch with My Masculine Side

Kenneth Milhander

In recent years, a lot of men have been working very hard to get in touch with their feminine side. You wouldn't know it from beer commercials, but men, who continue to be taught and socialized to be uncaring, unfeeling, unemotional robots, have found that compassion, nurturing, and altruism are also male attributes and do not threaten or inhibit the male mystique. For men who were raised in a male-dominated, autocratic, authoritarian home, such soul searching can only benefit and broaden their personal feelings and their relationships with their spouse and children.

This is what Judaism has always taught. Beginning with the God-image, Judaism blended the powerful, dominant, warrior type of deity with the notion that God is also compassionate, just, warm, and loving. As societies developed, though, men and women stuck to traditional roles and up until very recently had to play out their gender image irrespective of internal feelings. So most of us who are adults today grew up in homes where men carried the image of the strong, dominant type, and women the image of the "weaker sex."

I grew up in a very different kind of home. My father suffers from Huntington's Disease, a neurological disorder. The onset of his disease occurred when I was young, in fact shortly after my birth, and because of it, he was not able to hold down a steady job or provide emotional support to his wife and family. Certainly, he was not able to play the male role in my life. I didn't know it at the time, but my father was sick; he acted irrationally and was emotionally unattached, though always very loving. My parents divorced when I was 11 years old, and although I saw my father regularly, there is no question that my mother played a more prominent role in my upbringing. Now that I am a father with two daughters, I realize that I missed out on something very special: a close relationship with my father.

Like I said, my father was always very loving, but because of his illness, he was unable to perform in a fatherly manner. My father didn't teach me how to tie a tie. My father didn't buy me my first car. My father didn't teach me about male sexuality or relationships with women and other men. Though my mother did the very best that she could, clearly she could not be my father as well as my mother. But what my mother did teach me was compassion, warmth, caring, gratitude, and giving, typically feminine attributes.

Growing up in a female-dominated home spilled over into my professional life as well. I have spent my entire working life in a synagogue environment. At the age of 13, my temple became for me a surrogate home. At Temple Emanuel of Beverly Hills, where I grew up and worked as a teenager and young adult, the rabbis and cantors were all men, but the educator with whom I most closely worked was a woman. Now as a Jewish professional in my own right here at Temple Beth Tikvah, the office is filled with women. And when I go home, there are only women to be found there too. So what's a guy to do? Obviously, I am one man who has no problem getting in touch with or expressing my feminine side. But finding or expressing my male side—now that is another story.

As opposed to many men today who are searching for their feminine side, I have had several recent opportunities to get in touch with my masculine side. Last September, I attended our temple's Men's Club Joke Breakfast and realized that was the first time I could remember being in a room with all men. Later in the week, I played poker with eight other members (yes, I am a full-fledged, dues-paying member!) of the Men's Club. Though I won a few games, which I attributed to beginners' luck, I ended the night five dollars short. But the camaraderie and friendship were worth much more than that.

In mid-October, I took a few days off and went to Primm, Nevada, with my father-in-law and brother-in-law. Every year they have gone to the Las Vegas area for fun and bonding, but I had never been able to go with them before. We had a great time and I hope to be able to go again next year. Being with "the fellas" has been a very new and different experience for me, one that has strengthened me in many ways.

Women are much better relating to other women than men are at relating to other men. I don't know if that is universally true or just my perception, but because I feel as though I have always lived in a feminine world, it has always been difficult for me to relate to other men. That is why I am so grateful for the new male friendships I have found and established since coming to Temple Beth Tikvah and Orange County. These relationships are based on friendship and mutual respect, and a sense of sharing an community. To borrow a sports metaphor, we are all on the same team, working together for a common goal and the common good. And speaking of joining the team, our Men's Club recently voted unanimously to join the NFTB, to support their good work and to give us here local opportunities to connect with all of you nationally and globally.

Joining the NFTB completes our temple's total affiliation with every national Reform organization available to us. Our Sisterhood has always been affiliated with Women of Reform Judaism, but for various reasons our men have historically rejected joining the NFTB. Today, perhaps more than ever, I believe affiliating and connecting are especially important for Jewish men.

It seems that in recent decades, men have relinquished some of their responsibility vis-à-vis the synagogue. As women have achieved equality as rabbis, cantors, Jewish educators, and synagogue leaders, a very welcome and positive addition to the Jewish world that was long overdue, many men have moved to the sidelines. Instead of working together with women in partnership in continuing God's unfading creation, I believe many men have simply given up on the synagogue as a place for them. But just as men play a crucial role in the family structure and in the upbringing of their children, men also play a vital role in the life of the synagogue.

Our young and not-so-young sons and daughters need to see men as active participants in synagogue life. We need to set an example for our children to show them that Judaism is important and that it is an integral part of who we are as men. We also need to show our spouses/partners and children that we can relate to other men on a variety of levels and that we are strengthened and strengthen each other when we are able to interact with other men.

That is why I am so very grateful for our temple's Men's Club, as I am for our Sisterhood. Each group provides important services and support to our Temple. And now that our Men's Club has voted unanimously to affiliate with NFTB, I hope that our Men's Club will take its rightful place in the life of our synagogue right next to and in partnership with our Sisterhood.

One of the most central hallmarks of Reform Judaism is equality, particularly equality between men and women. As women have achieved long-overdue prominence in synagogue life, some men have taken a backseat. In some programs at Hebrew Union College–Jewish Institute of Religion women even outnumber men by a large margin. And in some communities many men have ceased to see the synagogue as a place for them.

Now is the time to realize that whether man or woman, we each have a part to play and an important stake in the life of our congregations. I hope your feelings of connection with your synagogue will be as strong as mine are and I hope the bonds of friendship and companionship between men of all ages will continue to strengthen and grow.

Lech Lecha: New Pathways for Jewish Men

Shawn Israel Zevit

> God said to Abram, *Lech lecha*
> [Go forth] from your native land
> and from your father's house
> to the land that I will show you . . .
> and you will be a blessing. . . ."
>
> (Genesis 12:1–2)

Like the reverberations from the "big bang" of Sinai, God's calling to journey into the unknown still echoes for us today. The quest to meet the yearning of the soul—where the desires of our heart intersect with the needs of the world in which we live—has not diminished with time.

This is a time of great excitement and challenge for the Jewish people as a whole and those of us who are Jewish men in particular. As the gender roles, expectations and hopes of men and women have shifted and stretched in contemporary society, it has become increasingly challenging to gain an understanding of where we are, even as we try to figure out where we are heading and give voice to our current experiences. Even more so our connection to, and definition of, what is Jewish, as well as what is male or masculine are in flux for the majority of Jewish men. We may feel the call to chart our unique path, connect to loved ones, and find our place in community and the world at large. Yet for many men today, having a clear and loving sense of our "Father's house" can be as problematic as finding our own identities and "calling" as men.

The particular challenges and opportunities facing Jewish men today resonate with the most ancient of Jewish callings, but the *"lech lecha"* (Gen. 12:1) of today requires a road map that is informed by the past, but not limited by it. Some of us may have been handed the richness of our faith, with its customs, rituals and insights and so can add our life stories to that of Abraham. However, for many Jewish men today this is not a given. We may have received little from our parents, or were antagonistic to what we experienced. Some Jewish men have experience in men's groups and movements but have been out of touch with their Jewish identity. Others are well grounded in their Jewish expression but have never explored being in a group of men, or have few or surface relationships with other men. Still others have had neither or very little of both.

At this time we are only beginning to see the need for Jewish men to find voice for our experience as the 21st century unfolds. These voices are informed by feminism, the larger Jewish men's movement, uniquely North American Jewish experiences, intermarriage, shift in family structures, technology and the media among other factors.

The complexity of issues facing Jewish men today and the rapidity of change we live in societally also call out for response. These include responding to our relationship to God, traditional and creative ritual, new men's midrash, sexuality and intimacy, internalized anti-semitism, feminism, the "Jewish Prince," raising and relating to children, physical health, competition and isolation, homophobia, cross-cultural connections, analysis of and understanding Jewish leadership, gender and men's studies, spiritual development, family, friendship, addictions, violence, work and money, creating and sustaining men's groups, Jews and the military, Israeli male identities, and the legacies we wish to leave behind to our sons and daughters and friends. This list is by no means complete, nor can any book or program cover all these areas extensively. However, what we are beginning here is a conversation about Jewish men's issues from a personal place largely un-nurtured in most men in our culture.

At the same time we have a history as Jewish men of passionate connection to community study, peoplehood, relationships and striving to live in God's image. The confluence of these issues and contemporary men's issues makes for a rich and unique mix that can be addressed by works about and for Jewish men. This includes the desire for a reconnection to longstanding Jewish traditions such as prayer, Torah study (either in discussions or enacted Bibliodrama), mikveh, developing new ritual expressions, as well as providing a place to deal with varied issues of concern to us as Jewish men in supportive environments (this can range from talk to prayer to play, etc.). For many men who have been active in the larger arena of men's work, there is often a lack of connection with their Jewish heritage, which is just beginning to be made available through such Jewish men's activities. Ultimately these themes attempt to balance personal identity and spiritual growth with a commitment to *tikkun olam* or renewal of the planet.

Men On the Move

In the late 1960's and especially in the 1970's men began to gather to address issues of dislocation, shifting male/female roles, their connection or disconnection to their masculinity and a myriad of other issues that included simply wanting to be close to each other at a basic level. As the '70's and '80's progressed it became apparent that there was no men's "movement," rather different streams of focus that men would and could rally around. The stream that gained the most notoriety was termed the "mytho-poetic" because of its open exploration of male spirituality and Jungian-based psychology. This stream, often identified by the media and public as "the" men's movement, attracted mostly heterosexual midlife men, who would delve into their masculinity and male psyche at retreats, support groups, council meetings and lectures. These would center around literature, mythology, art, creativity, drumming, and rituals, some borrowed from Native American traditions. There were even gatherings and trainings in deepening positive male identity and relationships under the wing of "New Warriors" training. Robert Bly, James Hillman, Michael Meade and Robert Moore have been among the many innovators in this area.

The pro-feminist/male affirmative stream grew up alongside the women's movement and was often termed "men's liberation." Men are encouraged to challenge and move beyond sexist, homophobic, class and race barriers. Women's rights, gay rights and other causes centered around groups that were marginilized in society are often emphasized. Harry Brod, Michael Kimmel,

Michael Kaufmann and John Stoltenberg are among the men that helped bring these men's issues to the fore. In Canada, after a violent attack on female students at a university, a "White Ribbon" campaign was organized to protest against, and work toward, ending male violence patterns.

The men's rights stream largely focuses on changing laws and the societal perception of men. Be it challenging issues around child custody, child support, rights of unmarried fathers, etc., the men's rights advocates tend to be more militant than other men's groups. Gatherings usually take the form of support groups, Father's Day events involving children, legal strategy sessions, and media campaigns. Warren Farrell's book about the "myth" of male power brought some notoriety to this male perspective.

More recent developments on the North American men's scene include addiction/recovery groups out of the twelve-step programs. These groups have attracted a large number of men who are looking for explicit places to deal with addiction issues and healing wounds from parental relationships. Not surprisingly, the renewed interest in spiritual matters, combined with a call to return to "family values" from the religious right, has given birth to large-scale gatherings such as "Promise Keepers." Stadiums double as religious sanctuaries where men are exhorted to overcome their failings and recommit to their families. Some uncertainty as to whether this is progressive or regressive is under debate, but the sheer numbers and passions exposed indicate an empty place in the soul that is being addressed. African-American/Canadian men and other men of color have also developed programs over the last decade. Men's chat rooms, web sites, magazines and media programs have also been sprouting in the 1990's.

Mensch amongst Men

As I mentioned earlier, the idea of gathering as men in a Jewish context is not an innovation. It is a long-standing tradition, with Jewish law historically mandating a minimum of ten men to form a "minyan" or official community. Even in North America many of us grew up within the framework of the "Brotherhood" or "Men's Club" of our synagogue, Jewish Community Center or B'nai Brith Lodge. If not ourselves, then many of us had parents who were active in these ways. In the last couple of decades, the attendance and participation in traditional forms of gathering in a Jewish context have not been able to maintain their membership at previous levels, or have expanded to include women's participation, or simply lost relevance for many Jewish men who are not connected to the institutions their parents may have been. The formal men's groups within Jewish institutional life continue to shift and try to meet contemporary needs, while many Jewish men have found a home in informal groups that meet once or twice a month in group members' homes. This was a natural outgrowth from the feminist model of women's groups and "Rosh Hodesh" groups for the new month, and the influence of the men's "movement" that began in the early 1970's.

Over time many of us began to try and articulate our vision to meet the need that so many Jewish men feel today. This includes, but is not limited to, our examining the heritage we have received, the state of current male identity and spirituality, and now, the still small voice that is drawing us into the future.

In 1993, at the Aleph Kallah in San Francisco, I was the only man to have signed up the first day for a workshop for Jewish men that was being facilitated by Yosaif August, an organizer of the first Jewish men's retreat held a few years previously. Yosaif and I reflected on the low turnout given the hundreds of people gathered in the hills of Berkeley, and the large attendance at courses which emphasized women's rituals and issues. We decided it was not a safe assumption to think Jewish men seeking a renewed connection with their Judaism would necessarily see their male forms of identity and spiritual expression as pressing. At least to make this an important item on the progressive Jewish agenda would take patience, authentic soul-searching, and a willingness to break through the barriers to intimacy, trust and connection many Jewish men carry like a backpack on the journey.

By the next day a few more names were added to the list, and we ended our week of "drashodrama" on Jacob and Esau with mutual blessings and commitments under Yosaif's guidance. He gathered a group of us together to begin an annual Jewish men's retreat at Elat Chayyim near Woodstock, New York. Before that Kallah, and certainly since then, thinking and action by courageous Jewish men have begun to create a greater interest in Jewish men's issues. Some thinkers including Rabbi Kerry Olitzky, Rabbi Rami Shapiro, Rabbi Arthur Waskow, Professor Harry Brod, R. Mordecai Liebling, Doug Barden, Alicia Ostriker, Barbara Brietman, Rabbi Charles Simon, Joel Grishaver, Peter Pitzele, and many other Jewish men and women have been writing about gender and Judaism.

A key question to understanding the movement towards new forms of expression for spirituality and identity is what draws us together. For many men it is the opportunity, structured and informal, for deep sharing with other men and deepening their connection to their Judaism. Some men have experience in men's groups, but have been out of touch with their Jewish identity. Others are well grounded in their Jewish expression, but while being liberal Jews, have never explored being in a group of men. Still others have had neither or a little of both.

We have also sought at such events to address the desire for a reconnection to longstanding Jewish traditions such as mikveh, Torah study (either in discussions or enacted bibliodrama), *Kiddush Levanah* (monthly celebration of the new moon and month which requires gathering outdoors for worship, study and sharing), developing new ritual expressions, as well as providing a place to deal with issues of concern to us as Jewish men in supportive environments (this can range from talk to prayer to play, etc.).

For many men who have been active in the larger men's work scene, there is often a lack of connection with their Jewish heritage, which is made available through such Jewish men's activities. The Reform movement's Temple Brotherhoods, the Conservative movement's Men's Clubs, Reconstructionist, Renewal, religious humanist and even some Orthodox men's circles have begun to restructure themselves or develop groups to address issues of concern to contemporary Jewish men. In all these locations there is much God-wrestling with the question of how to find contemporary, authentic expression of faith and tradition as male Jews, while acknowledging the confusion many Jewish men are struggling with today.

Unlike the past, where gathering as men was linked to dominance over and exclusion of women and gay men from equal participation in many facets of Judaism, our present gathering uses these opportunities to deepen our connections so we can build a richer, more compassionate community together. I have experienced much enthusiastic support from female colleagues and women in various communities for the work we are taking on, and this has been very encouraging in the early stages of this journey.

Along with weekly to monthly men's groups that have been in existence for a number of years, a group of us have also begun meeting to celebrate the new month at *Kiddush Levanah* gatherings. Here a combination of an evening of study of text and/or discussion about a particular issue is followed by a trip outside to a nearby park where we can sing and exchange blessings or mark transitions (these have ranged from new fatherhood, bar mitzvah, and marriage to healing prayers for ill friends and family). This ritual adds a Jewish spiritual dimension to our connecting as men.

If anything, building trust between us and learning how to relate to each other as men beyond the avenues previously afforded are allowing us an opportunity to push past competition, insecurities and fears. Forging a compassionate, relevant and authentic spiritual life deepens this dimension so that our renewed Jewish expression enhances and supports our journeys as men in an age of rapid change in roles and expectations. Guilt, feelings of shame, inadequacy and blaming others are the surest way to keep the baggage we drag along stuck in place. The assertion of identities and spiritual expression must neither be dominating and abusive nor so passive and apologetic that it leads to a total flattening of behavior that de-energizes and immobilizes.

As previous hierarchical power structures and roles are being challenged and transformed, albeit painfully slowly at times, men have often isolated themselves to face these changes alone. This pattern can reinforce a resistance to change and cause a backlash against the perceived and/or real agents of change. The ways in which Jewish men are seeking ways to deepen their connection to each other, to women, to people of all faiths and backgrounds will help to realign relationships in community. We must create these connections in such a way that values what is rich and meaningful in the past, and allows us to work together and support each other in creative, compassionate and insightful ways towards a healthy future.

Like a stone in still waters, so the ripples of the actions of Jewish men and women over the past 30 years have begun to hit the banks of the "mainstream" and resonate back to the center of initiation. In the past few years an array of workshops and courses were held at various retreats, synagogues, Jewish Community Centers and campuses, ranging from courses on Jewish men and Torah, gay men, mikveh, *Kiddush Levanah*, local men's groups, Men's Stories: Lives and Legends of the Bible, Men and Work, health issues and more. These all indicate the time is ripe for concrete exploration and action. Issues such as our relation to God, ritual, sexual integrity, relationships with women, children, physical health, competition and isolation, homophobia, cross-cultural connections, spiritual development, family, friendship, addictions, violence, work and the legacies we wish to leave behind to our sons and daughters and friends have all been earmarked by our annual retreat planning group as areas of discussion and exploration in the evolution of Jewish male identity and spiritual expression. These themes are part of a balancing of personal spiritual growth and a commitment to *tikkun olam*.

The Jewish spiritual technology available to us in rich and diverse ways makes this work unique. We have sacred texts that allow us to explore our own individual and collective path, ritual providing us with a context, and an opportunity to be creative in meeting new issues and needs as they arise. We also share a core value of *tikkun olam*, where the needs of the community in the time in which we live are as paramount as the flowering of our individual soul life. I recall a story my grandfather Aaron told me of their seven-year stay in Israel, when he and my grandmother Rose, *z"l*, attended a local Orthodox synagogue. The *mechitsa* was actually the balcony, above which the women would gather, with the men sitting below near the bimah. One Simchat Torah the men were dancing with the Torah on the main level, circling joyfully around the chapel.

My grandfather became disturbed that his wife and other women were denied this opportunity and asked the rabbi present whether there was a law against women dancing with the Torah as well. The rabbi shrugged his shoulders, whereupon my grandfather took the Torah upstairs to the women, who reacted with shock and joy, and with many in tears touched the Torah for the first time in their lives. This courageous, creative act was not the act of a radical, but it was a radical act, an action in which his sense of justice called him to a place he had never known.

Sharing personal and collective stories can be a meeting ground for us as men and Jews, "male Jews" as Harry Brod would say. This is but the beginning of a conversation, not the definition of what Jewish men feel, need, or can experience. We can all find a starting place to articulate our own unique lives as Jewish men.

Genesis 1:27 states, "And God created humans in God's image . . . male and female, God created them. God blessed them. . . ." Like the charge to Abram to become all that he might become, to grow into Abraham in a new place he knew not and then be blessed, so we are asked to expand our self-image to more fully reflect the imaging of God in our lives. Ultimately, this can only be achieved by trust, and with determination and compassion, we can chart a new course into unknown places. Then we will come to know the blessing we inherently are meant to be.

Men and Leadership in Reform Congregations: More Questions Than Answers

Dale Glasser

Throughout our long and varied history as a people, trends and practices within the Jewish community have mirrored those of the larger societies in which we have lived. Our liturgical history is filled with pieces that reflect our journey, from the rich warm sounds of Sephardim to the German drinking song melodies we now claim as our own. Nowhere has this been more true than in our Reform Jewish practices in America over the last two centuries. From Isaac Mayer Wise's *Minhag America* to the protest-inspired tunes that became our own in the last half of the twentieth century, we continue to blend our host culture with our ancient traditions.

As in worship, our congregational governance and involvement patterns also reflect the larger society. Post-emancipation, the organization of the Jewish community has mirrored the institutions and practices of our larger community. The exclusion of Hebrew from our earliest American rituals and holding Sabbath services on Sunday were attempts to blend in with our non-Jewish American neighbors. The structure devised in order to provide services to new immigrants and needy members of our community mirrored those structures established by secular and other religious and ethnic groups in North America.

As involvement patterns and the sociology of belonging have developed and changed in the greater society over the past century, so too have the patterns of involvement and belonging in our congregations. One place where this change has been felt is in the participation of men in leadership roles in our congregations. In congregational leadership, as in society at large, old distinctions have been blurred as the glass ceiling has been shattered, and women now hold positions of top leadership in government, politics, academia, and business. These changes necessitate a new perspective that requires new questions, even if new answers remain elusive. Primary among those questions is this one: What are some of the challenges and opportunities presented by this reality, and how might congregations respond to these challenges and opportunities?

The late rabbi and psychotherapist Edwin Friedman suggests that one way to understand congregations is to view them as systems—that is, as organizations where each part is connected to the others and as communities that develop their own culture and patterns of interaction over time. A systems approach indicates that previous patterns of interaction are often predictive of future patterns and that in order to create positive, long-term change, one must address not just individual issues but must also understand the intricate interrelationships between all parts of the synagogue system.[1]

This approach suggests that the decrease in men's involvement in leadership may well be tied to changes in other areas of synagogue life. If progressive Jewish education in the last half of the previous century has focused on holiday celebrations and our place in the modern world, it has not taught basic prayer skills. This resultant lack of knowledge and skills has resulted in clogging one potential path for male involvement in synagogue leadership. If someone is not familiar or comfortable with the language and rules of a system, he is unlikely to try to become a leader within it. If traditional men's club involvement is no longer appealing or seen as an avenue for involvement, another resource for moving men into synagogue leadership has been limited. While significant efforts have been made, many congregations have not been fully responsive to the multiplicity of family configurations that have emerged in twenty-first-century North America. The increase in single-parent families and two-parent working families has had an impact on male availability for involvement in congregational leadership. In male-female, two-parent families, even as women have moved fully into the workforce, women continue to be the primary caretakers of children and the primary interface with both congregational early childhood programs and religious school educators. There is an increasing possibility, therefore, that these women will be identified through their involvement as potential leaders. Established ideas about gender roles in congregational leadership impact the way present leaders and potential leaders envision their roles.

In *The Story of the Synagogue*, a textbook used in many Reform classrooms during the last half of the twentieth century, the roles of men and women in congregational leadership are clearly delineated:

> You may join the special clubs for men and women, the Brotherhood or the Sisterhood. The men have Sunday breakfast meetings for synagogue affairs, or to hear famous speakers, or to hear about Jews in other lands. Men and women may join the Community Council as representatives of the synagogue to meet with church people and others. Men usually take care of the finances of the synagogue. They may be elected as officers of the synagogue. And they may give their time to youth groups, to coaching sports, or to singing.
>
> The women will do many of the things the men do, but they will also have special activities, like sewing groups, or bazaars, or a book and gift shop. They may have a group to discuss family education. They may volunteer to bake cakes or to make decorations for parties at the synagogue.[2]

Women's roles in society at large have clearly changed since this was written. It is less clear how men have adapted to having roles that were once exclusively their own, filled by competent and capable women.

These issues are also reflected in recent writings about both the women's movement and also numerous articles about how Jews connect with organized Jewish life.

Many participants in the women's movement today refer to the "third wave of feminism." The first wave refers to the feminist movement of the nineteenth through early twentieth centuries, which dealt mainly with the suffrage movement. The second wave, from the 1960s to the 1980s, strongly influenced by Betty Friedan's *The Feminine Mystique*, was focused on inequalities in the legal system and other societal structures. The third wave of feminism, which began in the 1990s and continues until the present, carries on the concerns of the second wave while also responding to what are perceived as its flaws and failures.

Yet, as Judith Lorber writes, "the revolution that would make women and men truly equal has not yet occurred. I argue that the reason is that gender divisions still deeply bifurcate the structure of modern society. Feminists want women and men to be equal, but few talk about doing away with gender divisions altogether."[3]

This concept is echoed in the writing of my colleague Doug Barden, executive director of Men of Reform Judaism (formerly the North American Federation of Temple Brotherhoods), when he suggests that "the challenge before the Reform Movement is creating gender differentiated space without reverting back to gender stratification . . . to give our congregants equal, but different opportunities to express themselves Jewishly, to continue their Jewish journey within Reform congregational settings."[4]

It is important to recognize that the roles men and women take in congregational leadership, and the satisfaction and success they feel in those roles affect ways in which men and women are socialized to talk with, and listen to, one another. In her book, *Talking from 9 To 5: Women and Men at Work*, Deborah Tannen writes that men and women learn to speak in particular ways,[5] and that "negotiating and other decision-making are based as much on ways of talking as on the content of the arguments."[6] Further, she writes that conversational rituals common among men include using opposition as banter, joking, teasing, and playful putdowns, and expending effort to avoid the one-down position in the interaction. Conversational rituals among women "are often ways of maintaining an appearance of equality, taking into account the effect of the exchange on the other person, and expending effort to downplay the speaker's authority so they can get the job done without flexing their muscles in an obvious way."[7]

These differences in communication style significantly affect the roles of and participation by both men and women in congregational leadership. Tannen's observation that "when females and males get together in groups, the females are more likely to change their styles to adapt to the presence of males"[8] suggests that even in congregational cultures dominated by males, females are socialized to adapt more easily than males would be to adapting to a female-dominated congregational culture. This fact is reinforced by Tannen's observation that "men are less likely to ask questions in a public situation where asking will reveal their lack of knowledge."[9]

Tannen's research about men's and women's roles is consistent with the writings of others who have studied contemporary Jews' connection with Jewish institutions. In *Rekindling the Flame*, Samuel Osherson writes, "For many men the feeling of not knowing is doubly humiliating. Since men are 'supposed' to know and be able to perform, going back into the synagogue after years away means feeling like both a failed Jew and a failed man."[10]

In *The Jew Within: Self, Family and Community in America*, Steven M. Cohen and Arnold M. Eisen suggest that "perhaps the greatest change affecting Jewish identity in the past half century is the expansion of roles available to women."[11] They further note that

> virtually every one of the Jews we interviewed [views their Jewish lives as a journey]. . . . The pasts they remember, the places they have been, are in their view indispensable to their own understanding of where they are right now, and so are indispensable to our understanding as well. . . . Only by hearing personal stories can one comprehend the Judaism wrapped up in those stories. These Jewish memories . . . are also the key to imagining the possibilities which lie ahead, both for the individuals concerned and for the American Jewish community they make up."[12]

Cohen and Eisen write that gender is one of three key factors promoting and inhibiting involvement:

> To a remarkable degree, the "action" where Jewish activity among the moderately affiliated is concerned now rests with women who undertake such activity either with or without the assistance of male partners. Given the centrality of ritual to our subjects, and the fact that so much of Jewish ritual takes place in the home and involves children, the predominance of women in undertaking Jewish practice is not surprising. Women retain primary responsibility for child-rearing even in two-career families.
>
> Conversation about and experiences of transcendence come more easily to women than to men . . . and the visibility of women rabbis, lay leaders, and communal professionals has galvanized and legitimized re-interpretation of the tradition and re-direction of institutions, both of which in turn attract women who might otherwise have remained aloof. We suspect that the very language of search and quest presumes a hesitancy with which the men we met were often uncomfortable."[13]

The expectations of, and roles fulfilled by, men and women in our society have changed significantly during the past fifty years. So, too, have the roles of men and women in our congregations and the opportunities for Jews to connect with their Judaism in North American society. In many cases, our congregational worship culture, involvement patterns, and governance models have not been as responsive to change.

These factors are among many that suggest it is time for a new paradigm of leadership in our congregations. If we are to create a culture of leadership in our congregations, if we are to continue to attract competent, compassionate, Jewishly-knowledgeable male and female lay leaders to partner with our clergy and professionals and sustain and nurture our congregational communities, then we must put forward some new opportunities.

As Jews, we are often taught to be more comfortable pursuing the questions, rather than pursuing THE answer. When considering the future of leadership in our Reform congregations and how to engage both men and women in meaningful roles, the answer may be found in discussing these and other appropriate questions:

- Can we acknowledge the changing nature of congregational leadership in ways that address the needs of our congregations and of all involved in that sacred partnership?
- Can we imagine ways to create and sustain sacred community in our congregations that build upon the needs and experiences of female and male leaders?
- Can we promote new models of leadership that include the study of texts and of Jewish models of leadership, which change perceptions and add to the leadership models that are considered normative?
- Can we provide congregational leaders with the skills to partner with female and male clergy in ways that will build and strengthen the congregation, while building upon the skills, talents, and perspectives that each leader brings to the table?
- Can we consciously provide opportunities for males to be involved without minimizing the important roles of women?
- Can we build upon the family experiences that shape perspectives on and involvement in Judaism?
- Can we proactively teach congregational leadership skills that venerate and honor current leaders, thus providing healthy role models for our teenage boys and girls?

- Can we normalize leadership journeys and position congregational leadership as an aspiration, recognizing leadership as a position of *kavod*, rather than something to be avoided at all costs?
- Can we use our anecdotal experiences and contemporary research findings to structure board meetings and temple activities to engage more men in participating?
- Can we identify what it will take to involve men and keep them involved in temple life?
- Can we ensure that men and women feel welcome in all aspects of synagogue life and have clear leadership paths and opportunities?
- Can we discern instances when it is important to minimize the differences and work from common ground from instances when it is important to acknowledge the differences as strengths, and as part of the diversity that we as Reform Jews value and honor?
- Can we find ways for men to tell their Jewish stories?
- Can we overcome the notion that it is not politically correct to advocate for men in the same ways as it is to advocate for women? Can we have this advocacy understood not as an attempt to turn back the clock, but to turn it ahead to a time when the contributions of both women and men are noted, encouraged, and valued.
- Can we address the challenge that some men—who may seek their involvement through governance rather than spirituality—have a difficult time understanding that the bottom line in congregations is relationships, creating Jewish memory, and connecting Jews with one another and with the Jewish community? Can we help them to understand that the question becomes not "Is the synagogue a business?," but rather "What business are we in?"
- Can the benchmarks used in corporate America, the lessons learned as men prepared for high-powered careers, be translated to the congregational setting?
- Can we identify what we want for our sons and daughters in their roles as congregational leaders and how that might build upon, yet differ from, what our grandparents experienced and what our parents wanted for us?

If we can, women and men together, begin to address these questions, we can ensure that our journey as a Jewish people continues, strengthened by our diversity; mindful of our common goals; and bolstered by healthy, spiritually fulfilling congregational communities.

The Role of Men in the Social Action Arena

Marla J. Feldman

Anecdotal Evidence

Though many program areas of Jewish life reflect a diminishing proportion of men, this trend seems to be less predominant in the social action arena. There are several events and organizations that we can use to gauge the participation of men, in contrast to women, in Reform Jewish social action at the national level: attendance at the biennial Consultation on Conscience run by the Religious Action Center (RAC) in Washington, DC, the membership of the Commission on Social Action (CSA) of Reform Judaism, and participation in national Mitzvah Corps programs. At some point, it would be valuable to do a more thorough study of levels of participation at local congregational programming, such as social action committees, mitzvah days, and advocacy activities, in order to determine if the trends are consistent.

The Consultation on Conscience takes place every other year, bringing together hundreds of social activists, rabbis, cantors, educators, and lay leaders from Reform congregations around the country. Participants hear from elected officials and policy experts on a wide range of issues of concern, lobby their legislators, and learn about best practices in social action programming. When one visually surveys the room, the impression is parity among men and women. Upon review of registration records over the past ten years, this trend proves true, with a very slight tilt toward women. The overall records since 1997 reveal 930 male participants compared to 990 female participants, or roughly 48.5 percent male and 51.5 percent female. Of the five Consultations surveyed (1997, 1999, 2001, 2003, and 2005), the percentage of men ranged from 43 percent to 54 percent.[1]

The CSA, established in 1953, is a "joint instrumentality" of the Central Conference of American Rabbis and the Union for Reform Judaism and its affiliates. This body has representatives of all the affiliates of Reform Judaism and is tasked with developing the public policy agenda of the Movement, serving as the board of the RAC. As one might expect, in the earliest years the Commission was comprised almost entirely of men. Records from 1963 indicate 43 men served on the Commission, along with 4 women; in 1971 there were 60 men and only 7 women. A major shift occurred by the 1980s as gender equality became a growing priority for the Commission. Nearly doubling in size, in 1980 there were 60 men and 47 women; in 1990 there were 69 men and 31 women. Today, there are 67 men and 66 women who serve on the CSA, and maintaining gender balance is a criterion for consideration of new members. The CSA, over its 50-year history, has managed to make room for women, without diminishing the number of men involved. And as of 2007, the Commission has achieved parity among men and women, with a long list of both men and women interested in joining its ranks.

Another national measure we can use to gauge participation of men in national social action programs is the Adult Mitzvah Corps program. Although these programs are, by design, small in number, the participation of men in recent years has ranged from half the participants to one-third. The 2003 (Burlington, VT), 2005 (New Orleans), and 2006 (New Orleans) programs had roughly the same number of men and women.[2] However in 2004 (Orange County, CA) and 2006 (Mississippi), only about one-third of the participants were men.[3] It is important to note that the programs with the largest percentage of men took place during the December holiday season, which may be an easier travel time for working adults and parents of school-age children. Of course, that would apply to men and women equally.

Analysis—Why This Trend May Be True

In examining gender trends today, it may be useful to reflect on earlier gender studies that emerged from women's and feminist studies during the 1970s and 1980s. Some of the classic discussions at that time examined and challenged the power hierarchies and models for success that restricted roles for women and expanded opportunities for men. Those studies asked questions such as: "What words would you use to describe a successful man?" (answers included: powerful, wealthy, authority figure, competitive, self-confident, famous, etc.) and "What are desirable characteristics for a woman?" (answers included: pretty, loving, caring, nurturing, tender, compassionate, etc.).

These classic studies revealed a male model for success defined by the competitive realm of the business world and a female model for success defined by the relational world of family. In this paradigm, for a man to be compassionate was to be weak; gentle was a metaphor for wimp, and being a team player doomed one to middle-management. For women, to be assertive was to be pushy, and to be competitive and independent was to be a "femi-nazi" in the parlance of Rush Limbaugh.

To be sure, the growing numbers of women in the workforce and changing social mores have mitigated these distinctions, but I would argue they have not entirely been eliminated. In fact, they may help explain the gender trends we see in the social action arena. If we look at the particular aspects of the social justice agenda in which the stereotypically feminine traits are more dominant, we see more women involved. For example, of the over nine hundred congregations in the Union, about two-thirds of the social action chairs are women; these are the individuals responsible for running the hands-on social action programs of collecting items for the needy, tutoring in schools, and volunteering in soup kitchens. Even more so, we find this trend in other program areas such as education, outreach, membership, caring committees, and, increasingly, ritual committees. This estrogen-enriched Judaism serves our congregations and our congregants well.

On the other hand, if we look at the competitive world of politics, where who you know is power and the winner takes all, we are likely to find a higher percentage of men. This testosterone-infused arena is, I suspect, a more comfortable and desirable setting for many men. For some, the political social justice agenda allows them to integrate their professional expertise, success, and contacts with their religious values. So, while men may join others in a mitzvah day, Habitat build, or other hands-on activities of the congregation, it is in that room on Capitol Hill where the RAC introduces them to future presidents, policy wonks, and movers and shakers—where the whiff of power is palpable—that they get a real charge. Admittedly, the women in the room (including me) feel this charge too!

This is not to disregard the importance, indeed the necessity, of the relational work of coalition building that is so crucial to success in a bipartisan political arena. In this work of coalition-building, we see the power of those estrogen-dominant traits of compromise, organizing, and relationship building. As might be expected, women are overwhelmingly predominant in the growing congregation-based community organizing model that has been so effectively implemented in many of our congregations. Yet in our increasingly partisan red state/blue state reality, one needs the classic male traits to believe one can really make a difference: sharp elbows, thick skins, and a very healthy ego.

D'var Acher

On a nonpolitical note, it is worthwhile to examine activities such as Habitat builds, mitzvah corps programs, rebuilding New Orleans, and other projects that require significant physical labor and consider the gender breakdown of participants. We might presume that such projects would particularly interest and engage men, because we assume men are more likely to have the necessary skills for and be better able to respond to the physicality of the work. While there is a higher proportion of men in these programs than in other types of congregational experiences, such as adult education programs, we still find more women then men participating (unless the activities are specifically planned by a Brotherhood or Men's Club). On the national weeklong mitzvah corps experiences, there is a surprisingly diverse range of participants, from entire families to mother-son or father-daughter teams to empty nesters. In fact, the largest cohort consistently is women in their fifties and sixties.

When asked what brought these women to such programs, most admit they do not have the skills but always wanted to try it, and we (the CSA) provided a safe environment for them to do so. Interestingly, the same rationale for participation applied to both men and women. It is clearly presumptuous to think that construction skills are comfortable for the average male member of a Reform congregation! Also of note: women in particular expressed a desire for low-cost, meaningful vacation opportunities in which they could travel alone but be part of a group. In contrast, most of the male participants in these programs have been accompanied by spouses or children.

Programmatic Response to the Hypothesis

Just as our educational programs must reach students with different learning styles, our social justice programs can and should provide opportunities for people with a wide range of interests and activity styles. Building projects and mitzvah corps programs will appeal to those seeking physical, hands-on opportunities to literally repair the world. Other opportunities, such as housing the homeless, interfaith programs, and tutoring will be attractive to those seeking to build relationships and provide healing to vulnerable populations in need of immediate relief. And bringing our social justice agenda into the halls of power will appeal to those who are energized by that environment, as well as those seeking long-term systemic change through the more intangible realm of policy development. Each of these models is important to the pursuit of justice, and in each of these types of programs we will find both men and women. Yet, as different types of programs are likely to engage varying percentages of male and female participants, a well-rounded social action program that involves a variety of skill sets and interests will likely yield the most balanced gender results.

Congregations seeking to increase the involvement of men might ramp up their social action programs in the following ways:

- Develop local mitzvah corps and building projects led by the Men's Club but open to the entire congregation.
- Hold a candidates' forum during the campaign season and invite elected officials to speak during the course of the year at Shabbat worship and special events.
- Host a community program on current "hot" political topics, with speakers on both sides of an issue, policy experts, and political leaders addressing the group, and invite comment by the audience.
- Invite individuals to participate in leadership meetings with elected officials in their home offices; reach out to those who have business and political contacts to help lobby those officials on the Reform Movement's policy priorities.
- Organize a delegation of members to attend the biennial Consultation on Conscience in Washington; hold delegation meetings before and after to develop a plan to bring the knowledge and experience back to the congregation.

Perhaps the most important lesson to learn from the social action arena is from the CSA. In recognizing the need to bring more women into its ranks, the Commission did not diminish the opportunities for men, as if it was a zero-sum game. Rather, it expanded is membership base, deliberately reaching out to women to establish the gender balance that is now normative. Should future membership trends necessitate a shift, Commission leadership will seek to recruit and cultivate male leadership so that the social justice arm of the Movement will continue to be a space occupied by both men and women equally.

Section V

Gender-Sensitive Worship

Introduction

The essays in this section approach the challenges found in creating worship experiences that are designed to meet men's needs. Some of these pieces will undoubtedly be controversial. Throughout most of Jewish history, it was Jewish men who filled the pews. One of Reform Judaism's most significant innovations was to introduce the concept of egalitarian seating from its inception. But now, as rabbis and cantors look out into the congregation on Shabbat, they see far more women than men. Some of the authors included here argue for the creation of exclusively male worship experiences, while others have fears about the possibility of going "backwards" by exploring this mode of prayer. The worship experiences experimented with and described here have taken place at URJ camps, synagogues, and gatherings. Each piece offers a unique insight into the challenge of creating a meaningful prayer experience for Jewish men.

Kevin Kleinman planned and ran the first all-male worship service held at Kutz Camp. In "Praying in the Velvet Sea," he recounts his feelings prior to the service, the actual content of the liturgy used, and how he and the campers reported feeling afterwards. Kleinman found that the all-male service allowed the campers to reach new and heightened levels of vigor and spiritual experience. Kleinman challenges those leading prayer to think about new ways to explore male worship and the depth of the male Jewish spiritual experience.

Lisa Lieberman Barzilai was part of a team that created a new *t'filah* experience for male staff and campers at Eisner Camp. In "A Different Worship Experience: Experimenting with Same-Sex Services at Eisner Camp," Lieberman Barzilai and Greg Weitzman discuss how they created a worship experience that allowed boys to explore the relationships they had had with their male role models and why those role models were so important in their lives. They struggled to create a safe, welcoming environment that invited participation without making campers or counselors too uncomfortable. Staff at Eisner Camp continue to experiment with single-gender worship experiences and their effects.

"Not for Men Only: A Model for Worship with Men in Mind," by Rabbi Victor Appell and Cantor Jonathan Comisar, challenges the single-gender model as the solution to the disappearance of men from the pews. Their experience came out of their attempt to create a men's worship opportunity at the Joint Commission on Worship, Music and Religious Living. Their team tried to create a worship experience that was comfortable to everyone, but mindful of men. In this piece, they recount the factors they considered in creating the service.

The selection "The Reluctant Man: A Conversation with Susan Weidman Schneider," originally printed in *Reform Judaism* magazine, lends another perspective. Weidman, in conversation with Aron Hirt-Manheimer, suggests that men need to be liberated to break the molds of worship, just as women began to do in the 1970s. Because women felt the need to create new rituals and rethink old ones as they gained access to the world of Jewish worship, Weidman writes that such creativity was freeing. Such creativity could likewise be freeing for men. A key element that Weidman suggests is opening dialogue for both women and men to openly discuss both positive and negative experiences in Judaism. This potential jumping-off point, based on a women's consciousness-raising model, could allow for male creativity and a voice that need not be politically incorrect or perceived as domineering.

Questions for Discussion

As you read each piece, consider the following questions:

1. How do you feel about the Reform Movement encouraging, even creating, single-sex worship experiences?
2. Do you accept the premise that men and women have different worship needs or experience worship differently? Why or why not? Is it possible that *sometimes* men and women have different worship needs?
3. Have you ever experienced a single-sex worship service, and if so, what are your thoughts on the experience?
4. If you have not experienced single-sex worship, does your inexperience prevent you from passing judgment about single-sex services?
5. Who are the male members of your congregation whom you could interview or survey to learn about their experience of the worship so that you can determine what needs are not being met? Note that you may have to seek out those who do not participate to determine why they are not participating.
6. Envision a forum or panel for your own community along the lines of Weidman's suggestion: "We're going to host a panel where women *and men* can speak about their feelings of exclusion or inclusion in synagogue life." How might you make this or a similar event a reality in your community?

Praying in the Velvet Sea

Kevin Kleinman

We gathered underneath the billowing willow trees beside the lake. The sky shone bright purple and orange behind us as the sun slowly descended. I began by singing a niggun *and playing guitar. First I sang alone, then others joined in, some recognizing the familiar melody, some catching on as it repeated itself. Several guys picked up the drums I had brought and joined in. The sounds grew more and more powerful until we filled the open space with our voices blending together, getting louder and stronger as we fed off the power of the group. The melody poured in, and the deep parts of our souls poured out. I felt proud of the young men for feeling comfortable enough to put their arms around the shoulders of their friends and bunkmates. There were no outsiders in this group; everyone was swept up, held together in the moment. Though these were the same prayers we'd been reciting each evening, tonight we really felt them as we prayed, sang, and danced away the last wisps of sunlight.*

When the program coordinator first approached me to lead an all-male service at Kutz Camp, I was honored, yet uncertain how to approach the task. After all, didn't this concept run counter to all of our Reform egalitarian progress? Why go backwards? With mixed feelings I recalled an Orthodox synagogue where my girlfriend and I had prayed in Israel. Our experiences were split by the *m'chitzah*, right down the center of the room separating men from women. Immediately upon entering, an exuberant group of *yeshivah bochers* grabbed me and pulled me into their circle. I was intoxicated by a sense of belonging. I felt connected to a long line of Jewish men who'd lived hundreds of years before me, whom I'd never even met but whose life had made this ecstasy possible! My egalitarian values seemed almost wimpy next to the joyful, ceiling-shaking, floor-trembling celebration before me.

I emerged from the men's section to meet up with my girlfriend, excited to share my experience and hear about hers. To my dismay, she was not glowing. In fact, she was scowling. Apparently, while we had been whooping it up over on the guy's side, her side was quiet and boring. The women's main excitement was watching the men dance. My heart sank as I realized that we had experienced the same synagogue in two completely different ways. In my version, I wondered: "Why can't our prayers be more like this?" In her version, she wondered: "Is this fair?"

As I mulled over this painful experience, I struggled with the idea of dividing men and women for the purpose of prayer. On one hand, it can be exclusive and disempowering to women. On the other hand, maybe accepting the challenge to lead an all-male service at Kutz Camp was an opportunity to create a new model for a movement struggling to find ways to keep men engaged with Judaism and Jewish practice. I could offer these young men the ecstatic praying I had experienced.

I decided to lead the all-male service. Though I remained uncertain of the outcome, I felt excited to bring some yeshivah, "ay-ya-yay," old-world, traditional foot stompin', *niggun* davening into this Reform Jewish space! Soon enough, as the sun set over the pagoda in which we were located, the group grew bigger, bolder, and more spirited. The free-form dance of the band Phish met the head-banging ecstasy of song session with Shlomo Carlebach's melodies pouring out into the purest form of song. "Cool" guys, "nerdy" guys, "loud" guys, and "quiet" guys yelled out Hebrew melodies together into the darkening sky and a new language of prayer was born.

The camaraderie that came from spending a few weeks living together singing, learning, dancing, and joking, and the use of familiar melodies, enabled an outpouring of prayer and song in this group of young men. I had intentionally guided the service in a way that was also meaningful to myself: rhythmic chanting to get our bodies moving juxtaposed with time for personal prayer and meditation. I was swept up in the momentum we created, and I felt pushed by the teens to play faster to keep up with their young, male voices. We sang wildly without fear of being off-key. We prayed frenetically with primal devotion. We danced openly with the knowledge that we were brothers. Being outdoors in an open field allowed us to release all of our energy. Not being confined by walls or rows of chairs allowed our prayers to flow and our bodies to move freely.

The young men at Kutz Camp were inspired by our all-male service. They asked me to lead more services throughout the remainder of the session at camp. Had there been more opportunities, I would have worked with them so that they could lead the services themselves. In addition, I think that if I were to lead a service like this again, I would have more percussion instruments available for people to play.

I can personally attest to the importance of male bonding at camp and within NFTY (North American Federation of Temple Youth). Ten years ago, I knew I would stay in touch with my bunkmates from Camp Harlam as we went to study at different colleges. Still, I couldn't have imagined then that I would someday be in rabbinical school with two of them or that we would gather regularly for music shows and each other's weddings. Every time the seven of us meet we still do our bunk cheer from the summer when we were C.I.T.s (counselors in training). In retrospect, I realize how safe we must have felt as young Jewish men dancing around singing Shabbat songs, hugging, and even crying in front of each other. I see now that these relationships helped to form my Jewish identity in a high school where I was one of a handful of Jews in a student body of three thousand students. They excited and empowered me. They gave me extra motivation to stay involved in Jewish life. While I am no longer close with anybody from high school, my camp and NFTY friendships continue to support and nourish me, as I know they will throughout my lifetime.

I can see myself in the young Jewish men I taught at Kutz Camp. As the Judaic studies director that summer, I noticed many male participants shared the same kinds of friendships and connections that I had enjoyed. They would toss around a Frisbee and sit outside playing guitar. I often saw them walking around in clusters talking enthusiastically about relationships, Judaism, and music, especially the band Phish. The difference now is that because Phish split up, they can only listen to recordings of concerts I actually *attended* with my friends from camp. I teased them about their love of a band they never actually saw live and encouraged them in their efforts to fit the words of the *Mi Chamochah* prayer into the tune of "Wading in the Velvet Sea," one of my favorite Phish songs.

I think about my own experiences as a participant and a leader in Reform Movement camping and youth groups and I realize just how important these programs are for shaping our identities as Jewish men. There are very few opportunities for liberal Jews to spend time in an all-male space. Traditionally the synagogue was where men formed a minyan—they prayed, learned, and talked about their lives. As the Reform Movement took hold on American Judaism, the synagogue was transformed into a place where families came and sat together, rather than in separate sections. This important change fundamentally altered the social dynamics of the worship experience. As a result, many men no longer spend isolated time together in small groups at shul; they socialize while golfing or going on trips together. Even as a rabbinic student I have more opportunities to catch up with my male classmates in the gym than in the sanctuary of Hebrew Union College. Although most congregations today have a Brotherhood, Brotherhoods often do not provide a natural outlet for spirituality and friendship, especially for teenagers. Temple youth groups, despite their great potential, often fall short in providing male bonding opportunities. Camps and NFTY are some of the only places where young men can be alone together in a Jewish environment. Sharing a room or cabin builds stronger friendships than sitting next to each other in Hebrew school. By planning overnight retreats or ski trips, temple youth groups can use this successful model of informal education to build and strengthen the relationships between their young men. Our teenagers may not get this sense of Jewish fraternity anywhere else.

Parents, clergy, and social commentators all agree that we are at or near crisis point with North American young men today: lack of healthy outlets for their confusion, fear, and questions result in repression and, often, violence. Youth groups and Jewish summer camps often provide an alternative model to handle life's challenges by creating a safe, accepting space where young Jewish men can explore and evolve into the men they wish to become.

It has been almost two years since that all-male service, and campers, staff, and clergy still talk about it. Such talk shows us that our young men are hungry for real ways to connect, and once they do, the connection stays with them long after the moment itself. It is our job to keep giving our young men reasons and ways to reconnect. We are slowly building a new vocabulary to give to them. A friend of mine has suggested reviving a New York synagogue basketball league; another one organized a Jewish battle of the bands. As the times shift and change, we must learn how to bring tradition to teenagers in a whole new way. We must keep thinking outside the box to create meaningful ways to engage the youth. This is our responsibility as Jewish educators, clergy, and role models. How will we meet the challenge?

Five Ways to Make Your Temple Youth Group's Prayer Experience More Male-Friendly

1. **Have outdoor services.** They challenge the norm and break the mold. Without being confined to a space, the energy can spread. Outdoor locations also allow for more opportunities to connect to the spirituality of nature.
2. **Arrange the room differently.** This will allow for the energy to flow differently than does the normative frontal setup of most sanctuaries.
3. **Encourage physical movements.** Reform prayer services often restrict mobility of the participants. Try to let the participants stand up, hold on to each other, and dance around the room.
4. **Bring musical instruments.** Instruments, particularly guitar and drums, add to the energy level in the room. They also provide a steady rhythm for the participants to sing and move to.
5. **Accept the chaos.** Loud, male energy is often seen as a distraction or a behavioral problem. Try to harness this energy by using simple, repetitive melodies that will enable the young men to focus their testosterone on the language of prayer rather than trying to disturb their friends.

A Different Worship Experience: Experimenting with Same-Sex Services at Eisner Camp

Lisa Lieberman Barzilai and Greg Weitzman

Weekday *t'filah* at Eisner Camp had become repetitive, rote, and somewhat boring. In an effort to make *t'filah* more meaningful for both campers and staff, we and the camp director, Louis Bordman, decided that we needed to experiment with our worship. Louis, the Eisner Limud directors, and we considered who was participating in our *t'filot* and what type of experience would have meaning to all who worshiped. During the discussions between the coordinators of the service, we explored a number of reasons why people experience worship differently. The varying experiences may be based on the type of day someone has already had, the experiences each person brings to *t'filot*, and one's unique personality. Part of our deliberation focused on the idea that males and females would approach *t'filah* differently if we were to create a worship experience for a single-sex group. This deliberation led to our decision to have separate-sex services at Eisner. The truth is that we had tried single-sex services in the past; however, previously, we did not place attention on what would happen during the services. This would be our first serious attempt at designing worship experiences directed at a single-sex group (male only and female only) at camp. We brought thought and intention to what would happen at the service. These services would also be part of a larger discussion of the *t'filah* experience at camp.

Our first serious attempt at same-sex services was during staff orientation. Before *t'filah* began, there were several different sports set up around the quad, and the young men were able to choose a game to play. This allowed the men the opportunity to bond in a way that they often do at camp, through sport. At a specified time, all the young men left the field and headed into the *beit k'neset*, house of prayer, an indoor location at camp that has wonderful acoustics. Earlier in the day, certain staff members had been prepped to aid in the facilitation of the service. They were also asked to think about a personal male role model and what it was about that individual that made him so important in their life.

The *t'filah* began as a regular evening service, but at a specific juncture the staff members shared their prepared stories. As the service progressed, the participants were allowed to stand when they felt comfortable enough to share. If no one was ready to share, then the service progressed. It was important for the participants to feel as though this was a safe space, a space to share with each other the male qualities that they felt they wanted to share with their campers, and more importantly, with each other. At times it seemed the *t'filah* was secondary to the stories and feelings shared, but we felt that a great prayerful experience could be had in hearing each other's words.

The service itself had tunes and songs that were chosen specifically for both their tones and the words within the song. We wanted the participants to be able to sing along to songs that were well in their range of voice. For this reason, we chose songs in lower octaves, specifically the musical keys of "E" and "A minor." We also chose songs based on what words would most resonate with males. In our search for songs with masculine meanings we were unsuccessful, but we felt as though the gender neutrality in the meanings of the songs we did choose combined with a masculine twist provided by the sharing between prayers was actually a positive.

Our choices showed how a service could be changed and modeled to fit each individual person's needs or, in our case, a group's needs. The stories and emotions expressed were incredibly powerful and led other participants to share their stories. The ability to share both words and emotions in a safe environment led to a more powerful experience than even we had thought would transpire. One counselor, an Israeli who recently returned from the army, stood and shared his experience serving with his best friend, who for him was a role model. He went on to describe how his friend's bravery and strength pushed the two of them through the hardest times, and his friend even saved his life. What stuck out the most was that his best friend was sitting next to him at the service. They had made it through the army and were together again at Eisner Camp.

Another counselor stood and spoke of his grandfather whom he never knew, who passed away during the Holocaust. His memories of him came from what his family has told him, but he felt as close to him as if he had lived with him for his entire life. He spoke of his bravery and resilience during the Holocaust, and how he sacrificed his life so that his children could make it out alive on the Kindertransport. The counselor moved himself to tears while speaking of the grandfather he never knew who gave his life so that he could live.

Following this experience we challenged ourselves to consider what from this experiment would be good to try with the campers and what might not work. It was clear that there was a great amount of trust built within the framework of staff orientation that might not exist among the campers, so we needed to be careful how we framed the *t'filah*. We determined that such services were probably not best for the youngest unit of campers. These campers, both male and female, take a while to acclimate to *t'filah* at camp, and too much experimentation and variation would be detrimental to their worship experience. The concept of sharing the positive male role models was something that we decided would still be a positive experience for the boys, so certain male staff members were asked to prepare stories to share during *t'filah*. Some faculty chose to share a story from the Torah to help set the experience in a positive and meaningful Judaic way; for example, a midrash was told about Jacob and his sons. There was also discussion among the staff and faculty who participated in the original all-male service about the type of music that would be chosen, as we had a sense that some things would work better than others.

At Eisner we have the culture of praying together as a unit or as an entire camp. We determined that this service would be best run only once a session, twice during the summer. The campers find the experience special not only by what transpires but also because they are given this opportunity only once during the session.

All in all we believe that the experiment had positive results. The males felt positively about who they were. They also expressed feeling more connected to *t'filah* and the other males, campers, and staff within their units. Campers expressed a desire to continue this kind of worship.

The young men felt that this type of *t'filah* created a different atmosphere. They felt more a part of a worship community, and they felt somehow more free to express their thoughts and emotions to others. This was the first step in our understanding of what a male worship experience can and should be. We are most interested in learning what research and others have to say that will enhance our *t'filah* experience, which we plan to continue.

Not for Men Only: A Model for Worship with Men in Mind

Victor S. Appell and Jonathan Comisar

A great deal of attention is being paid to the flight of men from organized Jewish life. From our summer camps and NFTY, we have statistics indicating that the flight begins even before adulthood. From HUC-JIR, we have reports on the percentage of male applicants to its various programs. Our congregations are experiencing fewer and fewer men participating in synagogue leadership and worship. The Joint Commission on Worship, Music and Religious Living dedicated much of its time during a meeting in March 2006 to exploring the relationship between men and worship in our synagogues. We, the authors, were asked by Rabbi Sue Ann Wasserman, director of the Department of Worship, Music, and Religious Living, to lead a weekday *Shacharit* service for members of the Commission, which included both men and women. We began the planning process by talking with Rabbi Sue Ann Wasserman, Cantor Lanie Katzew, and Rabbi Kim Geringer.

Given that the service was, in some way, meant to address male spirituality, we began to explore ways in which men lead services and how men experience worship. Are there some things in worship that have a particular resonance for men? While we were not sure that we had answers to this question, or that we knew what we wanted this service to be, we knew what we did not want it to be.

We did not want it to be a "men's service." For us, this conjured up the image of a room full of men, maybe even exclusively men, led by men. In such a service the preponderance of readings would address what could be perceived as male issues. Such a service can be very powerful, and certainly has its place on the spectrum of Reform Jewish worship, but we were interested in exploring models that could be replicated in a congregational setting.

It became clear for us that we wanted to craft an experience that would be comfortable for everyone, but might specifically have in mind the spiritual needs and comfort levels of the men who were worshiping with us that day. Like most services, ours would be filled with beautiful music and inspired readings, but we wanted to find music and readings that spoke specifically to men's spiritual needs. These elements would create what we hoped would be moments of consciousness, those "aha" moments when what it means to be both Jewish and male would become abundantly clear.

Music would be an important aspect of the service. While many of the great composers of Jewish liturgical music and many of the great cantors have been men, we did not assume that any music, simply because it was composed by a man, would resonate with the men with whom we would be worshiping. Something we realized early in this process was that we had not paid enough attention, when leading worship in other settings, to whether the men in the congregation were singing as much as the women. We had not paid attention to whether we were hearing men's and women's voices equally, or if men sang some songs but not others.

In selecting music, we asked if men were more inhibited when it came to singing out loud. If so, this might mean that men were more comfortable singing within a more narrow range of music, with a stronger and easier beat. Interestingly enough, some of the music that we felt would most resonate with men was written by women. Small percussion instruments were handed out to the congregation. These have been used with success at other men's gatherings, including Jewish worship geared for men. The male worshipers were active participants in the worship. They sang with full voice and enthusiastically used the instruments.

While we did include readings from other sources in the service, our task was to use *Mishkan T'filah*, the new Reform siddur, for our worship. Given that language can be a barrier for some, we wanted to be sensitive to identifying those readings that might be most accessible for men. We did not feel that the service would be enhanced by using traditional male images of God, and we did not feel that congregations would find that to be an appropriate model. Not only were we concerned that male images of God might alienate some of the female worshipers, but given the prevalence of inclusive language in Reform synagogues, we were not sure that male images would resonate with men.

On each two-page spread in the siddur we gave much thought to which of the readings—the Hebrew, the translation, or the two interpretive readings—might resonate more with men. In selecting readings, we sought to have a balance between familiar Hebrew prayers and English translations and readings. Choosing among the interpretive readings was largely subjective. We would read each of the alternatives and imagine which might resonate particularly with men. For example, when selecting an interpretive reading from the pages for the prayer *Elohai N'shamah*, we chose the reading that included, "Praise God in market and workplace, with computer, with hammer and nails."

Another aspect that we considered was seating. The chapel in which this service would take place had movable, individual seats. We wondered if any particular seating configuration would be more comfortable for men. Would men be more comfortable if they sat with other men? Such an arrangement would essentially be creating a *m'chitzah*, and we did not want to in any way equate male spirituality with Orthodox Judaism. If our concern was creating a comfortable atmosphere, keeping the space as familiar as possible seemed one way in which to accomplish this. The seats were arranged in semicircular rows, and worshipers sat where they were comfortable. This model of seating is used by many congregations with movable seating and we felt in terms of the physical space that replicating something familiar would facilitate meeting the spiritual needs of the worshipers.

We began the service by explaining that in preparing this service, we wondered ourselves just what male spirituality is and how, through worship, it might be possible to speak to the spiritual needs of Jewish men. Even though the traditional siddur may have been written by men, with other men in mind, and even though up until recently the music of Jewish worship was written by men, that did not mean that Jewish men today in Reform congregations find worship compelling or able to address their spiritual needs. For many Jewish men, even thinking about their spiritual needs is so new that they may not yet even have the vocabulary to express those needs. They may not know why one arrangement of seats makes them feel more at ease than another; they just know it does.

Our challenge is to support our congregants, and not just those who are men, in this endeavor. We can begin by letting go of preconceived notions and by experimenting and taking chances. We examined every aspect of the worship experience, from the musical settings and the use of instruments to the arrangement of the physical space and the choice of readings. If one reading doesn't work, we can try another next time. Creating worship that responds to the spiritual needs is neither easy nor quick. It is not as simple as rearranging the chairs. It does, however, take patience, commitment, and a willingness to take chances. Was our worship service a success? While the worshipers certainly participated and offered positive feedback, this service was designed to begin the conversation, not to provide the answers. Most importantly, we can work to create an atmosphere where these questions can be asked and where everyone can work together to find the answers.

The Reluctant Man

A Conversation with Susan Weidman Schneider

Some Reform leaders have observed a decline in men's involvement in synagogue life. Have you noticed this trend as well?

In my travels to Reform congregations around the country, I've seen as many men as women at services. But male participation seems to decline when innovative programming is introduced. Let me give you one example. I was recently at an erev Shabbat service at Temple Micah in Washington where the dancer/choreographer Liz Lerman led congregants in a spontaneously choreographed dance midrash which she created after watching how individual congregants moved and gestured while they discussed a text. The experience was pretty thrilling to me, and an unusual way to celebrate Kabbalat Shabbat, but it required a willingness to give oneself over to it. The unconventional Shabbat program had been widely publicized in the community, and although men were present, they were greatly outnumbered by women and not as enthusiastic.

If we are seeing some diminution in men's participation, it's coming at a time when women are finding an inspiring elasticity and room for growth in Jewish tradition. We're living in a time when Jewish women's study, scholarship, adult education, and spirituality groups are flowering.

What do you think is the source of this Jewish renaissance among women?

As children, many of these women didn't have the same Jewish educational opportunities as their brothers—they didn't become a bat mitzvah, for example. And while in the earlier years of the women's movement some women were reluctant to accept a public role in services, now many women are saying, "Yes, I want this for myself, and I want to do it differently." Increasingly, women are exploring and stretching the tradition in a fashion that's both enriching to their heritage and personally engaging.

They're *owning* their Judaism; they're not passive participants. And because many weren't taught these Jewish practices in childhood, they're by and large free of communal expectations, and therefore not afraid to say, "You know, I don't have even the remotest idea of how to perform that function." And once they've learned how to give a *d'var Torah* or chant from the Torah or lead a discussion group, they're thrilled to be doing something new, making change.

Men, on the other hand, are often expected to know all about Jewish history, Israel, Hebrew, ritual, the rhythms of the prayer service—to be masterfully proficient in our performance-oriented religion. I think many men are uncomfortable with this cultural expectation, but don't feel free to say so. Maybe what's needed is a gentler way of teaching boys and men, so they're not afraid to reveal their discomforts.

Women are also generally more inclined to want to share knowledge and experience. It's how most of us have been socialized. I remember attending one Simchat Torah celebration at a Long Island temple where just about equal numbers of men and women got called up, row by row, to march with the Torah through the sanctuary. The men picked up the Torah, quickly made their way up the aisle to the back, walked around, and came back. The women stopped at every row and leaned the Torah towards the congregation so people could kiss it; they wanted everybody to be included. So, too, when it comes to Jewish knowledge, women are teaching other women, and the learning doesn't feel competitive—the beginner's sense that it's perfectly okay to make mistakes, to fall and get up again. Many men, I think, still suffer from what my husband's sister calls "perfect report card syndrome"—anything less than an A+, you're a failure. With that comes a haunting sense of shame . . . so some Jewish boys and men just back off and avoid Jewish experiences.

Nowadays, you're saying, women are, on the whole, more comfortable expressing themselves Jewishly.
Yes. Ever since the 1970s, a time when men were much more resistant to changes in the content and the rhythm of worship services, Jewish women have been at the forefront of creating new liturgies, ceremonies, and rituals to mark the landmarks of our lives. At *Lilith* we see a lot of these—new rituals for becoming pregnant, blessing the birth of a daughter, turning fifty or sixty, separating from a marriage, launching a loved one to college, healing from abuse, or marking the end of cancer treatments. They're also writing psalms on healing, *midrashim* on biblical women, poems about their Jewish grandmothers. Forging intimate connections between traditional Judaism and the complex issues of modern life has helped them become more knowledgeable and engaged Jews. In addition, with the publication of feminist *haggadot*, women are talking, for example, about women's roles in the Exodus narrative: Miriam, who colluded with Pharaoh's daughter to save Moses; the midwives Shifra and Puah, who saved newborn Jewish sons; the four *daughters;* and more—broadening the Passover theme of liberation.

What do you think Jewish men can learn from these innovations?
I believe that women are demonstrating how it is possible to own the tradition in personal and resonant ways. Men can do this too, perhaps using the women's consciousness-raising model to talk about the times when they've felt alienated from Jewish traditions and the times they've felt authentically connected, maybe at a wedding, or a son's bar mitzvah. Celebrating a Jewish lifecycle event in a community of family and friends can feel very buoyant, pleasurable, and spiritual.

Of course, just as women's personal stories can be negative, so can men's. A man may have had an unpleasant experience at his bar mitzvah, sat down or stood up at the wrong time or tripped over something in front of the crowd. But until he tells his story, there's no way to figure out how it can be recast. If he speaks frankly and specifically about what he hasn't liked about attending synagogue—beyond "It's boring" or "It's not meeting my needs"—and is willing to take his own emotional and spiritual pulse, to be introspective and share his discoveries with other men, he may develop, over time, a more satisfying relationship with Judaism.

But some men don't seem comfortable discussing their Jewish needs openly, partly because focusing on "men's issues" isn't "politically correct."
This is a paradoxical problem. Some women may raise objections when men assert themselves because it seems like those who still have a great deal of power are trying to wield even more

power. And there's plenty of evidence that women are still being shut out. I just opened up a book called *Fifty Key Jewish Thinkers*, published in 1997, and not a single woman is included. There are still Jewish academic conferences with all-male panels, and it has been an uphill battle to make sure women are considered when leadership slots open up in Jewish organizations. So I'm sure there's a not-too-deeply-buried feeling among some women that men who raise issues like the "feminization of the synagogue" are attempting to endorse a male dominance of so much of Jewish life.

Rabbi Jeffrey Salkin, for one, fears bringing up gender issues could cause a backlash.

There are strategic ways of reframing the Jewish female/male issue. Avoidance surely is not one of them. The conversation needs to be opened, even if it's going to rock the boat. Congregations might begin by simply announcing, "We're going to host a panel where women and men can speak about their feelings of exclusion or inclusion in synagogue life."

The first woman rabbi in America, Sally Priesand, recently announced her retirement from the pulpit. Isn't it interesting that we are talking about what's happening with Jewish men just as we approach this milestone?

I think Rabbi Priesand's retirement gives us a benchmark. She was ordained in 1972. Considering what women have accomplished in the past three incredibly liberating decades, we realize that men, too, could be liberated from certain cultural inhibitions that have tied them down. If they can free themselves from these inhibitions, they may find themselves more comfortable and fulfilled in a religious setting. Judaism will be enriched as well.

Section VI

Adult Education: Men Welcome

Introduction

In this section Dr. Lisa Grant offers us a look at her research regarding Jewish learning in the life of adult Jewish males. In "Jewish Men and Adult Jewish Learning," she concludes that "attracting men requires creative rethinking to imagine topics, venues, and methods of instruction that will be more appealing and connected to men's lives and concerns." The other contributors to this section are men who are leading successful adult learning experiences. They are fulfilling, perhaps unknowingly, many of the suggestions that Dr. Grant makes. These authors add their personal experiences and insights, emphasizing the great need for effective Jewish learning venues for men.

Rabbi Howard Jaffe's Achim group asks itself, "For What Do Men's Souls Hunger?" Refusing to believe that men only connect through activity, Achim offers the opportunity for men to create lasting connections through conversation and dialogue. The group has touched the lives of dozens if not hundreds of Rabbi Jaffe's male congregants. The group allows them to ask the questions of ultimate importance in their lives. In addition to the group, Rabbi Jaffe also provides examples of two programs that have been successfully run in his congregation.

Rabbi Jerry David writes from the front lines of creative programming that attempts to involve men. He believes that Jews-by-choice provide the ideal model for all Jews. In order to find real meaning, Jews must participate in in-depth learning and self-exploration. Rabbi David offered his congregants the opportunity to relearn the Torah they had learned as children. A key policy is to make sure not to shame those who had not yet revisited the lessons of the Torah as adults. Rabbi David has had four years of successful programming to date, changing the lives of many of his male congregants in the process.

In "Yes, We Are Our Brother's Keeper, and He Is Ours!" Rabbi Dan Moskovitz describes how he began his men's study group as part of a personal need that emerged from a moment of crisis in his own life. The study group allows participants to truly connect with each other in a safe place to share the stories of their lives. Rabbi Moskovitz's process for creating this space involves agreement by all participants on a set of ground rules for each meeting so that men know what to expect. Rabbi Moskovitz provides one of the discussion guides that he has used successfully in his men's study group.

Questions for Discussion

As you read each piece, consider the following questions:

1. Do Dr. Grant's findings contradict or support the anecdotes of the rabbis leading men's study groups? How or how not?
2. Are there possibilities for you to create safe learning environments to allow for men's participation in Jewish learning? What would you like to see in your congregation?

3. Why do you think the programs described in this section allow men to support each other through the complexity of their lives? Can you think of other ways to achieve this goal?
4. What outreach opportunities can be found in welcoming men in new ways, tailored to men's lives, struggles, and needs?

Jewish Men and Adult Jewish Learning

Lisa D. Grant

Jewish study is a normative and integral part of Jewish life. Jewish study deepens meaning and understanding of Jewish beliefs and practices. It provides people with the language of Jewish discourse, which in turn allows learners of all types to shape their own Jewish narrative. Without study, Jews lack the basis for informed choice or the ability to teach the next generation, which is also a central obligation of Jewish tradition. Without study, Judaism's meaning becomes diluted.

For much of the twentieth century, adult Jewish study hardly figured in the lives of even those American Jews most active and engaged in synagogue life and the broader Jewish community. In the last few decades however, communal attention to Jewish education has increased significantly, perhaps marked most notably by the watershed 1990 National Jewish Population Study. Since that time, adult Jewish learning has gained an increasingly prominent place on the religious and communal agenda. This is manifest in a wide variety of learning programs in synagogues and in the integration of Jewish study as part of the organizational life within the Jewish communal world as well. Overall enrollment rates in these programs vary greatly from synagogue to synagogue, but one thing remains steady throughout: for the most part, among Reform and Conservative Jews, far more women than men engage in Jewish learning.

The research is consistent in documenting this imbalance. Key findings can be distilled from a variety of studies (Cohen 1998; NJPS 2001; Cohen and Davidson 2001; Grant 2003; Grant, Schuster, Woocher, and Cohen 2004; Keysar and Kosmin 2004; Grant and Schuster 2006):

- Across all age groups, and regardless of employment status, more Jewish women than Jewish men participate in adult Jewish learning activities.
- The greater the number of class sessions, the greater the gender imbalance. In other words, women are far more likely than men to sign up for multiple session courses.
- A great proportion of men who do sign up for long-term adult Jewish learning programs come with their wives.
- Far more women than men attend adult and parent education programs related to Jewish family education.
- More balanced numbers of men and women can be seen at one-off programs and scholar-in-residence type lectures.
- The more prestigious the speaker, the more likely men are to attend.

- Certain topics and venues remain more popular with men, such as "downtown lunch and learn" programs, Talmud study, and contemporary issues such as bio-medical ethics and the Israeli-Palestinian conflict.

Setting the Data in Context

These data need to be understood in terms of their relationship to other patterns of religious belief, belonging, and behavior. Women participate in religious life in greater numbers than males in the overall American population in terms of a variety of different measures, including attendance at worship, belief in God, and participation in religious education. Likewise, females outnumber males in participation in many aspects of Jewish life, beginning in adolescence and continuing across the life span. For example:

1. Among Reform and Conservative Jewish adolescents, females outnumber males in their participation in Jewish youth groups, Jewish summer camps, college Hillel programs, Israel experience programs, and many ritual activities (Halbertal and Cohen 2001; Keysar and Kosmin 2004; Friedman, Kane, and Stollman 2005).
2. The current gender mix of rabbinical students at Hebrew Union College is approximately 30 percent male and 70 percent female; there is an even higher proportion of females in the School of Sacred Music. Anecdotally, we know similar patterns exist in graduate programs of Jewish communal service.
3. In a recent study of young adult children of intermarried couples, ninety people voluntarily responded to a request to be interviewed (with an offer of a $75 stipend for their time); 39 percent were male and 61 percent were female (Beck 2005).

Simply put, it appears that women act on being Jewish more than men. Thus, it should be no surprise that we see similar patterns in Jewish learning. This is reinforced by a recent study of the Jews on Long Island in New York (2006). Here, four hundred respondents were asked to respond to the following question: "There are many ways of being Jewish. How important is being Jewish, to you, in terms of. . . ." They were then asked to assess the importance imbued to a list of different Jewish beliefs and behaviors. Based on chi-square tests of statistical significance, gender differences arose in four key domains, as shown in Table 1. This table presents the percentage of respondents who noted that this dimension of being Jewish was "very important" to them. Two of these domains relate directly to Jewish learning, and a third relates to Jewish practice.

These data should not be taken to suggest that women consider being Jewish more important than do men, rather only that they value certain Jewish behaviors more than do men. Indeed, in this same study, there were a number of areas where there was no statistically significant difference between the genders in terms of their ranking of importance of certain Jewish values, as shown in Table 2. Again, the table presents the percentage of respondents noting that this dimension was "very important" to them. While the gender difference by percentages does not appear

Table 1. Dimensions where there is a statistically significant gender difference

	Males	Females
Celebrating Jewish holidays	53%	79%
Giving one's children and grandchildren a Jewish education	61	77
Learning about Jewish history and culture	37.5	44.5
Believing in God	48	65

Table 2. Dimensions where gender difference is *not* statistically significant

	Males	Females
Supporting Israel	54%	60%
Remembering the Holocaust	81	89
Leading an ethical and moral life	81	87
Giving to charity	49	58
Studying Jewish texts	13	18

to be much different between the two tables, the test of statistical significance is gauged against the full range of responses and the numbers of people responding to the question. For presentation purposes, only the "very important" responses are given. The key point to note is that women seem to consider Jewish learning a more important priority than do men.

It is also important to contextualize these data about gender mix in terms of the relationship between those adults who participate in Jewish learning versus those who do not participate. While Jewish religious and educational leaders recognize the crucial role adult Jewish learning can play in increasing Jewish literacy and engagement in Jewish life, there are still relatively few people, regardless of gender, who participate in ongoing Jewish learning, and these are typically among the most highly affiliated. Likewise, adult Jewish learners are typically more highly educated than average American Jews (Grant et al. 2004). Studies report a range between 10 percent and 25 percent of Jewish adults who engage in "structured Jewish learning activities," such as attending a lecture, taking a class, going to a study group, or studying Jewish texts. Thus, it appears that formal study just is not a high priority among most American Jews. The Long Island study documents this quite clearly. As shown in Table 2 above, quite a small percentage of both men and women consider studying Jewish texts as a "very important" way to be Jewish. Indeed, this dimension of being Jewish received the lowest ranking in the entire list. Thus, the challenge is not only to address the gender imbalance in adult Jewish learning, but also to make Jewish learning more attractive and accessible to a broader population altogether.

Reasons for Men's Lower Rates of Participation

In addition to the trends about women being more actively involved in religious life in general, several other factors may contribute to the even greater disparity between the genders in the adult Jewish learning classroom. Studies of adult Jewish learners consistently report that the major motivation for participation in Jewish learning activities is to "grow as a Jew" (Schuster and Grant 2005). However, the appeal of Jewish learning frequently derives from the opportunity the learner has to come together with other Jews and to feel socially connected to a Jewish community. Thus, both the primary and secondary motivations for adult Jewish learning are spiritual and relational in nature, aspects of life that tend to be more important to women's development than to men's (Gilligan 1993, Hayes and Flannery 2000).

In a related vein, women tend to be more comfortable revealing their vulnerabilities and ignorance than are men. As we see in Table 2, the proportion of men and women begins to equalize in more advanced Jewish learning classes, or in programs that are predominantly lecture-style where there is no expectation for participation and community-building. Those classes that explore introductory level material and/or involve dialogue and personal meaning-making are much more likely to attract a female audience.

Another feature that draws women more than men is the tendency for women to feel a greater sense of responsibility in transmitting Jewish knowledge, practice, and values to the next generation. While in today's world, more and more men do take on significant child-rearing roles, overall women remain the primary parent in terms of caring for the health, education, and well-being of the child. Thus, the impulse toward generativity is felt more greatly by women than men.

Another factor is that women tend to have somewhat more flexible lifestyles and work schedules, which provides them with somewhat more discretionary time. This, coupled with their motivation for social interaction and impulse toward generativity, may be strong reasons for why more women make time in their lives for Jewish learning than do men.

Indeed, it may be that men are as interested in Jewish learning as women, but either they do not want to participate in a formal class or are unwilling to commit to the time away from work and other more self-directed (or competitive) leisure activities such as sports and independent learning. For instance, the Long Island study showed that all adults engaged in much higher rates of independent study than in formal learning. When asked what types of Jewish learning activities they had engaged in within the past two years, 78 percent of Jewish adults report that they regularly read about Israel or some aspect of Judaism or Jewish life, 58 percent report they visited Jewish Web sites on the Internet, and 53 percent read a nonfiction book; in contrast only 24 percent participated in a Jewish study group within the last two years (Grant and Schuster 2006). Thus, it appears that Jewish adults as a whole are more likely to engage in private and personal study than they are in formal classroom study.

There also is a historical reason for the greater numbers of women in adult Jewish learning. Gender parity in Jewish education has only recently been achieved for the youngest cohort of Jewish adults (ages 18–34). For all other age cohorts, males received more Jewish education as children than females (Ukeles, Miller, & Beck 2006). Thus, many midlife and older Jewish adult women had no formal Jewish education as children. Many of the staples of synagogue-based adult learning programming implicitly meet these women's needs to make up for lost opportunities, with course such as:

1. Hebrew literacy and adult *b'nei mitzvah* to enhance participation in worship.
2. Introduction to Judaism.
3. How-to courses that are often the focus of family education programming.

Conclusion

The research findings are also clear in telling us that interest in a fuller range of Jewish topics increases as an individual becomes involved in Jewish learning activities.

In other words, the more a Jewish adult learns, the more she or he wants to learn about more aspects of Judaism and Jewish life and to renegotiate Jewish meaning in personally relevant ways. The challenge for engaging both men and women in Jewish learning is getting them to begin the process. Attracting men requires creative rethinking to imagine topics, venues, and methods of instruction that will be more appealing and connected to men's lives and concerns.

References

Beck, Pearl. 2005. *A flame still burns: The dimensions and determinants of Jewish identity among young adult children of the intermarried.* New York: Jewish Outreach Institute.

Cohen, Steven M., and Aryeh Davidson. 2001. *Adult Jewish learning in America: Current patterns and prospects for growth*. New York: The Florence G. Heller/JCC Association Research Center and the Jewish Theological Seminary.

Friedman, M., M. Kane, and M. Stollman. 2005. URJ young men's project: Young men and their presence in the Reform Movement. A project of the Union for Reform Judaism Youth Division and the North American Federation of Temple Brotherhoods.

Gilligan, Carol. 1993. *In a different voice: Psychological theory and women's development*. Reissue ed. Cambridge: Harvard University Press.

Grant, Lisa, D. 2003. Jewish Learners and Learning at the Skirball Center. Evaluation report conducted for the Skirball Center for Adult Jewish Learning at Temple Emanu-El, New York.

Grant, Lisa D., Diane T. Schuster, Meredith Woocher, and Steven M. Cohen. 2004. *A journey of heart and mind: Transformative Jewish learning in adulthood*. New York: JTS Press.

Grant, Lisa D., and Diane T. Schuster. 2006. The impact of J Learn on the Long Island Jewish Community: Baseline year findings—2005–2006. Report prepared for the UJA-Federation of New York.

Halbertal, Tova, and Steven M. Cohen. 2001. Gender variations in Jewish identity: Practices and attitudes in Conservative congregations. *Contemporary Jewry* 22: 37–64.

Hayes, Elisabeth, and Daniele Flannery. 2000. *Women as learners: The significance of gender in adult learning*. San Francisco: Jossey-Bass.

Keysar, A., and B. Kosmin. 2004. *"Eight-Up:" The College Years: The Jewish Engagement of Young Adults Raised in Conservative Synagogues, 1995–2003*. New York: Jewish Theological Seminary.

Schuster, D. T., and L. Grant. 2005. Adult Jewish learning: What do we know? What do we need to know? *Journal of Jewish Education* 71 (2): 179–200.

Ukeles, J., R. Miller, and P. Beck. 2006. *Young Jewish Adults in the United States Today*. New York: American Jewish Committee.

For What Do Men's Souls Hunger?

Howard Jaffe

For what do men's souls hunger? That is the foundational question that led to the establishment of Achim, the men's program of Temple Isaiah, Lexington, Massachusetts. Achim has touched dozens, perhaps hundreds of men directly, and many more indirectly, by providing an opportunity for Jewish men to bond not through activity, as we are so often told is the modality for male connection, but by talking—openly, honestly, sometimes unreservedly, often to their own surprise almost always meaningfully.

What surprised me most about Achim was that two dozen men who had never done so before signed up to spend a weekend together when the first retreat was announced. Our congregation is not tiny, but it is not huge, either—a bit more than eight hundred households—a large enough group from which to draw a critical mass, but small enough that everyone waited to see if it would really fly. The idea came out of a collaboration between one of our members, then the CEO of a midsized technology company, and one of our rabbis. The man who brought the idea forward had been a member of the synagogue for a number of years but not especially active, himself. He has three kids, the oldest of whom was in high school at the time, and he had found participation in our family education program enjoyable and interesting enough, but he had never gotten involved much beyond that. His wife, on the other hand, was a committee chair, sat on the temple board, and seemed, like a number of other women, to build a large part of her life around the synagogue.

The demographics of our congregation are such that there are a number of men, mostly retired, who spend meaningful amounts of time around the building. This includes a cadre who work in our well-used and well-tended library, and others who are involved in our senior adult group. Our adult education program has been successful in reaching men and women, and we have been blessed to have men in many key leadership programs and appropriately represented on the board. But it was clear that at our congregation, as in so many others, the deep connections between individuals happened far more often between women than between men.

We discovered something gratifying and a bit surprising: given the opportunity to do so in a safe, physically comfortable, and uncompromisingly Jewish setting, we were able to give men the chance to talk with each other about things they rarely discussed with anyone. One of the key ingredients was the setting: a university-owned retreat center about forty-five minutes away in an area that few had reason to travel to—far enough and unfamiliar enough territory to be a retreat, close enough that everyone could arrive easily and not have to factor in travel time and energy. The setting is not plush, but it is pretty and very comfortable (it is often used as a venue for weddings, including the wedding of the daughter of one of our members who is a regular participant). There's no roughing it at the facility—good food, a cash bar at night, and padded couches and chairs created more of a large country house than a rustic lodge feel and, I think, contributed to the general feeling of comfort with each other that was quickly established at the first retreat and continues through all Achim events. Even though there were other groups using different parts of the facility, we had our own spaces at all times, contributing to the sense of intimacy that began to develop.

Our Achim worshiped on Friday night and Saturday morning, and made *Havdalah* on Saturday night. But the primary Jewish component of each of the retreats has been the discussion around a chosen theme, based on Jewish texts. And it was in this context that we learned the answer to our initial question: For what do men's souls hunger? At least, for what do our Jewish men's souls hunger? And we discovered the answer: to relate to each other in the context of the master narrative that they share as Jewish men. Men who rarely, if ever, had the context or opportunity to do so talked about the most meaningful, and usually private, details of their lives as they contrasted them to the stories of Jewish men from across the ages and the teachings of our tradition of what it means to be a Jewish man. We learned, not surprisingly, that they were less interested in learning about the Talmud than they were in how a particular passage from the Talmud inspired or challenged them. And when they engaged with the ideas, they engaged with each other and formed an authentic community.

There was time for touch football, but there was also time for singing. And men who otherwise did not have a setting such as this explored more deeply and perhaps more honestly what it meant to be husbands, sons, fathers, and brothers. One of my favorite stories to come out of an Achim retreat was about a weekend around these various roles we play. All of those who signed up agreed to talk about the topic, as long as "we don't talk about our fathers." And guess what— all weekend long, everyone talked about their fathers. During one retreat, one man decided to try out his Hebrew name for the weekend and asked his fellow Achim to call him by that name for the entire weekend. It was a powerful experience for him and for others who began to think more about their own identity.

What made the original retreats, and now the ongoing gatherings (more about those in a moment) successful, I believe, is the intentional creation of a community of meaning. The structured discussions (mostly led by a rabbi) were not merely sharing sessions, but opportunities for the exploration of purpose and self-review. That notion continues to guide and inform the program.

The annual retreat takes place in the same venue each year, though the length has varied due to a combination of logistical necessity and experimentation. There have been one-night retreats, two-night retreats, and one-day (Shabbat morning through evening) retreats; each has its pluses and minuses. In addition to the retreats, our Achim gather several times a year for dinner and for other structured gatherings, including at least one *kallah*, a half-day Sunday gathering at the temple similar to the retreats. As this is being written, plans are in the works for a spring *kallah* on the topic "Have We Left Slavery Behind or Is Our Freedom an Illusion? Seeing the Haggadah in a New Light."

Participation is open to anyone who is interested, on a first-come, first-served basis. Keeping the numbers limited enables the group to have the kind of conversation that has become the standard, and the limit is strictly observed. Here is an excerpt from the publicity: "All Men of Temple Isaiah (or men who are not members of the Temple) are invited to the FIFTH Annual Spring Kallah sponsored by the Temple Isaiah Achim Men's Group. Discussion will be drawn from excerpts from the Haggadah and possibly other Judaic texts, but we want discussion to be open, freewheeling and relevant to our contemporary lives. Enrollment is limited to the first thirty (30) men who RSVP. By the way—no rabbis at this event. It is all to be led by members of the group."

Not everyone who has participated in the Achim programs has become more active in the temple, and that is fine. It is difficult to say this with authority, but my sense is that just about everyone has come closer to and, for some, more comfortable with their Judaism. I will take that every time. In addition, new, strong, and often cross-generational friendships have evolved (while few of the participants are/were fathers of young children, the age range spans close to fifty years). The result, of course, is that there are many recognized and many more unrecognized ways in which relationships have been facilitated and deepened as a result of these new connections. And most of all, these Jewish men have the opportunity to celebrate and explore what it means to be a Jewish man in the presence and fraternity of others who, like them, care to know and understand what that means.

Following are the outlines of two Achim programs run at Temple Isaiah, "Our Roles as Fathers" and "The God of My Father."

Our Roles as Fathers

Time: 1.5 hours

Goals:

For participants to consider their own obligations as fathers
To view how Judaism views the role and obligations of a father
To explore Jewish biblical narratives with an eye to the father-son relationships explored within

Set Induction:

Ask participants to think for a few minutes about their children and their roles as father. Ask them to share the roles that they have as father (list on board).

Hand out Jewish texts that describe the role and obligations of a parent.

Kiddushin 29a: "Our Rabbis taught: The father is bound in respect of his son, to circumcise, redeem, teach him Torah, take a wife for him, and teach him a craft. Some say, to teach him to swim too."

Discuss:

In what ways did your father do this for you?
In what ways do you do this for your children?

Akeidat Yitzchak

Read *Akeidat Yitzchak* together:

The *Akeidah*—Genesis Chapter 22

1. And it came to pass after these things, that God tested Abraham, and said to him, "Abraham;" and he said, "Behold, here I am." 2. And he said, "Take now your son, your only son Isaac, whom you love, and go to the land of Moriah; and offer him there for a burnt offering upon one of the mountains which I will tell you." 3. And Abraham rose up early in the morning, and saddled his ass, and took two of his young men with him, and Isaac his son, and broke the wood for the burnt offering, and rose up, and went to the place of which God had told him. 4. Then on the third day Abraham lifted up his eyes, and saw the place far away. 5. And Abraham said to his young

men, "Stay here with the ass; and I and the lad will go yonder and worship, and come back to you." 6. And Abraham took the wood of the burnt offering, and laid it upon Isaac his son; and he took the fire in his hand, and a knife; and they went both of them together. 7. And Isaac spoke to Abraham his father, and said, "My father"; and he said, "Here am I, my son." And he said, "Behold the fire and the wood; but where is the lamb for a burnt offering?" 8. And Abraham said, "My son, God will provide himself a lamb for a burnt offering"; so they went both of them together. 9. And they came to the place which God had told him; and Abraham built an altar there, and laid the wood in order, and bound Isaac his son, and laid him on the altar upon the wood. 10. And Abraham stretched out his hand, and took the knife to slay his son. 11. And the angel of *Adonai* called to him from heaven, and said, "Abraham, Abraham"; and he said, "Here am I." 12. And he said, "Lay not your hand upon the lad, nor do anything to him; for now I know that you fear God, seeing that you did not withhold your son, your only son from me." 13. And Abraham lifted up his eyes, and looked, and behold behind him a ram caught in a thicket by his horns; and Abraham went and took the ram, and offered him up for a burnt offering in place of his son. 14. And Abraham called the name of that place Adonai-Yireh; as it is said to this day, In the Mount of *Adonai* it shall be seen. 15. The angel of *Adonai* called to Abraham a second time from heaven, 16. and said, "By Myself I swear, *Adonai* declares: Because you have done this and have not withheld your son, your favored one, 17. I will bestow My blessing upon you and make your descendants as numerous as the stars of heaven and the sands on the seashore; and your descendants shall seize the gates of their foes. 18. All the nations of the earth shall bless themselves by your descendants, because you have obeyed My command." 19. Abraham then returned to his servants, and they departed together for Beer-sheba; and Abraham stayed in Beer-sheba.

Large-group questions:
1. What do we (or don't we) learn about parenting from these texts?
2. Imagine you are Abraham; how might you have handled this situation differently?

Bibliodrama: We are going to make midrash by becoming some of these characters and adding our voices to theirs. In small groups, I am going to ask you to become either Abraham, Isaac, or one of the servants. What is important is that you speak in character but that you speak as yourself in the present. You know your past but not your future.

1. Set the scene:
    a. Get into groups of three—Abraham, Yitzchak, one of the servants.
    b. Triangle chairs: actor, director, observer
       Text: "5. And Abraham said to his young men, Stay here with the ass; and I and the lad will go yonder and worship, and come back to you. 6. And Abraham took the wood of the burnt offering, and laid it upon Isaac his son; and he took the fire in his hand, and a knife; and they went both of them together."

    And Abraham, what are you thinking?
    And Isaac, what are you thinking?
    And Mr. Servant, what are you making of this entire scene?
2. Switch
3. Write two to three sentences as your character expressing what you have learned about yourself.
4. Share with the entire group: hear from the Abrahams, the Isaacs, and the servants.

Small-group Questions:
1. Do you, in any way, see yourself (as a father or as a son) reflected in the *Akeidah* text? If so, how? If not, why not?
   a. How do you respond to this text as a father?
   b. How do you respond to this text as a son?
2. Can you think of a time in your life when you might have treated your child(ren) in a similar way to how Abraham treated Isaac? Do you feel that you may have, in some way, sacrificed your child? For what?
3. If you could rewrite the past, what, if anything, might you have done differently as a parent? What do you wish your father did differently with you? Can you change the past?

Gather to share discoveries with the large group.

A Final Thought: From Rabbi Norman Cohen, *Voices From Genesis*

Commenting on the *Akeidah*—Genesis 22:

At the denouement of the episode, Isaac was awakened to the fragility of life and to his father's true nature. He was no longer the naïve young person who thought that his father could do no wrong and in whom Isaac had total confidence, assuming that his judgment and his ability to protect his son were impeccable. He now saw Abraham as a human being, with the same frailties as every other person. In discovering his father's humanness, he discovered himself. This was a powerful moment of maturation for Isaac, as it is for every young adult who witnesses his or her parents' frailty for the first time. Isaac would never be the same. The mark of this experience would remain with him throughout his entire life. What he had seen and felt would shape his whole being.

The Isaac who ascended Mount Moriah with his father did not come down from the mountain. A more mature, wiser Isaac descended in his place—one who, having experienced a near-death trauma at the hand of his father, was no longer umbilically connected to him. Isaac had become an individual in his own right.

Large-group questions:
1. How did you feel when you discovered your father's frailties? How did you respond?
2. Have your children discovered your own frailties? If so, how did they respond? How did you respond? If not, what sort of thoughts have you had about this impending moment for your child?
3. When our children discover our frailties do our obligations as fathers change? If so, how?

Activity: Write a letter to your child(ren) explaining why you made the choices that you made when you and they were younger. Or alternatively, write a letter to your father telling him some of the things you wish he had done for you.

Stories of Our Elders

This would probably work best as a fireside chat format:
- Pass out index cards to all the participants. Have them write a question they would like to ask a man who is older than they: something they always wanted to ask their father or an older man (or if their father is deceased, something they wish they had asked).

- Ask two to three older members of the community to attend the retreat. Ask them in advance to prepare some introductory thoughts on who they are and one or two things they have learned or gleaned from life.
- Have a moderator (rabbi) ask the senior members the questions and see where it goes.

The God of My Father

I. God as Father
(God, no matter what we do with language, is gendered. The question is, how do we portray that gender? As Jeff Salkin writes, "When your daughter stubs her toes, she does not run into the house yelling, 'Parent! Parent!'")

Read Mary Daly quote: "If God in his heaven is a father ruling his people, then it is the nature of things and according to the divine play and the order of the universe that society be male-dominated."

Ken Woodward (It's hard to be a father):

"These are tough times to be a father. The media are full of stories about abusive fathers, fatherless children, and deadbeat dads—and about New Fathers who are trying to do better. But in general this is an age when fathers get little respect, and you don't have to look farther than the biggest father figure of them all, God. Few theologians these days seem to want a God who takes charge, assumes responsibility, fights for his children, makes demands, risks rebuffs, punishes as well as forgives. In a word, a father."

    a. Prayers: How do these prayers portray God?
        i. *Avinu Malkeinu*
        ii. *Anim Z'mirot*

How does a fatherly image of God teach men about fatherhood?
1. The Jewish God is not oppressive.
2. God is firm and fair, active when necessary, and compassionate when desirable. The Jewish God is a creative combination of distance and intimacy, of the urge to love and the need to control.

Exodus 34:6–7: "*Adonai, Adonai,* a God compassionate and gracious, slow to anger, abounding in kindness and faithfulness, extending kindness to the thousandth generation, forgiving iniquity, transgression, and sin—yet not remitting all punishment."

3. God can be wrong—and loves it (*Bava Metzia* 59b):
It has been taught: On that day R. Eliezer brought forward every imaginable argument, but they did not accept them. Said he to them: "If the halachah agrees with me, let this carob-tree prove it!" Thereupon the carob-tree was torn a hundred cubits out of its place—others affirm, four hundred cubits. "No proof can be brought from a carob-tree," they retorted. Again he said to them: "If the halachah agrees with me, let the stream of water prove it!"
Whereupon the stream of water flowed backwards—"No proof can be brought from a stream of water," they rejoined. Again he urged: "If the halachah agrees with me, let the walls of the schoolhouse prove it," whereupon the walls inclined to fall. But R. Joshua rebuked them, saying: "When scholars are engaged in a halachic dispute, what right have you to interfere?" Hence they did not fall, in honor of R. Joshua, nor did they resume the upright, in honor of R. Eliezer; and they are still standing thus inclined. Again he said to them: "If the halachah agrees with me, let it be proved from heaven!" Whereupon a Heavenly Voice cried out: "Why do you dispute with R. Eliezer, seeing that in all

matters the halachah agrees with him!" But R. Joshua arose and exclaimed: "It is not in heaven." What did he mean by this?—Said R. Jeremiah: "That the Torah had already been given at Mount Sinai; we pay no attention to a Heavenly Voice, because You have long since written in the Torah at Mount Sinai, After the majority must one incline." R. Nathan met Elijah and asked him: "What did the Holy One, Blessed be God, do in that hour?"—"God laughed [with joy]," he replied, saying, "My sons have defeated Me, My sons have defeated Me."

4. God weeps (*Eichah Rabbah* 24):

God said: "So long as I am within the Holy Temple, the peoples of the world will be unable to touch it. However, I will shut My eyes and swear that I will have nothing to do with it again till the messianic end of time. Meanwhile, let the enemies [the Romans] come and devastate it." At once the Romans entered the Temple and burned it. After it was burned, the Holy One said: "I have no dwelling place in the Land of Israel. So I shall remove My Presence from it and go unto My former residence [the heavens]."

God wept and said: "Woe is Me! For Israel's sake I caused My Presence to dwell below. But now that Israel sinned and I am returning to My former place, I have, heaven forbid, become a laughingstock of the nations, an object of derision for mortals."

In that instant, the angel Metatron came, fell upon his face, and spoke before the Holy One: "Master of the universe, let me weep, but You must not weep." God replied: "If you do not let Me weep, I will go into a place where you have no authority to enter and weep there."

5. God nurtures (Deuteronomy 32:10): "He found him in a desert land, and in the waste howling wilderness; he led him about, he instructed him, he kept him as the apple of his eye."

II. The God of My Father
   a. When is the phrase "The God of My Father" used in Torah? What is its purpose/power?
      i. Genesis 26:24—God appears to Isaac: protection and blessing.
      ii. Genesis 28:13-15—God as cheerleader, booster, protector, comforter. "I will never leave you."
      iii. Genesis 46:1-4—Don't be afraid to go to a scary and dark place because I will be with you and I will bring you up.
      iv. Exodus 3:6-14—Figuring out just who this God is (Ehyeh Asher Ehyeh). It's always somewhat ambiguous.
      v. I Chronicles 28:9—God is always there but you must maintain your part of the relationship.

III. For Small-Group Discussions:

The God/Gods of my father . . .

1. Did my father have an understanding of God? What was it? How did he share it with me?
2. What were some of my father's gods? (What was really important to him?) What or whom did he worship? Why? How do I feel about his choices?
3. How did he consciously and unconsciously make these gods known to me?
4. Are his gods my gods? Which are different? Why?

IV. Individual Writing Exercises:
   1. What are my gods?
   2. What of my gods do I want to pass on to my children or someone whom I mentor and care for?
   3. If someone asked my children what is important to me (i.e., what are your father's gods?) what would they say? How would I feel about their answers?
   4. What do I hope they come to see is of importance to me? How have I let them know this? How do I continue to let them know?

A True Homecoming

Jerry David

I was in third grade or maybe fourth when I went to services with my friend, Gary, at his Orthodox shul. We are both children of Holocaust survivors, but while his family clung to tradition, mine tried to escape it. I was trying to follow the service but, to this day, I remember that uncomfortable, sinking feeling of being lost and confused—a stranger in a strange place. I also had this growing awareness that the older kids sitting near me were pointing at me, talking about me and laughing—or so it seemed. Just then the *shamash* towered over me, grabbed my siddur, and turned it right side up! "Here, try this," he barked.

I swore then I was not going to remain ignorant in my own Judaism. I succeeded in my demand that my parents join a synagogue—a Reform temple, where my rabbi served as a mentor and role model. Years later, I became a rabbi myself.

The prevailing philosophy of my rabbinate is to "meet people where they are and grow together." I have served the same congregation, Temple Emanuel of Cherry Hill, since my ordination thirty-three years ago, and have taught Introduction to Judaism for most of that time. Perhaps the greatest strength of our congregation is the diversity of our membership. I have been especially inspired by Jews-by-choice, who bring to us their passion and their deep commitment to Judaism, as well as their questions, doubts, and love of learning.

Read these heartfelt words from one Jew-by-choice as he stood on our bimah and became part of Judaism and the Jewish people. Bob has allowed me to share his personal words:

> I have thought of this moment since I was a child and, yet, I am startled by the suddenness of it. I have been reading and learning for years, and now, what I know seems inadequate. I have pictured myself standing here, on the bimah, many times and . . . at this moment, I am overwhelmed. None of this should surprise me, as I have lived my life trying to bring dissonant parts of my "self" together. When I was a very little boy, my father told me—"Live each day so that at night, lying in bed, you can look back over your day and be able to say that, in some small way, you have made the world a better place"! So, I have come to this day, bringing my own special mixture and perspective to my faith. For myself, Judaism is living out the timeless covenant with God and God's law—living personally and as part of the people ISRAEL. The essence of that covenant lies in the unshakable truth that each unique individual life has value. I am one with the message of Judaism and the long, tragic yet proud history of our people. My wandering is over—I have come home.

I was moved by Bob's sense of having arrived at home in becoming a Jew, as I have been by working with many Jews-by-choice. And then five years ago I had an epiphany. Jews-by-choice participate in in-depth learning and self-exploration, but what about the rest of us? And what about, specifically, our men? What about *our* wandering? Are we "at home" as Jews? What are we doing about our Judaism? So many of the men I meet are quick to assure me that yes, they are Jewish, but, no, they don't do much, if anything about it. They leave that to their wives and kids. At the same time, many also acknowledge that they have everything in life they ever dreamed of and they still come up empty. Something is lacking; something is missing. Could it even be that they feel, as I once did, alien in synagogue? The late Abraham Heschel once said that every Jew is a messenger for a great tradition, and the tragedy of the modern Jew is that he is a messenger who forgot the message.

I was determined to help us recapture that message. Therefore, I sent out a personal appeal to our men to join me on a Jewish journey. The letter read:

> As your rabbi, I am always searching for ways to share my love of Judaism and Torah with you. The Torah is our guide for living, and I continue to read, learn and discuss its lessons.
>
> Many boys had the opportunity to study Torah when they were young. When they speak of the lessons they learned, it is from the perspective of their young lives. If you did not have the opportunity to attend religious school as a child, or if you did but would like the chance to be reintroduced to the lessons of our heritage, I have a wonderful plan in mind. I am personally inviting you to join a class of men who meet regularly to learn and talk together. We view the lessons of the Torah through an adult lens. As men, we look forward and backward in history and discuss the implications of the Torah's lessons. In addition, there will be a track that could culminate in an adult bar mitzvah, if you should elect to do so. I want to stress that no prior knowledge is necessary to become part of this exciting class, just the enthusiasm to join together with a group of men to discuss Judaism and its relevance in your life and in the world today.

To my surprise, I struck a curious, responsive chord. At that first organizational meeting, fifty men attended and we spent the next several hours sharing our Jewish memories. From that larger group, twenty-five men began a course of study that is now in its fourth year.

The first year's agenda mirrored a basic Introduction to Judaism course. The second year focused on Joseph Telushkin's *Jewish Literacy*, and the third year explored Joseph Telushkin's *Jewish Wisdom*. Presently, we use *Living Torah*. However, the texts were really a pretext for the lively discussions, insightful questions, and emotional responses.

The class often begins with a sharing of an article that might relate to the scheduled topic or a personal situation one might be dealing with. We then delve into the text by taking turns reading passages, which generates more discussion and lively debate. I have been referred to as the coach; and if this is the case, my team has no set strategy, although we always touch base with Judaism.

The second year culminated in an adult bar mitzvah, during which ten of our men read Torah (for the first time). This past year, we conducted our first ever men's seder. The men's seder is from the male perspective, but then one might say, the traditional seder always was. However, what makes this seder different is the element of personal reflection and recounting of sacred memories. Our seder begins with introductions based on one's Hebrew or Yiddish name, and the meanings of those names, and concludes with an Israeli wine tasting.

I am including one reflection as an example of what some of the men are seeking and finding. In this particular case, Greg Bruno has remained Catholic, but has helped to raise his children Jewishly and takes an active role in congregational life.

When first invited, I decided to attend "The Men's Study Group" in an effort to fulfill my responsibility as the father of two Jewish children. Your invitation offered me the chance to develop an understanding of the Torah from a purely Jewish perspective. Having been raised in a non-Jewish home, I was void of any Jewish religious experience. Your class helps me to develop an understanding of Torah while also providing me the opportunity to interact with Jewish men and to hear their thoughts relative to their unique religious beliefs and experiences.

I find myself wanting to return because of those Jewish men and their individual experiences and thoughts. Those men, who exhibit a sincere interest and knowledge of their faith and are willing to share their beliefs, experiences, and thoughts within the group have provided me a place to contemplate and learn Jewish faith. My parents passed on to me, apparently without my knowledge, a desire for faith and religion. The men of this group have in some sense become surrogate parents, guiding, affirming and enlightening me, and also at the same time evolving into a brotherhood.

Rarely have I been able to contemplate or even openly discuss the concepts, lessons and possibilities found in Torah, let alone speak to those thoughts and ideas in an arena safe from critics. Thanks for the initial invitation and thanks for the ongoing experience.

On a personal note, I have, in turn, derived intense satisfaction, understanding, and joy from this exciting and rewarding learning experience. As a rabbi, a teacher, a spiritual guide, I strive to create a comfortable and safe setting in which these men can explore, question, and learn about our Judaism. The environment is welcoming, open, and accepting, and the classes often take on a life of their own. No one feels alienated, no one is embarrassed.

The message that I have gained from this exploration into men's study is that we all need to be Jews-by-choice, choosing to learn our traditions, choosing to live our faith, so that we also can affirm, "My wandering is over—I have come home."

Yes, We Are Our Brother's Keeper, and He Is Ours!

The Origins of a Jewish Men's Group

Dan Moskovitz

I began leading a monthly men's discussion group at my congregation about four years ago. These evenings, which at first I held in my living room, began with a simple question that came out of a profound personal need. My marriage of eight years had just ended in divorce, and I was living alone for the first time since college. I was wondering what it means to be a man in our world today and if Judaism had any insights. I turned first to my dad, who had taught me many important things in life—how to tie a tie, to field a ground ball, to use a circular saw, to work hard, to respect women, to make *Kiddush* on Friday night. He was still there for me, but my questions were deeper now, and so were my needs.

How do we cope with the male drive to succeed? How do we keep a marriage alive? How do we find some balance between work and home? How do we confront our mortality? Why is it so hard for men to make new friends? A few years later, when I remarried and became a father, the number of questions only increased.

Like so many things in life, true insight comes not in finding the answer but in seeking it. Learning comes through asking questions and then, of course, in listening: listening to those who have been there before, listening to those who struggle and seek with you, and, above all, listening to yourself. As men, our pride, machismo, or just plain arrogance often drowns out that still small voice inside us. Like the fourth son at the seder table, we often don't even know how to ask a question.

As true as the generalizations above may be, it is interesting to note that a careful reading of the Torah shows that the very first question asked by a human being is Cain's incredulous parry back to God: "Am I my brother's keeper?" (Genesis 4:9). It is, of course, the most fundamental of questions a man can ask: Am I responsible for anyone but myself? Men seem to be hardwired for independence and self-determination; so to ask the question, even rhetorically, is, for most men, admitting a level of emotional vulnerability that is as uncomfortable as standing too close to the mohel at a *b'rit*. Yet, as I soon discovered in our men's group, it is when we are most uncomfortable that we are most open to question and to listen. When we strip away our defenses and competitiveness, what each of us finds beneath is our inner-man.

The monthly meetings began with getting to know each other and affirming that this was a safe place to share our stories. We started with a simple but powerful exercise: we had to introduce ourselves to the other guys without saying what we did for a living. As men, so often we define ourselves by what we do, how we provide for our families. It's probably deeply connected with our hunter-gatherer nature, and it certainly feeds our competitiveness with each other.

I felt this group would only work if we could retrain ourselves to change this damaging and isolating pattern. We had to teach ourselves to see other men as brothers, with good things to give and good things to receive. To take part in a men's group is to answer yes to Cain's question of God—Yes! I am my brother's keeper, and he is mine!

Like any relationship, there would need to be a set of implied and explicit rules so we could ask and answer questions in safety. We may indeed be our brother's keeper, but if Cain and Abel are any example (among many examples), brothers don't always get along with each other. With this in mind I established four ground rules for the group:

1. Confidentiality. What happens in Vegas stays in Vegas. What is said here stays here.
2. No put-downs of others or talking about people by name who are not here—including wives or bosses, present and former specifically.
3. Hear each other out. Let a man finish. The emphasis is on listening to each other speaking from our hearts, rather than interrupting with argument or well-meaning advice. We get plenty of that in our normal lives.
4. You don't have to speak, but when you do, use "I statements." No b.s. Say what you mean, what you feel, and don't talk too long.

Our topics were obvious, if only by how uncomfortable it was to talk about them.

- Why Do We Work So Hard?
- What Kind of Fathers We Had. What Kind of Fathers We Are.
- Being a Husband: How Has Your Partner Influenced the Way You Think?
- The Buddy System: Man's Search for Friends.
- Relationships I: Being a Supporting Actor.
- Relationships II: Parents and their Children.
- The Big Guy with the Beard: Man and God.
- When Did You Realize You Were a Man? A Journey of Self-Discovery.
- All in the Family: Our Fathers, Our Brothers.
- SEX—Let's Talk about It.
- Being a Mensch: Our Male Character.
- Power and the Male Identity.
- Being a Man: Moral Outrage and In-Rage.
- Where Are You Going? Why Men Don't Ask for Directions.

Our meetings would follow a basic format. After gathering and greeting each other, we would sit in a circle and do a formal check-in. Each guy would introduce himself, even if there was no one new in the group, and just share whatever was going on in his life. Men talked about work, their children, trips they were planning or just returned from, and often what they were struggling with. There was no cross talk in this check-in period, but after everyone went around, I would then ask if anyone had a similar experience as what had been shared and if they wanted to share that experience and insights gained from it. In this way men could learn from each other without feeling lectured to or judged by the others.

We would then turn to our topic for the evening. I would introduce the subject, usually with a contemporary anecdote or vignette from my research and then ask leading questions that would bring us to a related Jewish text and more questions for discussion. The goal was dialogue with each other and an inner dialogue with ourselves. The hope was that through the lens of our tradition and the shared experiences and insights of the other men, we could uncover truths that we had hidden from ourselves and maybe some we had never known.

We would end each session by standing and gathering in a circle with our arms around each other's shoulders. There, in the familiar embrace of a football huddle, we would recite a blessing together. *Baruch atah Adonai, Eloheinu Melech haolam, she-asani ben chorin / Blessed are You Adonai our God, Master of the universe, who has made me a free man!* The blessing was fitting and appropriate, for what greater expression of freedom is there than the freedom to ask questions, even if we ultimately are asking them of ourselves.

We have been meeting for four years now. The group has changed some; members have come and gone, and some have come back again. But change was the whole point. Some have found answers to their questions; others have found more questions; but we have all learned how to ask—and that, for men, is no small thing.

On the following page is an example of one of the discussion guides used during our monthly men's group. I hope you find it useful in developing your own materials and, ultimately, asking your own questions.

Being a Supporting Actor: Temple Judea Men's Group

Text 1

And Israel said to Joseph, Are not your brothers feeding the flock in Shechem? Come, and I will send you to them. And he said to him, Here am I. And he said to him, Go, I beg you, see whether it is well with your brothers, and well with the flocks; and bring me word again. So he sent him out from the valley of Hebron, and he came to Shechem. And a certain man found him, and, behold, he was wandering in the field; and the man asked him, saying, What do you seek? And he said, I seek my brothers; tell me, I beg you, where they feed their flocks. And the man said, They have departed from here; for I heard them say, Let us go to Dothan. And Joseph went after his brothers, and found them in Dothan. (Genesis 37:13–17)

Questions for Discussion

- What's the rest of the story—what happens between Joseph and his brothers?
- What is the significance of the man that Joseph meets?

Commentary

In the language of Hollywood, the unnamed man plays a bit part. In the vocabulary of life, however, his influence is far more than that of a bit player. He is the character upon which everything depends: He is "the right guy, in the right place, at the right time." Some commentators see the man as an angel sent into Joseph's life to make sure that he meets up with his brothers and fulfills his destiny of saving the Jewish people. They might be right if we understand an angel to be not a winged figure from heaven but a messenger sent into our lives to nudge us in the direction we need to go.

Questions for Discussion

- Have you ever encountered an "angel" as described above?
- Have you ever been an "angel" in the life of someone else?

Text 2

The Talmud tells of one of the sages who was close to death. His students gathered around his bed, urging him to leave them with one last bit of wisdom. He said to them, "May you fear God as much as you fear men." The students were perplexed. One of them said, "Master, has illness confused your mind? Surely you mean to say that we should fear God *more* than we fear people." "No, my son," the sage replied, "so many people do things of which they know God disapproves but go to great lengths to hide them from their neighbors. If only they feared God as much." (BT *B'rachot* 28b)

Commentary

Sometimes it takes more than one person to nudge us in the right direction; sometimes it takes the pressure of the group. In that way the community plays a supporting role in shaping the arch of our personal and professional life. Communal pressure, the combined force of people banding together, for good or for ill, will do as much if not more to shape our future than all of our dreams and expectations.

Questions for Discussion

- How is God a supporting actor/influence in your actions?
- In what ways does God's supporting role differ from that of friends/family?
- How do the standards/expectations of your community influence your personal behavior?

Text 3

Each lifetime is the pieces of a jigsaw puzzle. For some, there are more pieces. For others, the puzzle is more difficult to assemble. But know this: you do not have within yourself all the pieces to your puzzle. Everyone carries with them at least one piece and probably many pieces to someone else's puzzle. Sometimes they know it; sometimes they don't know it. And when you present your piece, which is worthless to you, to another, whether you know it or not, whether they know it or not, you are a messenger from the Most High. (Rabbi Lawrence Kushner, *Honey from the Rock*, pp. 69–70)[1]

Commentary

Often it is just one person or a small group of people that have the most profound impact on a life. These people are "invested" in the well-being of the other, their success or failure is bound up in the success or failure of the other. They need not be equals, in fact often they are not, but as part of a team each depends on the other for some immeasurable aspect of their own success. They are our supporting actors, and we may be theirs.

Questions for Discussion

- How are you a supporting actor in the life of those close to you? What missing piece do you bring?
- If you were to cast the supporting actors in your life, who would they be? What missing piece do they bring to you?
- Hollywood gives awards for supporting actors. How do you acknowledge the contribution of your supporting actors in your life?

Section VII

Gender Boundaries Blur: Alternative Masculinities

Introduction

This section asks us to keep in mind the complex gender identities and sexual relationships that make up our community today. While prior sections challenge and support various notions of masculinity, here we explore and remain mindful of masculinities in a day and age when gender is largely understood as a construct. The Reform Movement prides itself on being a welcoming movement to GLBTU Jews. As we consider how to involve men in our communities in new ways, we must honor the spectrum of men in our Movement, including our gay, bisexual, transgender, and undefined brothers.

Craig Rosen's piece "Gender, Stereotypes, and Sexuality" explores the needs of those men who do not identify as straight. Rosen challenges us to create communities and programming that allow all who enter to be comfortable. He raises our awareness that we may perpetuate negative or narrowly conceptualized male gender stereotypes without realizing it. If we do so, we will leave some men feeling ashamed and alone without realizing what we have done. All programming must be aware that it embraces rather than excludes the gay male community.

Rachel Van Thyn's "Girls and Boys: What About Everyone Else? Supporting Our Trans Community" acknowledges the struggle to make room for transgender individuals within our community. While this book has largely been focused on meeting "male needs," Van Thyn reminds us that there are people who identify with a gender other than their biological one. We must recognize that we often do not question our basic assumptions when it comes to our historical understanding of masculinity. Meeting the needs of our trans congregants will help us ensure we do not prejudge members of our community due to their biology.

When considering these issues, we recommend you turn to the new edition of *Kulanu: All of Us, A Program for Congregations Implementing Gay, Lesbian, Bisexual, and Transgender Inclusion*, Revised and Updated Edition (URJ Press, 2007).

Questions for Discussion

As you read each piece, consider the following questions:

1. How might we envision a space that men of all orientations find safe?
2. How can the variety of challenges and joys that men of varying experiences and orientations face be used to develop an overall richer men's experience in our communities?
3. What can we learn from the Reconstructionst and Jewish Renewal communities, who have long incorporated GLBTU members in the full spectrum of their programming and activities with great success?

Gender, Stereotypes, and Sexuality

Craig Rosen

Our congregations today are a microcosm of society. We are blessed to have so many families be a part of what it is that we offer. In recent years, though, there has been a steady decline in participation from men and boys in many aspects of our congregational programming. Why is this happening? What might we do to bring this population back into our doors? Is there a new understanding that we must reach to better know who these males are? Do certain gender stereotypes of men and boys dictate what it is that we are or are not programming for them? What is the role of sexuality and sexual orientation when talking about gender?

The question of gender is at the most basic level quite easy to distinguish. God created both sexes, men and women. But when examining this in depth, we know that it's not so clear-cut. Of course we can distinguish one another by our genetic makeup or our body characteristics, but beyond the biological differences we have sociological differences as well. We have certain stereotypes that exist for both males and females. Typical male/female stereotypes though do not always hold true. While these labels attempt to classify the particular gender, they are not always accurate.

When we think of men and boys, many of these stereotypes come to mind. A majority of our stereotypes come from the media. According to the report *Boys to Men: Media Messages About Masculinity*, written by Children Now, a national child advocacy organization, the five most popular stereotypes of male characters are the Joker, the Jock, the Strong Silent Type, the Big Shot, and the Action Hero.[1] Of course, I can think of those men and boys in our congregation who fit each one of these stereotypes. There are also a large number who do not. These labels carry a certain connotation with them. They tend to dictate how we treat one another and what we may expect from one another. By having these stereotypes, men and boys who do not live up to society's expectations often feel left out, different, and inadequate. Labels and stereotypes have a tendency to segregate rather than unite those who are affected.

Take, for example, those men and boys in our congregations and institutions who may not identify with the popular male stereotypes. How do they feel when they enter our doors? Are our synagogues and camps doing all they can to welcome these men and boys, or are we making them feel as though they don't belong?

Oftentimes, without thought, we perpetuate the male gender labels by creating programs or activities that promote the masculine stereotype. We place certain expectations on boys to be successful and strong. For men, we expect them to be the breadwinners of the family, the head of the household. For years, many of the programs we offered in our synagogues and camps supported these labels. Judaism was a male-dominated religion. We speak of our Patriarchs, the prophets, and the Rabbis and know that all of these males played an important role in shaping our religion. We speak of the warriors and those who fought in battles throughout our history. It's the strong male and the wise male whom we hold high above the others. Does this exclude a large group of men and boys who may not see themselves as the strong warrior or the wise scholar? Are we being open to all types of males, or are we allowing those masculine stereotypes to dictate who and what it is we are programming for?

A conversation about gender is not complete until we consider those who don't necessarily fit the typical male stereotype. Within the last decade or so our society has become more tolerant toward gay, bisexual, and transgendered individuals. Some of our congregations have also become more open to accepting these men. Those that are have changed their mission statements to become more welcoming and inclusive. When teaching about families in school, they teach that there are all kinds of family units. Some of our rabbis in these congregations perform same-sex unions. This openness toward those who are homosexual has proven to be a wonderful thing for this community of Jewish men. There is a feeling of belonging that many of these men never had while growing up. To be welcomed and accepted for who they are is something that they can only hope for. Of course this is not to say that these men are not strong or wise or in any way don't fit many of the masculine stereotypes as well. The difference is in their sexual orientation, but for that reason alone society looks down on them and does not grant them equal status. Not all of our congregations are as open and as accepting.

Growing up in a major congregation in Los Angeles, I was very involved in my synagogue. My rabbi, cantor, and directors of education did a wonderful job at allowing me opportunities for leadership. I was the "Temple Kid"—most congregants knew me, and I knew most congregants. I was the junior youth group advisor, in the choir and the dance troupe, a counselor at camp, and I worked as an usher for High Holy Days. In high school, I became a teacher and worked along with the educator to create weekend retreats.

Throughout all of this, though, there was always something that I had to hide. I never discussed the fact that I was gay, and for years I actually fought it off because it wasn't the Jewish way to be. According to all that I was taught, I was to date women, get married, and have children. At summer camp, when all the guys in the bunk were talking about the girls, I remained silent or pretended to have a secret crush as well. It was uncomfortable, and I always felt less of a man because of these experiences. My life was intertwined with my Judaism, but at the same time I was held back from being myself because of my religion. I never really fit in. I'm sure I'm not the only one who had this experience. In our congregations today there are most certainly other boys and men who must be embraced and accepted for who they are.

On the whole, Reform Judaism is miles ahead of society in accepting the gay community. Just as the struggle for women's rights was embraced by the Reform Movement years ago, it's now time for homosexual men to be embraced and accepted, as well as, of course, gay women or any members of the GLBT world. Just as women have now gained equal status in our congregations, it is my hope that one day soon the gay, lesbian, bisexual, and transgender community will also be granted equal status in all of our congregations and in our country. Temple boards, Men's Clubs, religious school staff, and congregants must be trained to be welcoming and understanding. If we begin in our own homes, hopefully we can continue to be a light to the nations. As long as society maintains the idea that gay men are not equal or don't count in conversations about masculinity, we cannot expect our congregants to accept and even understand what a gay/bi/transgendered male might feel in our congregation.

Some may argue that perhaps the reverse is happening. Could this openness to embracing the homosexual male be that which is driving the heterosexual men away from the synagogue? Is it possible that our congregations have become so welcoming to those men who do not fit the typical stereotype that we're losing the majority who do?

I honestly don't think so. By accepting and embracing the gay community, we can only strengthen the entire community of men. We can and should continue to support programs that promote masculinity in our congregations. The Brotherhood or Men's Clubs should plan a variety of events that will attract men of all types. We must recognize that within the male gender, there are many levels of masculinity and often that plays a role in how we treat one another. There are plenty of heterosexual males in our communities who happen to be effeminate. Let us be open to welcoming men of all types and embracing those who want to join us and actively seek out and create programs for those who may be different.

It is with this new attitude that we can increase participation so that our institutions can grow stronger. We must be open to a new definition of who a man is. We may be heterosexual or homosexual, gay, straight, bisexual, or transgendered, the bottom line is we're all men. We must not feed into the stereotypes that persist within our society, but rather accept that each of us is unique and has something to offer.

Girls and Boys: What About Everyone Else? Supporting Our Trans Community

Rachel Van Thyn

While we consider the issue of men's involvement, or lack thereof, in our Jewish community, let us not forgot the men who are not so easily categorized. At the beginning of the twenty-first century, as gender lines in America slowly reveal themselves to be an artifice, we must remain aware and responsive. Let us not forget our gay men, our transgender men, or our men who define their gender outside of such categories, for all the men of our Jewish community are *our* men, to be welcomed, appreciated, and included.

As the Reform Movement takes another step toward a progressive future, we are faced with some important challenges and questions. This book aims to tackle the question of how to encourage men and boys—those who identify as being male and were assigned a male gender at birth—in our Movement. But if we are to be truly welcoming and progressive, we need to acknowledge that even in our step forward, we may be leaving some of our members behind. It is vital that as a community we understand that in our attempt to be inclusive, we may actually be excluding people. In our efforts to incorporate some, we may be shutting out others

What follows are some helpful ideas for considering the needs of all men and of all people—everyone within our community. As we move into the future, we want to be welcoming to the full spectrum of gender identity in all its holiness, lest we be left behind in outdated and constricted ways of thinking.

Throughout our lives we are identified and split up by various factors. It could be by our marital status, our hometown, or our profession. Beginning in our childhood and adolescent years, we are often labeled and sectioned off based on our gender. Many people believe that there are only two choices in terms of gender. You're either a boy or a girl; there isn't room for anything else, and the very notion seems to be a source of confusion, jokes, and ignorant comments. In reality, there are people who identify as having a gender that is different from how people "read" them (as in, what judgment people make when they physically look at or speak to someone) or identify as having multiple genders, no gender, or different genders throughout their lives.

Being transgendered isn't just a phenomenon happening in the Jewish world nor is it an example of "political correctness gone too far," as some people might suggest. It is a reality in our society—one that is finally getting people to sit up and take notice. On the front page of the

New York Times on December 2, 2006, there was an article about transgender children and the ongoing debate about how to best support people who are either questioning their gender or who identify as a gender other than the one they were assigned at birth. The article addressed if parents should encourage cross-dressing and how parents, guardians, teachers, and friends could support a child's choices and feelings.

But before we go any further, let's define a few, but certainly not all, relevant terms:

Transgender/trans: Used most often as an umbrella term. Some commonly held definitions: (1) Someone whose behavior or expression does not match their assigned sex. (2) Some use it to describe a gender outside of the man/woman binary. (3) Some use it to describe the condition of having no gender or multiple genders. (4) Some definitions also include people who perform gender or play with it. (The term continues to evolve.)

Non-transman: A person who has been assigned a male gender identity at birth and someone who identifies as being a man.

Non-transwoman: A person who has been assigned a female gender identity at birth and someone who identifies as a woman.[1]

The language and concepts can be a little confusing at first, but they are important to understand. Also, a common misconception is that being a transperson has something to do with your sexual orientation. It does not. The gender that a person identifies as has nothing to do with whom a person is attracted to. You might think that it is only adults that question their gender. However, sometimes children at a very young age recognize that they don't feel right in their bodies or that they would rather dress in a way that seems in opposition to their assigned gender.

This is in no way meant to be the final word on gender identity and transgender issues. There are many resources available on the Web and in print that raise awareness and bring to light issues the trans community faces. I encourage you to learn more about these topics on your own. In 2007, URJ Press published *Kulanu: All of Us: A Program and Resource Guide for Gay, Lesbian, Bisexual, and Transgender Inclusion,* Revised and Expanded Edition. This work focuses on GLBT inclusion within the synagogue and is a necessary resource for any synagogue dealing with this issue. Additional resources include the works of Leslie Feinberg, Riki Wilchins, Emi Koyama, and Pat Califa. Other good books include *My Gender Workbook* by Kate Bornstein, *The Last Time I Wore a Dress* by Daphne Scholinski, and *Invisible Lives: The Erasure of Transsexual and Transgendered People* by Vivian Namaste. The following are wonderful resources on the Web: **www.eminism.org** and **www.Trans-Health.com.**

The important question for us is how do we make space for transpeople in our community? What kind of choices should we make in our programming to include this important group and make everyone feel welcome? When we split children or teens into groups during a program, must we split them by gender? Could we split people up by height or hair color or sneaker color? There are valid reasons to do so by gender, but what happens to those who identify as transgender when we do that? What kind of a message are we sending when we reinforce the either/or gender split? Splitting the group in ways other than gender can avoid creating a binary situation in which people may be uncomfortable about which group they're put into.

Another thing to keep in mind is not to assume that you know how a person identifies. If someone refers to themselves as "she," "he," or "they," honor their choices. If someone refers to themselves by a different name than what you're used to, honor that as well. Stand up for people when offensive jokes and comments are made about a person's gender, perceived or otherwise. If you are having people fill out a form and want to know the gender of the person writing, don't only give options of "male" or "female." Include "transgender" or "two-spirited."

There are, of course, other larger issues that as a Movement we will have to consider—ones that go beyond honoring a person's name choice. How can we incorporate transpeople into our camping movement, our youth movements, and programming in our synagogues? So much of those systems are based on being either male or female. What about our Brotherhoods and Sisterhoods? What role can they play in creating a sense of welcome and inclusion?

Educating yourself and others is the most important step, the first step of many. Do not expect transpeople to educate you. The onus is not on them to explain things. It is your responsibility to learn and to help nurture our community. We need to start expanding our minds and seeing the realities of our ever-changing world. If we don't, we run the risk of losing vital members of our community.

Conclusion

Beginning the Discussion: A Guide for Congregational Conversations

Doug Barden

In the preceding essays and articles, my professional colleagues have focused on specific congregational or Movement venues where the absence of adolescent and adult men has been noted, and they have made excellent specific suggestions on how best to bring them back. But we recognize that the initiation and promotion of programs and activities that focus on meeting the diverse needs of men have to be handled with sensitivity, as our goals are to reengage our brothers, not to disenfranchise our sisters. A series of beginning conversations are in order to ensure fuller congregational support and greater ownership by more lay people, both men and women. Only in this way will the introduction of new programs and activities of interest to more men be eventually institutionalized and become intrinsic elements of a future egalitarian but, when appropriate, gender-differentiated congregational Reform culture.

The following is a more detailed guide on just how to begin those needed conversations within our congregations. The essay borrows extensively (and with permission) from a pamphlet entitled "*Panim el Panim* (Face to Face)" created by the URJ Department of Worship and Religious Living. In addition, some of the ideas presented in this conclusion were adapted from *Cultivating the Future: Long-Range Planning for Congregations* and *Hear, O Israel: Creating Meaningful Congregational Mission Statements*, both of which are publications produced by the URJ Department of Synagogue Management.

There is an effective organizational and communication tool that will permit congregational leaders to approach the gender issues with the kind of sensitivity that will not only generate better information on how best to proceed, but will also increase goodwill and build a sense of community throughout the congregational membership. The tool is one many of you are well familiar with in the business world: the focus group. It is a group technique that is equally applicable across a wide spectrum of synagogue matters, including the discussion of gender-related issues.

Introduction to the Guide

Increasingly, more and more lay and professional leaders of our congregations note situations similar to the following:

- The temple introduces a new series of adult education programs. The following month the temple bulletin reports great "success": over sixty people showed up. Unfortunately, fifty of these are women, only ten are men, and of the ten men, most came with their spouse.
- Saturday Torah study has a good combination of men and women, though all the men are over sixty.
- Good turnouts of men occur when their children are heavily invested/involved in a temple venue; otherwise "parenting" is a euphemism for "my wife handles that."
- While many men continue to serve on various temple committees, increasingly the committee chairmanships and the key officer positions (with the noted exception of treasurer) are held by women. The ratio of men to women in these leadership positions is extremely disproportionate to the ratio of men to women who are members of the congregation.
- The temple's youth group has no problem attracting young women to participate and assume an active role. Young men who are active in the youth group are scarce.
- More young women than men are confirmed each year.
- The temple leadership, men and women, lay and professional over time unconsciously lower their expectations with regard to men's participation in various temple venues. They are not disappointed.

If any parts of this list sound familiar, it may be that your temple community is failing to encourage and enlist the full participation of a large segment of its community: the adolescent and adult men. In order to rectify the situation, it is helpful to first figure out why this decline has occurred.

Questions to Consider

- How much recognition or attention has ever been given to the men's participation by the congregational leadership?
- How much of the decline in men's involvement is a function of the temple not offering what the men want or need?
- How much of the decline is because your temple's reputation is such that it is seen as a place where women's needs are given much attention, perhaps at the expense of men's?
- How much of the decline is not within the control of the temple but rather that many men of your temple are just too busy to give time/energy/effort to their synagogue?
- How much of the decline is simply due to men not knowing what they want from their temple, therefore they don't know how to ask for it, and subsequently they only know they are dissatisfied and frustrated, and express their disappointment by absenting themselves entirely.
- Some combination of all of the above.

A Suggested Vehicle to Begin the Congregational Conversation about Gender: The Focus Group

In this context, a focus group is a series of small meetings in which congregants can discuss issues of men's inclusion or gender issues more generally. It is likely to yield deep and comprehensive information regarding members' thoughts and feelings about utilizing various limited temple resources (i.e., people, time, and finances) to initiate and promote various activities or programs with an explicit goal of increasing men's participation. If focus groups are skillfully facilitated, they can help more congregants articulate what it is that they need in order to feel comfortable with the concept; they can help other congregants articulate what it is that they are looking for from the temple leadership; and finally, it can provide insight, assistance, and direction to those responsible for designing the appropriate congregational activities.

Well-structured focus groups allow the participants to hear and reflect on the feelings of others, to appreciate the diversity of views that exist within their community, and to clarify their own expectations. In addition, focus groups can encourage and support the process, perhaps initiated by the local organized men's group, of greater partnership between professionals and laypeople.

Getting Focus Groups Started

- A focus group meeting is a gathering of not more than twelve people. It can be held in someone's home, in the synagogue, or even at a restaurant (if privacy can be secured).
- The goal is to find a place that allows the participants to express their feelings about gender comfortably and share them openly with others.
- In order to elicit the broadest participation possible, hosts or group facilitators should invite congregants personally. The importance of "I was personally invited by the rabbi or temple president" cannot be overstated.
- It is preferable that the guests at each meeting are representative of the entire membership (young couples, empty nesters, single, etc.) so that different points of view are expressed. Structuring meetings in this way can produce a valuable bonus: Individuals who may not have ordinarily had the opportunity to meet will connect. These new bonds will strengthen the sense of community within the congregation. But it will also be important to recognize that different generations may have a different take on the gender situation and therefore have very different recommendations or suggestions for implementing congregational activities and programs. The specific issue of male teen involvement, for example, is an important subset and should probably be treated as requiring its own distinct series of focus groups with appropriate attendees.
- If the meetings are to take place in the synagogue, schedule them at a time when congregants are normally there; for example, when parents drop their children off for nursery school or when senior citizens are engaged in activities that interest them. Doing this will facilitate the broadest participation possible, although it will also limit the contact between various congregant groups.
- It is very important to clarify how the views and opinions that are voiced in focus groups will be used and who will ultimately make gender-programming-related decisions. Will the ideas expressed by the groups be considered advisory in nature? Will the clergy, the board, or someone else make the final decisions? Explaining the process by which decisions will eventually be made reduces the possibility of misunderstanding, disappointment, or anger later on.

Who Is Responsible for Conducting These Focus Groups?

In many congregations, the Brotherhood or Men's Club is probably the group historically identified with men's programming activities. However, there are many congregations where that organized men's element is missing, and having the necessary skills and experience to facilitate this focus group does not correlate to being a member of the Brotherhood. Thus, the facilitator of the focus group might be a member of the Brotherhood or the rabbi, the cantor, a board member, or a layperson with a particular expertise in leading groups. If a Brotherhood or Men's Club exists within the temple, but the facilitator is not a member, we encourage that one member of the Brotherhood be present at each focus group meeting.

Selecting Your Facilitator

The role of the facilitator is critical to the success of the focus group. The facilitator is responsible for ensuring that participants get heard and for monitoring group process. Ideally, this person is trained in the fine art of facilitating meetings. This includes knowing how to manage time; being sensitive to and encouraging of participants who may be hesitant to speak; being capable of controlling group monopolizers; and possessing the ability to create a nonjudgmental, open, and accepting group environment. Many people have these skills. You might look for someone with a background in social work, psychology, or organizational behavior/development.

A Blueprint for Congregational Focus Groups: Aspects of a Focus Group Meeting

First read the following information carefully, noting the items that might be relevant to your congregation. Then go back and construct the program, utilizing the suggestions that will best serve your needs.

Pre-Meeting Preparation

- Establish the date and time of your meeting with all the relevant congregational professionals. Don't forget to check the master congregational schedule! Personally invite the participants. At the same time, do not hesitate to advertise and solicit from the bimah, in your temple bulletin, or in weekly e-mails that a series of focus groups is being planned and conducted in the coming weeks. You may obtain names of people who have never responded to a temple program before.
- In planning the session's length, allow for approximately two hours.
- Consider the arrangement of your meeting space. A good room setup for such a meeting consists of chairs arranged around tables that are put together in an open square or simply chairs arranged in circles. Have paper, pens, flip charts, markers, tape, name tags, etc., available.
- Sharing food is a great way to break down barriers among meeting participants and to create a sense of community. Depending on the time of day, consider providing beverages and light snacks. Give the participants time to eat and schmooze before beginning the meeting. Recite the *Motzi* together before starting to eat.
- Establish roles. You will need a facilitator. You may also wish to appoint someone as the timekeeper and someone else as the note taker.
- Be sure to order sufficient copies of *The Gender Gap: A Congregational Guide for Beginning the Conversation about Men's Involvement in Synagogue Life* for distribution before the meeting.

Introduction and Opening Ritual or Prayer

- Beginning the meeting with a brief ritual or a prayer elevates what is about to take place to a higher level. It signifies that this gathering is not like other, conventional gatherings, such as PTA or work meetings. An opening prayer or ritual frames the ensuing discussion within a Jewish context so that participants are instilled with the awareness that this meeting serves a sacred purpose. Ideas for an opening include:
  - A five-minute *d'var Torah*
  - A song
  - Reading a poem or a piece of prose that is linked thematically to the purpose of the meeting
  - Excerpting a passage from one of the articles in *The Gender Gap*.
- Say the following: "When we look at the communal life of our congregation, we see much that is successful and fulfilling. But we also see problems, reflected in the lower-than-hoped-for attendance by many men in various congregational venues, including our weekly services, adult education programs, social action programs, *b'nei mitzvah* programs, confirmation classes, youth group, and even in our board rooms. However, we believe that many more of our male members, our husbands, our sons, our fathers, and our grandfathers, sincerely want the temple to be a place that will uplift and engage them, will motivate them to be better people, will connect them to a community of other seekers, and will help them find their place in this world. In order for us to help make this happen as a community, we have to do three things:
  - Recognize that we may not be fully taking into account the differences between Jewish men and women's attitudes, behaviors, and expectations toward the temple community.
  - Recognize that change is difficult, especially one that may on the surface appear to be an overreaction to the increased participation of more and more women in the past three decades and thus an attempt to set the egalitarian clock back thirty years.
  - Build a stronger partnership between congregants and clergy. We've chosen to meet together in this way because we believe that through focus groups, we can best understand the needs of the adolescent and adult males of our community. This is a first step."

Checking In

When the focus group participants gather, some or many of them may not know one another. In order to facilitate a sense of community, begin the meeting by having the participants introduce themselves. Break the ice by asking everyone to respond briefly to a question. The questions can be lighthearted or serious. It's important to consider how well the participants know one another, if at all. Ask one question or combine two of them, depending on the size and needs of your group and the allotted time. Questions can include the following:

- How long have you been a member of the congregation?
- In what ways have you been involved in the synagogue up to now?
- What is something surprising that we might learn about you?
- What is one aspect of your experience in this congregation that you find fulfilling?
- What do you hope to accomplish in this meeting?
- What are your fears or concerns regarding this meeting?

Study a Section from *The Gender Gap* Together

Select one of the sections from this book; reread the introduction for that section, and focus on the questions that are raised at the beginning of each section.

Introduce the Group Leaders

- The facilitator ensures that everyone is heard and keeps the group on track.
- The note taker records ideas on a flip chart and transcribes them after the meeting for future reference.
- The timekeeper watches the time to ensure that the group completes its task and apprises the participants of the remaining time.

Establish the Ground Rules for the Discussion

The following are suggested guidelines for focus group discussion:

- All ideas are valid.
- There should be no judging of ideas as good or bad.
- Piggybacking off someone else's idea is fine.
- The more ideas, the better.
- Hear people out. Wait for the person speaking to finish before jumping in.

The Discussion Itself

The focus group process provides an opportunity to move beyond simple yes or no, like or dislike answers. The facilitator should present a series of questions about gender and then actively encourage the participants to think more deeply about the implications of their views, to critically examine their positions, and to challenge commonly held assumptions. All of this needs to be done in an atmosphere of mutual respect, courtesy, and civility. If your congregation is implementing the focus groups for the purpose of addressing a particular segment of the male membership (e.g., post–bar mitzvah male teenagers or fathers you only see during the High Holy Days and while they are dropping their kids off at Hebrew school on Sundays), the facilitator should develop questions that pertain directly to the subject under consideration.

Reflection and Conclusion

- Summarize briefly the topics that were addressed and the range of views that were expressed in the focus group meeting.
- Invite the participants to offer a few last words or final thoughts.
- Establish the next steps to be taken in this process. Will there be a follow-up meeting, a written report, or a review of the findings by the board? Make sure that the participants know how their views will be assimilated and what they can expect to take place in the coming weeks and months (see below).
- Read a poem or offer a prayer. Help the participants to transition from this experience back to their everyday lives.

After the Focus Group and Beyond: Communicate, Communicate, and Communicate

- Send a brief but personal handwritten note of thanks to those who attended the focus group meeting.

- Summarize the findings of the focus group in writing. Present them to the relevant synagogue group, such as the Brotherhood, or board of trustees.
- If changes are going to be made as a result of the meeting(s) of the focus group, send this information to every household.
- Publish the findings in the synagogue bulletin.
- Let the congregants know what the next steps will be. If certain matters will be referred to committees, tell the focus group members which committees will be handling which issues. Give an approximate time frame for the making of decisions.
- When changes are going to be implemented, explain via a letter and the bulletin when and how those changes will occur.

Sharing Your Congregational Experiences with Others

Please share your experiences with other members and leaders of the Reform Movement. Others can learn from both your successful and your not-so-successful experiences. Congregational experiences with using focus groups and then implementing new programs and activities for adolescent and adult men of our community will be collated and shared by MRJ and URJ through various Movement communication vehicles. Please send your material to MRJ, 633 Third Avenue, New York, NY 10017 or via e-mail to mrj@urj.org. Thank you.

Endnotes

Introduction to *The Gender Gap*

1. Susannah Heschel, *On Being a Jewish Feminist: A Reader* (New York: Schocken Books, 1983), p. xxxiv.
2. Ibid., p. xxxv.
3. "Dear Reader," *Keeping Posted* 25, no.5 (February 1980): 2.
4. Doug Barden, *Wrestling with Jacob and Esau: Fighting the Flight of Men; A Modern Day Crisis for the Reform Movement* (New York: North American Federation of Temple Brotherhoods, 2005), p. 6.
5. Steven M. Cohen and Arnold M. Eisen, *The Jew Within: Self, Family and Community in America* (Bloomington: Indiana University Press, 2000).
6. Ibid., pp. 183–184.
7. Ibid., p. 206.
8. Ibid.
9. Ibid., p. 202.
10. Ibid.
11. Ibid., p. 207.
12. Charles Kadushin and others, "Being a Jewish Teenager in America: Trying to Make It" (Brandeis University, December 2000).
13. Ibid., p. iv.
14. Ibid., p. v.
15. Ibid., p. 24.
16. Ibid., p. 68.
17. Ibid.
18. Michael S. Friedman, Molly Kane, and Melissa Zalkin Stollman, "URJ Young Men's Project: Young Men and Their Presence in the Reform Movement" (URJ Youth Division, NFTB, August 2005).
19. Ibid., p. 5.
20. Ibid., p. 8.

Man Enough

1. Frank Pittman, *Man Enough: Fathers, Sons, and the Search for Masculinity* (New York: G. P. Putnam's Sons, 1993), p. xx.
2. David D. Gilmore, *Manhood in the Making* (New Haven: Yale University Press, 1990), p. 7.

3. Doug Barden, *Wrestling With Jacob and Esau: Fighting the Flight of Men; A Modern Day Crisis for the Reform Movement* (New York: North American Federation of Temple Brotherhoods, 2005).
4. David Murrow, *Why Men Hate Going to Church* (Nashville: Thomas Nelson Books, 2005), p. 7.
5. Ibid, p. 14.
6. Jeffrey Salkin, *Searching for My Brothers: Jewish Men in a Gentile World* (New York: G. P. Putnam's Sons, 1999).

Connecting Men to Judaism: The Need for Comprehensive Cultural Shift

1. Kevin Sack, "Poll Finds Optimistic Outlook, but Enduring Racial Division," *New York Times*, July 11, 2000. In a national poll that asked, "Has too much been made of the problems facing black people, has too little been made, or is it about right?" 10 percent of blacks said "Too Much," while 33 percent of whites said the same. When asked, "Who has a better chance of getting ahead in today's society?" 57 percent of blacks said "White People," while only 32 percent of whites said the same. These kinds of splits were consistent throughout the survey.

Where Do We Go from Here? One Woman's Perspective

1. Aviva Cantor, *Jewish Women, Jewish Men: The Legacy of Patriarchy in Jewish Life* (San Francisco: Harper San Francisco, 1995), pp. 92–93.

Men and Leadership in Reform Congregations: More Questions Than Answers

1. Edwin Friedman, "Generation to Generation: Family Process in Church and Synagogue," *The Guilford Press,* July 19, 1985.
2. Meyer Levin and Toby K. Kurzband, *The Story of the Synagogue* (New York: Behrman House, 1957), p. 185.
3. Judith Lorber, "Using Gender to Undo Gender: A Feminist Degendering Movement," *Feminist Theory* l, no. 1: 79–95 (2000).
4. Doug Barden, *Wrestling with Jacob and Esau: Fighting the Flight of Men: A Modern Day Crisis for the Reform Movement* (New York: North American Federation of Temple Brotherhoods, 2005), p. 34.
5. Deborah Tannen, *Talking from 9 to 5: Women and Men at Work* (New York: Quill, 2001), p. 15.
6. Ibid., p. 34.
7. Ibid., p. 23.
8. Ibid., p. 119.
9. Ibid., p. 26.
10. Samuel Osherson, *Rekindling the Flame: How Jews Are Coming Back to Their Faith* (New York: Harcourt, 2001), p. 102.
11. Steven M. Cohen and Arnold M. Eisen, *The Jew Within: Self, Family and Community in America* (Bloomington: Indiana University Press, 2000), p. 33.
12. Ibid., p. 15.
13. Ibid., p. 206.

The Role of Men in the Social Action Arena

1. It should be noted that this is not a scientific survey since gender is not noted in the records; consequently, in providing these statistics we made assumptions about names that were not clearly gender-specific. We also included those who were registered as "spouse" but did not attend all events, which likely skews the results in favor of women, although that is an assumption that we cannot test with our current records.
2. In 2003 there were 13 men and 13 women; in 2005 there were 9 men and 10 women; in 2006 there were 16 men and 18 women.
3. In 2004 there were 8 men and 13 women; in 2006 there were 7 men and 14 women.

Yes, We Are Our Brother's Keeper, and He Is Ours!

1. Lawrence Kushner, *Honey from the Rock: An Introduction to Jewish Mysticism* (Woodstock, VT: Jewish Lights, 1990), pp. 69–70.

Gender, Stereotypes, and Sexuality

1. Children Now, "Boys to Men: Conference Report on Media Messages about Masculinity" (1999), http://publications.children.org/publications/media/boystomen_1999.cfm.

Girls and Boys: What About Everyone Else? Supporting Our Trans Community

1. These definitions are from the Survivor Project, a nonprofit organization that supports intersex and trans survivors of domestic and sexual violence through action, advocacy, and education. (www.survivorproject.org/basic.html).

Bibliography

General

Faludi, Susan. *Stiffed: The Betrayal of the American Man.* New York: Wm. Morrow & Co., 1999.

Gurian, Michael. *Boys and Girls Learn Differently: A Guide for Teachers and Parents.* San Francisco: Jossey-Bass, 2001.

Levin, Meyer, and Toby K. Kurzband. *The Story of the Synagogue.* New York: Behrman House, 1957.

Putnam, Robert D. *Bowling Alone: The Collapse and Revival of American Community.* New York: Simon & Schuster, 2000.

Ravitch, Diane. *The Language Police: How Pressure Groups Restrict What Students Learn.* New York: Knopf, 2003.

Roof, Wade. *Generation of Seekers: The Spiritual Journeys of the Baby Boom Generation.* San Francisco: HarperSanFrancisco, 1993.

Men's Work/Men's Movement

Baraff, Alvin. *Men Talk: How Men Really Feel about Women, Sex, Relationships, and Themselves.* New York: Dutton, 1991.

Black, J. Nelson. *Becoming a New Man: Daily Spiritual Workouts.* Orlando, FL: Creation House, 1997.

Bliss, Shepherd. "Men, Men's Groups, and Men's Movements." Review of, *A Circle of Men*, by Bill Kauth. www.menweb.org/mengrbk.htm.

Boyd, Stephen B. *The Men We Long to Be: Beyond Domination to a New Christian Understanding of Manhood.* San Francisco: HarperSanFrancisco, 1995.

Cose, Ellis. "In the Trenches: An Interview with Stephen Johnson." *Whole Life Times*, August 1994.

Cose, Ellis. *A Man's World: How Real Is Male Privilege—and How High Is Its Price?* New York: HarperCollins, 1995.

Dana, Howard. "The Spiritual Needs of Men." *MaleCall* 11, no. 2 (Winter 2000).

David, Robert G. "Understanding Manhood in America: The Elusive Quest for the Ideal in Masculinity." *Heredom* 10 (2002).

Diamond, Jed. *The Whole Man Program: Reinvigorating Your Body, Mind, and Spirit after 40.* New York: John Wiley & Sons, 2002.

Doyle, James, and Sam Femiano. "Reflections on the Early History of the American Men's Studies Association and Reflections on the Evolution of the Field." http://mensstudies.org/history.html.

Fanning, Patrick. *Being A Man: A Guide to the New Masculinity.* Oakland, CA: New Harbinger, 1993.

Fleshler, Daniel. "Newsflash: Men Want Football, Pizza, Beer and Yes, Sex." *Forward,* March 9, 2001.

Friedman, Michael S., Molly Kane, and Melissa Zalkin Stollman. "URJ Young Men's Project: Young Men and Their Presence in the Reform Movement." URJ Youth Division and National Federation of Temple Brotherhoods, 2005.

Gratch, Alon. *If Men Could Talk—Here's What They'd Say.* Boston: Little Brown, 2001.

Halberstam, David. "Men without Women." *GQ,* September 2002.

Jaeger, Jim. "Male Spirituality?" *MaleCall* 11, no. 2 (Winter 2004).

James, David C. *What Are They Saying about Masculine Spirituality?* New York: Paulist Press, 1996.

Johnson, Stephen. "Natural Allies: In Search of a Mentor" *Man!,* Spring 1992.

Johnson, Stephen. "The Quest for the Masculine Soul." *Whole Life Times,* August 1995.

Kauth, Bill. *A Circle of Men.* New York: St. Martin's Press, 1992.

Keen, Sam. *Fire in the Belly: On Being a Man.* New York: Bantam Books, 1991.

Kimmel, Michael. *Manhood in America: A Cultural History.* New York: Free Press, 1996.

Korda, Michael. *Man to Man: Surviving Prostate Cancer.* New York: Random House, 1996.

Levinson, Daniel J. *The Seasons of a Man's Life.,* New York: Knopf, 1978.

Liebman, Wayne. *Tending the Fire: The Ritual Men's Group.* St. Paul, MN: Ally Press, 1991.

McGrath, Tom. "Is Men's Spirituality Out of the Woods?" *U. S. Catholics*, April 2002.

Pasick, Robert. "Men." *Detroit News,* December 26, 1992.

Pittman, F. "Why the Men's Movement Isn't So Funny." *Psychology Today*, January 1992.

Pogrebin, Robin. "Magazines Reassess What It Is Men Really Want." *New York Times*, December 9, 1996.

Real, Terrence. *I Don't Want to Talk About It: Overcoming the Secret Legacy of Male Depression.* New York: Scribner, 1997.

Schocke, Doug. "Men's Movement History and the Term 'Masculist.'" www.shocke.com.

Sheehy, Gail. *Understanding Men's Passages: Discovering the New Map of Men's Lives.* New York: Random House, 1998.

Sommers, Christina Hoff. "Where the Boys Are." http://www.menweb.org/sommersboys.htm, 2000.

Mythopoetic

Arnold, Patrick. *Wildmen, Warriors, and Kings: Masculine Spirituality and the Bible.* New York: Crossroad, 1992.

Atteberry, Mark. *The Samson Syndrome: What You Can Learn from the Baddest Boy in the Bible.* Nashville: Thomas Nelson, 2003.

Bly, Robert. *Iron John: A Book about Men.* Cambridge, MA: DaCapo Press, 2004.

Giles, Doug. "Where Are God's Warriors and Wild Men?" www.freerepublic.com, April 17, 2004.

Moore, Robert, and Douglas Gillette. *King, Warrior, Magician, Lover: Rediscovering the Archetypes of the Mature Masculine.* San Francisco: HarperSanFrancisco, 1991.

Osterhaus, James. *Bonds of Iron.* Chicago: Moody Press, 1994.

Rohr, Richard, and Joseph Martos. *The Wild Man's Journey: Reflections on Male Spirituality.* Cincinnati: St. Anthony Messenger Press, 1996.

Feminism/Jewish Feminism

Asher, Jeffrey. "The Matriarchy Rules." *The Ottawa Citizen*, December 2001.
Butler-Bodon, Tom. "Critique of *Men Are from Mars, Women Are from Venus*." http://www.butler-bowdon.com.
Eskenazi, Tamara Cohn, and Andrea Weiss, eds. *The Torah: A Women's Commentary*. New York: URJ Press, 2007.
Gillman, Neil. "The Feminist Critic of God Language." In *The Way into Encountering God in Judaism*. Woodstock, VT: Jewish Lights, 2000.
Goldstein, Elyse M. *Seek Her Out*. New York: UAHC Press, 2003.
Heschel, Susannah. *On Being a Jewish Feminist*. New York: Schocken Books, 1983.
Johnson, Allan G. *The Gender Knot: Unraveling our Patriarchal Legacy*. Philadelphia: Temple University Press, 2005.
Knuth, Elizabeth. "'Male Spirituality': A Feminist Evaluation." http://www.users.csbsju.edu, May 1993.
Lorber, Judith. "Using Gender to Undo Gender: A Feminist Degendering Movement." *Feminist Theory* 1 (2000): 79–95.
Peskowitz, Miriam, and Laura Levitt, eds. *Judaism Since Gender*. New York: Routledge, 1997.
Plaskow, Judith. "God: Some Feminist Questions—Why Female Pronouns for God May Not Be Enough." *Sh'ma*, January 9, 1987.
Plaskow, Judith. *Standing Again at Sinai: Judaism from a Feminist Perspective*. San Francisco: HarperSanFrancisco, 1990.
Prell, Riv-Ellen. *Fighting to Become Americans: Assimilation and the Trouble Between Jewish Women and Jewish Men*. Boston: Beacon Press, 1999.
Schulman, Edith, "Are Women's Organizations a Thing of the Past?" *Jewish Herald Voice*, Houston, September 1996.

Jewish/Sociology/Studies

Cahill, Thomas. *The Gifts of the Jews*. New York: Doubleday, 1998.
Cohen, Steven M., and Arnold M. Eisen. *The Jew Within: Self, Family and Community in America*. Bloomington: Indiana University Press, 2000.
Dershowitz, Alan M. *The Vanishing American Jew*. Boston: Little, Brown, 1997.
Hartman, Moshe, and Harriet Hartman. *Gender Equality and American Jews*. Albany: SUNY Press, 1996.
Reimer, Joseph. *Succeeding at Jewish Education: How One Synagogue Made It Work*. Philadelphia: Jewish Publication Society, 1997.
Schiffman, Lisa. *Generation J*. San Francisco: HarperSanFrancisco, 2000.
Schuster, Diane Tickton. *Jewish Lives, Jewish Learning: Adult Jewish Learning in Theory and Practice*. New York: UAHC Press, 2003.
Tannen, Deborah. *Talking from 9 to 5: Women and Men at Work*. New York: Quill, 2001.
United Jewish Communities. National Jewish Population Survey. http://www.ujc.org/content_NJPS.

Jewish/Spirituality/Non-Gender Specific

Braverman, Nachum. "Chauvinistic Judaism." http://www.aish.com, March 12, 2000.

Cohen, Norman J. *Hineini in Our Lives.* Woodstock, VT: Jewish Lights, 2003.
Cohen, Norman J. *Self, Struggle and Change: Family Conflict Stories in Genesis and Their Healing Insights for Our Lives.* Woodstock, VT: Jewish Lights, 1995.
Kelner, Shaul. "Birthright Israel and the Creation of Ritual." *Contact,* Spring 2002.
Kushner, Lawrence. *Honey from the Rock: An Introduction to Jewish Mysticism.* Woodstock, VT: Jewish Lights, 1990.
Kushner, Lawrence. *Invisible Lines of Connection.* Woodstock, VT: Jewish Lights, 1996.
Matt, Daniel. *The Essential Kaballah.* San Francisco: HarperSanFrancisco, 1995.
Mitelman, Geoffrey, Joel Kushner, and Richard Address, eds. *Kulanu: All of Us; A Program for Congregations Implementing Gay, Lesbian, Bisexual, and Transgender Inclusion.* Revised and Updated Edition. New York: URJ Press, 2007.
Niebuhr, Gustave. "Putting Life's Trials in a Sacred Context." *New York Times,* February 9, 1997.
Noson, Reb. *Healing Leaves.* Deerfield Beach, FL: Simcha Press, 2000.
Olitzky, Kerry M., and Daniel Judson, eds. *The Rituals & Practices of a Jewish Life.* Woodstock, VT: Jewish Lights, 2002.
Osherson, Samuel. *Rekindling the Flame: How Jews Are Coming Back to Their Faith.* New York: Harcourt, 2001.
Person, Hara E., ed. *The Mitzvah of Healing.* New York: UAHC Press, 2003.
Salkin, Jeffrey. *Being God's Partner: How to Find the Hidden Link between Spirituality and Your Work.* Woodstock, VT: Jewish Lights, 1994.
Shapiro, Rami. *Hasidic Tales.* Woodstock, VT: SkyLight Paths, 2004.
Sonsino, Rifat. *The Many Faces of God: A Reader of Modern Jewish Theologies.* New York: URJ Press, 2004.
Sonsino, Rifat. *Six Jewish Spiritual Paths: A Rationalist Looks at Spirituality.* Woodstock, VT: Jewish Lights, 2000.
Wolf, Arnold Jacob. "Against Spirituality: Personal Spirituality versus Social Connectedness through Religion." *Judaism,* Summer 2001.

Specific to Jewish Men

Alexiou, Alice Sparberg. "Jewish Movement Seeks to Reconnect Men to the Faith." http://www.beliefnet.com/story/20/story_2070.html, July 25, 2004.
Barden, Doug. *Wrestling with Jacob and Esau: Fighting the Flight of Men; A Modern Day Crisis for the Reform Movement.* New York: North American Federation of Temple Brotherhoods, 2005.
Boyarin, Daniel. *Unheroic Conduct: The Rise of Heterosexuality and the Invention of the Jewish Man.* Berkeley, CA: University of California Press, 1997.
Brod, Harry, ed. *A Mensch Among Men: Explorations in Jewish Masculinity.* Freedom, CA: Crossing Press, 1988.
Children Now. "Boys to Men: Conference Report on Media Messages about Masculinity." Children Now. http://publications.children.org/publications/media/boystomen_1999.cfm.
Grishaver, Joel Lurie. *The Bonding of Isaac: Stories and Essays about Gender and Jewish Spirituality.* Los Angeles: Alef Design Group, 1997.
Kadushin, Charles, Shaul Kelner, Leonard Saxe, Archie Brodsky, Amy Adamczyk, and Rebecca Stern. "Being a Jewish Teenager in America: Trying to Make It." Waltham, MA: Cohen Center for Modern Jewish Studies, Brandies University, 2000.
Kessler, E. J., "Now Hear This: 'Voices of Men' As Shuls Go Feminine, Does a Backlash Brew?" *Forward,* August 1, 1997.

Klagsbrun, Francine. Editorial. *Moment,* December 1997.
Michelson, Brian. "Jewish Men Step Forward." *Manzine.* http://www.manhood.com.au/
Mulchin, Andrew. "Real Men Read Rashi." *B'nai B'rith Monthly*, November 1998.
Olitzky, Kerry M. *From Your Father's House: Reflections for Modern Jewish Men.* Philadelphia: Jewish Publication Society, 1999.
Rosenblatt, Gary. "A Synagogue of Their Own." *Jewish Journal of Greater Los Angeles*, May 15, 1998.
Salkin, Jeffrey. "Jewish Macho." *Reform Judaism Magazine,* Spring 1998.
Salkin, Jeffrey. *Searching for My Brothers: Jewish Men in a Gentile World.* New York: G. P. Putnam's Sons, 1999.
Surrence, Matthew. "Getting Down in the Menschhood with Jewish Males." *Jewish Bulletin of Northern California*, February 21, 1997.
Susskin, Yisroel. *Jews Are from Sinai, not Mars or Venus.* http://www.chabad.org/library, 2004.
Taller, Michael. "Jewish Men: Outside, Looking In—Painfully." *Jewish Exponent*, March 20, 1997.
Zoll, Rachel. "Looking for a Few Good Jewish Men: Leadership in Much of American Reform Movement Falling Mostly to Women." *Washington Post*, May 22, 2004.
Zoll, Rachel. "Reform Embraces Women, But Where Are All the Men? *South Florida Sun-Sentinel*, June 18, 2004.

Fathers

Brenner, Daniel. "Honoring Our Fathers." http://www.beliefnet.com/story/81/story_8168_1.html.
Fuchs, Lawrence. *Beyond Patriarchy: Jewish Fathers and Families.* Hanover, NH: Brandeis University Press, 2000.
Kane, Courtney. "Men Are Becoming the Target of the Gender Sneer." *New York Times,* January 28, 2005.
Osherson, Samuel. *Finding Our Fathers.* Chicago: Contemporary Books, 2001.
Ostriker, Alicia Suskin. *The Nakedness of the Fathers: Biblical Visions and Revisions.* New Brunswick, NJ: Rutgers University Press, 1994.
Pitzele, Peter. *Our Fathers' Wells: A Personal Encounter with the Myths of Genesis.* San Francisco: HarperSanFrancisco, 1996.
Tierney, John. "The Doofus Dad." *New York Times*, June 18, 2005.
Tuffs, Allan C. *And You Shall Teach Them To Your Sons.* New York: UAHC Press, 1997.

Christian Perspective

Alexander, Bill. *A Man's Book of the Spirit: Daily Meditations for a Mindful Life.* New York: Avon Books, 1994.
"Creating Groups for Men Within Your ITU Congregation." *InterConnections* 3, no. 4 (August 2000).
Edelen, Dan. "Another Look at the Church's Missing Men." *Cerulean Sanctum,* April 20, 2005. http://www.dedelen.com/2005/04/another-look-at-churchs-missing-men.html.
Editors of *Religion Today*. "Men Shun 'Feminized' Churches." http://www.shatterdmen.com, April 5, 2000.

House, Polly. "Male-Friendly Men's Ministries Spur Church Growth." http://www.lifeway.com.

Nuechterlein, James. "The Feminist Church?—Book Review." *The Public Interest*, Fall 1999.

Olshine, David. "Boys Will Be Boys: Rites of Passage and Male Teens." Youth Specialties. http://www.youthspecialties.com/articles/topics/gender/boys.php

Oppenheimer, Mark. "Forum: The Variety of Religious Experience—Vive la Difference." *Pittsburgh Post-Gazette,* August 10, 2003.

Owen-Towle, Tom. *Brother-Spirit: Men Joining Together in Quest for Intimacy and Ultimacy.* Bald Eagle Mountain Press, 1991.

Owen-Towle, Tom. *New Men, Deeper Hungers.* Rev. ed. San Diego: UU Men's Network, 2000.

Podles, Leon J. "Missing Fathers of the Church: The Feminization of the Church and the Need for Christian Fatherhood." *Touchstone Magazine*, January/February 2001.

Ritchie, Cinthia. "Where Are the Guys on Sunday?" *Providence Journal*, April 30, 2005.

Roncone, Gene. "Encouraging Male Involvement in Children's Ministries." *Enrichment Journal of Assemblies of God USA*, Summer 2001.

"Where Are All the Men?" http://www.churchformen.com/allmen.php.

Biographies of Contributors

Rabbi Victor S. Appell, a native New Yorker, grew up in the Reform Movement. In high school, he served as a regional NFTY president and spent three summers on the staff of URJ Joseph Eisner Camp in Great Barrington, Massachusetts. After a decade-long career in sales and marketing, Appell decided to pursue a lifelong dream of becoming a rabbi and was ordained from Hebrew Union College–Jewish Institute of Religion in 1999. For four years he served as assistant and then associate rabbi of Temple Jeremiah in Northfield, Illinois. For two years Appell served Temple Emanu-El in Edison, New Jersey. In July of 2005 he joined the staff of the Union for Reform Judaism as the Small Congregations Specialist in the Department of Synagogue Management. Appell, his partner, and their two children live in Metuchen, New Jersey.

Lisa Lieberman Barzilai has a master's degree in Jewish education from HUC-JIR in Los Angeles. She is currently the regional educator for the URJ Greater New York Council. Additionally Lieberman Barzilai is the education director for the URJ Crane Lake and Eisner Camps. She serves on the Executive Committee for the National Association of Temple Educators (NATE).

Doug Barden assumed the position of executive director of the Men of Reform Judaism (formerly the North American Federation of Temple Brotherhoods) in February 1994. In early 2006 he authored *Wrestling with Jacob and Esau: Fighting the Flight of Men; A Modern Day Crisis for the Reform Movement*.

Debra Nussbaum Cohen is an award-winning journalist on staff at the *New York Jewish Week*, where she writes about religion, spirituality, Jewish identity, and philanthropy. She is also a freelance contributor to the *New York Times*, *New York* magazine, the *Wall Street Journal*, *Village Voice*, and many other publications. Nussbaum Cohen is author of *Celebrating Your New Jewish Daughter: Creating Jewish Ways to Welcome Baby Girls into the Covenant* and lives in Brooklyn with her husband and three children.

Rabbi Marla J. Feldman is the director of the Commission on Social Action of Reform Judaism, which develops public policy for the Reform Movement and oversees the work of the Religious Action Center of Reform Judaism. In addition, Feldman directs the Union for Reform Judaism's Department of Social Action. Feldman is both a Reform rabbi (HUC-JIR, New York, 1985) and a lawyer (University of Florida, 1993). She is the author of Reform Movement action manuals, including *Speak Truth to Power* and *K'hilat Tzedek: Creating Communities of Justice*. Her articles, op-eds, and modern midrash have appeared in Jewish publications and newspapers throughout the country.

Jason Freedman recently served as regional director of youth for the URJ's Southeast Council and assistant director at URJ Camp Coleman. He is currently enrolled at Dartmouth's Tuck School of Business, studying ways organizations can better address the needs of the world.

Michael Geller is a communications/public relations professional based in Manhattan. His involvement in the Jewish community includes work on secular Jewish identity, young Jewish involvement, Israel and GLBT matters, as well as his service as former editor of Men of Reform Judaism's *Achim* magazine. He has a master's degree in political thought/Jewish studies and was one of the writers of the acclaimed off-Broadway show *The Kafka Project*.

Dale Glasser has served as the director of the Union for Reform Judaism's Ida and Howard Wilkoff Department of Synagogue Management since 1996. He holds a bachelor of arts degree in comparative culture, a master of science degree in counseling, a master of social work degree, and a master of arts degree in Jewish communal service from Hebrew Union College. He has spoken and presented workshops throughout North America and has served as contributor and executive editor of the UAHC/NATA *The Temple Management Manual*, a more than 700-page resource for congregations, and over twenty other department publications. His volunteer experience includes serving as a congregational president and as a member of the board of directors of the Jewish Federation Council of Greater Los Angeles. Glasser lives in Westchester County, New York, with his wife of thirty years. They are the parents of two brilliant and adorable children.

Rabbi Elyse Goldstein is the rabbinic director/*rosh yeshivah* of Kolel: The Adult Centre for Liberal Jewish Learning in Toronto, and has been since its inception in 1991. She is the author of *Seek Her Out: A Textual Approach to Women and Judaism* (UAHC Press) and *ReVisions: Seeing Torah through a Feminist Lens*, and the editor of *The Women's Torah Commentary* and *The Women's Haftarah Commentary*. She is recognized as a leading voice in the fields of Jewish adult education and women and Judaism.

Art Grand is chair of the Reform Movement's Commission on Worship, Music and Religious Living and president of the URJ's Pacific Central West Council. He has two Ph.D. candidates in his family, his wife and his son. His daughter, an avid guitarist, is about to graduate high school. Grand is a longtime member of Temple Or Rishon in Orangevale, California.

Lisa D. Grant is associate professor of Jewish education at the Hebrew Union College–Jewish Institute of Religion, New York. Her research interests include adult Jewish learning, professional development of Jewish educators, and the role Israel plays in American Jewish life.

Rabbi Michael Garret Holzman is an associate rabbi and the director of the Youth Learning Program at Congregation Rodeph Shalom in Philadelphia, Pennsylvania. He is a graduate of Washington University in St. Louis, and the Hebrew Union College–Jewish Institute of Religion in New York. Michael is also the editor of *The Still Small Voice: Reflections on Being a Jewish Man* (URJ Press). He lives outside Philadelphia with his wife, Nicole, and their children, Avi and Talia.

Biographies of Contributors

Howard L. Jaffe is senior rabbi of Temple Isaiah, Lexington, Massachusetts. He is a past president of the Minnesota Rabbinical Association, the New Jersey Association of Reform Rabbis, and the Boston Area Reform Rabbis. He currently serves as vice chair of the URJ/CCAR Commission on Outreach and Synagogue Community.

Dana Jennings is an editor for the *New York Times* and the author of the forthcoming *Sing Me Back Home: Love, Death and Country Music*. He is a member of Temple Ner Tamid in Bloomfield, New Jersey.

Shaul Kelner is assistant professor of sociology and Jewish studies at Vanderbilt University. He has conducted research on a variety of aspects of Jewish education, the most recent of which appears in *Family Matters: Jewish Education in an Age of Choice*, edited by Jack Wertheimer.

Kevin Kleinman is a rabbinical student at Hebrew Union College–Jewish Institute of Religion in New York. A graduate of Brandeis University, he spent two years as a program coordinator at the Teva Learning Center, a Jewish environmental education program. Kleinman grew up in Woodbridge, Virginia, and retains his membership at Temple B'nai Shalom in Fairfax Station, Virginia. Recently he directed Kutz Camp's Teva Outdoor Experience, a new program that combined outdoor adventure and Jewish environmental awareness.

Rabbi Kenneth Milhander serves as the spiritual leader at Temple Beth Tikvah in Fullerton, California. He was ordained in 1995 from Hebrew Union College–Jewish Institute of Religion and holds an M.A. from the University of Judaism and a B.A. from UCLA. His "Kaddish for September 11th" (written on the first anniversary of the terrorist attacks) has been used widely by congregations each year. Milhander lives in Orange County, California with his wife, Laura, and four children.

Rabbi Dan Moskovitz was ordained at Hebrew Union College–Jewish Institute of Religion in 2000 and also holds a master's degree in Jewish education from HUC-JIR. He is a rabbi at Temple Judea in Tarzana, California, where as part of his rabbinate he continues to lead a monthly men's discussion group and a variety of men's programming. Moskovitz is also the coauthor of the forthcoming *The Man Seder: A Passover Seder Experience for Jewish Men* (MRJ, 2008). He is married to Sharon Mishler, and they are the proud parents of Judah.

Rabbi Stephen S. Pearce is senior rabbi of Congregation Emanu-El of San Francisco. From 2001 to 2003, he served as editor of the *Journal of the Central Conference of American Rabbis*. He is author of *Flash of Insight: Metaphor and Narrative in Therapy*, and coauthor with Bishop William E. Swing, former Episcopal bishop of California, and Father John P. Schlegel, past president of the University of San Francisco, of *Building Wisdom's House: A Book of Values for Our Time*. For a decade, he authored "Torah Thoughts" columns available at jewishsf.com. The April 2, 2007 issue of *Newsweek* magazine ranked Pearce as one of the fifty most influential rabbis in America.

Rabbi Mindy Avra Portnoy, rabbi of Temple Sinai in Washington, D.C., was ordained by the Hebrew Union College–Jewish Institute of Religion. She is a graduate of Yale University and the author of four children's books, including *Ima on the Bima (My Mommy Is a Rabbi)*, *Matzah Ball*, and *Where Do People Go When They Die?* Her next children's book, to be published in 2008, will be about children of divorced parents. Portnoy is married and the mother of two adult children.

Craig Rosen was born and raised in Van Nuys, California. As an accomplished educator/youth worker, Rosen has served as the regional director for NFTY in the Pacific Southwest Council office of the URJ. He also was the program director for the JCC of Seattle and served seven years as the director of education for Congregation B'nai B'rith in Santa Barbara, California. Rosen currently serves as the director of lifelong learning at Congregation Ner Tamid in Henderson, Nevada. He also begins his second term on the national board of NATE (National Association of Temple Educators), and his article on engaging college-age teachers for religious school was published in the 2006 spring edition of *Torah at the Center*.

Evie Levy Rotstein, Ed.D., is the director of the Leadership Institute for Congregational Educators, a joint endeavor sponsored by the New York School of Education at Hebrew Union College–Jewish Institute of Religion and the Davidson School of Education at the Jewish Theological Seminary. She is an adjunct professor at HUC-JIR and JTS and a consultant for the ECE (Experiment in Congregational Education) RE-IMAGINE Project.

Rabbi Jeffrey K. Salkin is the founding rabbi and executive director of Kol Echad: Making Judaism Matter, a trans-denominational learning community in Atlanta, Georgia. A well-known teacher and writer, he is the author of several books on Jewish spirituality. His most recent book is *A Dream of Zion: American Jews Reflect on Why Israel Matters to Them*.

Leonard Saxe is professor of Jewish community research and social policy at Brandeis University. He serves as director of the Cohen Center for Modern Jewish Studies and the Steinhardt Social Research Institute. Saxe is an author and/or editor of nearly 250 publications. He has been a Science Fellow for the United States Congress and was a Fulbright Professor at Haifa University, Israel. In 1989, he was awarded the American Psychological Association's prize for Distinguished Contributions to Psychology in the Public Interest (Early Career). He teaches in the Hornstein Program for Jewish Professional Leadership and at the Heller School for Social Policy and Management.

Rabbi Joel E. Soffin served for twenty-seven years as the rabbi of Temple Shalom in Succasunna, New Jersey, where he is now rabbi emeritus. In retirement, he is the Social Action Rabbinical Scholar-in-Residence at the Barnert Temple in Franklin Lakes, New Jersey. His worldwide social action projects continue through the URJ Adult Mitzvah Corps and the Jewish Helping Hands Foundation.

Melissa Zalkin Stollman, a recipient of the Mandel Fellowship, is in the rabbinical and education programs at the Hebrew Union College–Jewish Institute of Religion in New York City. She has also served the Union for Reform Judaism in several capacities most recently as the regional advisor for NFTY's New York Area Region. In the past Zalkin Stollman has worked with KESHER students as a staff member of the URJ College Department and the Association of Reform Zionists of America. When not meeting with high school and college students, or pursuing her passion for Israel, she be found song leading, creating photo albums, and working with her scrapbooking company.

Rabbi Allan C. Tuffs was born in Vancouver, British Columbia, and is the father of Gabe, Abbie, and Danny Tuffs. He was ordained at Hebrew Union College–Jewish Institute of Religion, New York, in 1982, holds a doctorate in ministry, and is a Senior Rabbinic Fellow at the Shalom Hartman Institute, Jerusalem, Israel. Tuffs is the author of *And You Teach Them to Your Sons: Biblical Tales* *for Fathers and Sons* (UAHC Press), as well as numerous articles relating to masculine spirituality from a Jewish point of view. He is the spiritual leader of Temple Beth El in Hollywood, Florida.

Rachel Van Thyn has previously held various positions in the Reform Movement, including working with the Youth Division and with ARZA. She currently works for AVODAH: The Jewish Service Corps. Originally from Canada, Rachel now lives in Brooklyn, New York. She wishes to thank both those that encouraged the inclusion of her piece and those that helped her to write it.

Greg Weitzman graduated from Hobart and William Smith Colleges in 2005 with a degree in biblical archaeology. He has been both a camper and staff member at URJ Eisner Camp since 1993. Currently, he is a full-time teacher and youth advisor at Central Synagogue in New York City. This is Weitzman's first publication for the Union for Reform Judaism.

Rabbi Daniel G. Zemel is the rabbi of Temple Micah in Washington, D.C. He loves his work, his family, and reading. He is married to Louise Sherman Zemel, and they have three children, Shira Michal, Adam Solomon, and Ronit Elana. Finally, and for him most significant, Zemel is a passionate fan of the Chicago White Sox and has not been the same since they won the 2005 World Series.

Rabbi Shawn Israel Zevit, www.rabbizevit.com, has over twenty-five years of experience in spiritual leadership, human relations training, educational arts, teaching, and performing. He is a founding member of Shabbat Unplugged, the Davenning Leaders' Training Institute, and Gratz College's "Melton Adult mini-school" and has released a number of musical recordings of original inspirational spiritual music. He has been involved with gender and men's issues in particular, starting in Toronto and later as part of the annual Jewish Men's Retreat at Elat Chayyim, where he is the guest faculty and rabbi. He has written pieces on Jewish men's issues for *The Reconstructionist*, *Achim* magazine, *The New Menorah*, and *From Our Father's House: Meditations for Jewish Men* and is one of the co-editors of a forthcoming book for Jewish men.